KATHARINE

BARNWELL

KATHARINE
BARNWELL

*How
One Woman
Revolutionized*
MODERN
MISSIONS

JORDAN K. MONSON

B&H
PUBLISHING®
BRENTWOOD, TENNESSEE

Published by B&H Publishing Group
Brentwood, Tennessee

Dewey Decimal Classification: B
Subject Heading: BARNWELL, KATHARINE
/ MISSIONARIES—BIOGRAPHY / WOMEN
TRANSLATORS

Cover design by B&H Publishing Group.
Cover photo by Michael Wharley, MW Photography Ltd.
Author photo by Amy Sprunger.

1 2 3 4 5 • 28 27 26 25

To all the missionaries whose stories remain untold.

CONTENTS

FOREWORD

Maybe you've never noticed this while watching a movie or reading a novel or streaming a televised series, but if you pay attention you might pick out, in almost every one of them, what's known to the author or screenwriter or script developers as a "point-of-view character." The job of this character is to be a stand-in for you, the reader or watcher. He or she is to discover information necessary to the plotline just as you do.

This kind of character is necessary because much of what we say or do in real-life is unarticulated, based on shared assumptions that don't need to be explained. So unless there's someone who's being surprised or being enlightened along with the reader/viewer, the narrative will end up with the schlocky dialogue along the lines of this: "As you know, captain, the suspect, your wife, is a wealthy heiress who has long resented her father for the way he gave her a lesser share in the family business, which, as you know, is an oil company located in Houston" or "As you know, Bzzynt-757, you and I are alien creatures from a solar system far from earth, and, as you know, we are on a journey far from our own galaxy to find a secret mineral on earth, which will fuel, as you well know, the power centers for our dying planet."

The point-of-view character—along with other things—saves us from all of that. As the character pieces things together, so can the audience. After all, if the readers or viewers already knew the plot and all its details, if there were nothing surprising or any mysteries to be solved, what would be the point of the story?

I write all of this because I suspect that in this little foreword you are reading, I am the point-of-view character—not for all of you but for those of you who aren't familiar with Katy Barnwell or the world she inhabits. Usually if I introduce a book, it's because I know something about the subject—maybe it's on the Bible, theology, cultural engagement or Christian ethics, the fiction of Wendell Berry, or the music of Merle Haggard. Not this time.

I admire those who translate the Bible into new languages, but I know almost nothing about how they do it. I am oblivious to the intricacies of Nigerian political and cultural divides and controversies. I respect those missionaries who carry the gospel into situations that could result in their own deaths, but my list of such heroes never included Katy Barnwell until this book. If it were not for this book, I would have never heard of her.

Some of you reading this book have followed the life and ministry of Katy Barnwell, so you know something of what to expect. But maybe you're like I was; you're coming at this with new eyes. Maybe, in some ways, we are at an advantage in reading this book. We get to follow the upward swings and downward troughs in this mission, as we learn bit by bit, page by page, just how remarkable this woman is.

Maybe you're the kind of person who, like me, is sometimes tempted to cynicism. Maybe you've seen the veil lifted a few too many times on the fallen human tendency to cruelty or lying or selfishness. Perhaps that leads you sometimes to wonder whether the way to survive the world is to have the lowest expectations possible.

Now, Jesus told us not to seek after signs. We have the only sign we need—the sign of Jonah in the One who is greater than Jonah (Luke 11:29–30). Sometimes, though, Jesus does allow us to see signs of life around us. Even when John the Baptist—discouraged to despair—sent his disciples to ask Jesus, "Are you the one who is to come, or shall we wait for another?" (Luke 7:20). Jesus said: "Go and tell John what you have seen and heard: the blind receive their sight, the lame walk, lepers are cleansed, and the deaf hear, the dead are raised up, the poor have good news preached to them" (7:22 RSV).

This book might be something of that kind of reminder for you. Despite all the scandals and collapses we see all around us, the Spirit is still alive and rustling through the world, calling and equipping disciples such as Katy Barnwell to lose their lives in order to find them. In the Jericho Road of this present age, sometimes all we see are the priests and Levites walking to the other side, but there are many Samaritans still on that road too.

The Bible not only is still the Word of God, but there are countless people who are hearing that Word for the first time—often because there are those who, like Katy Barnwell, still believe in carrying it to the poor and to the brokenhearted, for of such is the kingdom of God.

As you read this story, maybe you will find yourself in the place of those hearing this Word for the first time. Maybe, like real-life "point-of-view characters," their experience will prompt you to hear it anew too. And maybe this book is one way God is changing your story—leading you to places and callings you never imagined. How can I know? You and I are just point-of-view characters for the storyline of the cosmos—the story of Jesus.

Maybe in reading Katy Barnwell's biography, you might just find the plot-twist of your own.

Dr. Russell Moore
Editor in Chief
Christianity Today

PREFACE

If it weren't for the terrorists, I would have met Katy ten years earlier.

In the early summer of 2012, I received my first Bible translation assignment over email. I would fly to Abuja, Nigeria, in two months' time to begin my on-the-job training. Under a senior Bible translation consultant, I would learn to train local translators, teach tricky biblical, linguistic, and translation concepts, and check Scripture translation for faithfulness and accuracy. For years to come, I would train under this same senior consultant until I achieved the coveted status of "Bible translation consultant."

Nervous, I scanned to the final lines of the email to unveil the name of my trainer—*Dr. Katharine Barnwell.*

A memory sparked. *That was the same person, right?* It must be. I'd seen her once before.

A year earlier, I sat at the ubiquitous round table of any hotel conference room, uneasily full on refined carbohydrates and questionable coffee. It was my first Bible translation conference. My job title was *translation consultant (in training) (intern)* in case my standing there could be any clearer.

A kind colleague leaned in my direction, signaling toward the hall's entrance. "Have you ever met the Michael Jordan of Bible translation?"

I creased my brow, eyeing the incomers. What kind of question was that? Did any of them fit that impressive bill? I frowned and shook my head.

"It's *her*, in the light blue." She pointed.

My head snapped back. "Her?"

My colleague's eyes went wide, almost too wide, while she nodded. "That's her."

The woman in the light blue, then in her mid-seventies, faltered slightly as she walked into the great hall. No doubt the early signs of osteoarthritis, which afflicts her in full force now. It's one of the few footholds old age has managed against her.

Stealing a glance around the room, I saw that half the conference hall watched her as well. One by one, the senior leaders I only dreamed of impressing approached her. They may as well have bowed before her. Who was she? And why was everybody so impressed with her?

I may have been the only soul there who didn't know. Well, besides the woman herself, so oddly unaware of her stature. Unaware that to many in the Bible translation movement, there may be no one in the history of the church who's had a greater influence on Bible translation—ever.

As I read that email a year later, I blinked hard at the words. Yes, that was her. Katy Barnwell. I didn't know it then, but she was not just one of the most influential Bible translators in church history; she is arguably one of the most influential missionaries ever. Period. And I had the fortune of apprenticing under her.

But something happened.

Shortly before my travel date, a distress call came from Nigeria. It was my colleague, a few years ahead of me on the same career path. He was working near Jos in the Middle Belt, the few-hundred-mile stretch where Nigeria's predominantly Muslim north and Christian south blur together.

In that troubled region, you'd be hard-pressed to find a single Christian who has not known church bombings or relatives maimed or killed. And, I'm ashamed to say, you'll scarcely meet a Muslim who has not endured the same.

The Middle Belt is ever fraught, ever tense. The work of the faithful can continue on there for months, sometimes years unharmed, and then tensions rise in a moment. A moment like the fall of 2012.

Word carried fast that there was an American Bible translator in the area. A hit was put out on his life. Receiving warning, my colleague fled just in time. But they pursued. He was hunted across the country until he could reach an international airport.

Hours later I got word. Neither I nor the other "in training" "interns" would be going to Nigeria. Not then. And not anytime soon. The seasoned veterans like Katy would stay on. God knows she'd seen much worse. But the rest of us would have to reroute, finding other projects, other trainers, and other directions for our entry into the craft.

I knew it then in part, but it would take years to fully grasp how much I had lost. Katy was renowned. She was the best—and favorite—trainer and shepherd of Bible translators for the last three generations. There was hardly a major Bible translation leader alive who wasn't trained on her methods, let alone face-to-face.

Still, decades later, any who have trained under Katy betray a twinkling in their eye when remembering her care, her shepherding. I knew she was good. I knew she was influential. But I didn't know how influential. And maybe it's a blessing I didn't know then.

I didn't know that many of the largest mission organizations in the world reinvented their methods based on her work, going on to reap a harvest markedly greater than before. I didn't know then that Katy enjoys more than one hundred times the influence of Billy Graham (see chapter 33). The heavyweights of heaven do not always stand in the order we imagine.

I didn't know then that there had been a great battle for the future of Bible translation. One camp fought to keep the West in the pilot's seat. The other fought to equip the global church to lead the work itself. The West would come alongside to help—not lead. The latter method won the day and is used all over the world in approximately 85 percent of the Bible translation work worldwide. Katy led that charge.

Her training, her students (and their students), and her books have trained thousands of Bible translators around the world. You'd be hard-pressed to find a dozen Bible translation projects on the face of the planet not swimming downstream of her work.

Estimates vary, but she's likely directly influenced upwards of three thousand Bible translation projects. Some have started Bible translation institutions, like William Cameron Townsend, who began Wycliffe and (what is now called) SIL.[1] His institutional influence will be greater. But nobody in church history holds a dim candle to Katy's *direct* influence on translation.

I didn't know then that the last sixty years had seen the greatest missiological shift since the early church. *From the West to the rest* was in its death throes. That runner was old, tired, injured. But a faster runner, a better runner, stood waiting ahead. The global church was ready. But somebody needed to pass the baton. More than any other Bible translation figure, it was Katy who passed the baton. She equipped the global church. She democratized Bible translation, sealing the coffin on the colonial era behind her.

Yes, I'd lost out on much. But through the mysterious workings of God, that was not the end of a friendship with Katy. More than a decade later, I had the honor of sitting with her in her English home. Of making her a meal. Of hearing her full story. I can't express the honor I felt at listening to the firsthand stories of a living legend so that I might write this book.

It may have been the loss of that initial assignment that made her influence stick in my mind. Whenever I had the chance, I asked Bible translation leaders about her. I read her books and articles. I paid closer attention when the old-timers described how they used to do things and how they do things so differently now. And at the center of those great changes, those great upheavals, stood Katy Barnwell.

Reading the pantheon of famous missionaries, the *best of* lists, I would furrow my brow. I knew a story like these. More impressive in breadth and reach. Yet her story remained untold. It was as if a Billy Graham—a Mother Teresa—had lived and worked, all without a chronicler. She was the forgotten missionary—or as I like to say, the greatest missionary you've never heard of.

Not only does she deserve a prominent place in the pantheon of *Great Missionaries,* but I believe she may be the last in that list. Not the last missionary. No, there won't be any end to those until his kingdom comes. What I mean is that she is the last great Western missionary.

The last five hundred years, the era of the "West to the rest" is over. The church is different now. Missionary work is different now—for the better. Now the whole church is reaching the whole world. Korean missionaries come to North America. Nigerian missionaries go to Europe as Europeans go to Nigeria. Brazilian missionaries go to Northern Africa. Chinese missionaries go to Japan. That old era is dead and buried, and Katy held the shovel.[2]

I think of it like this:

My young children play a game, familiar to many from childhood. In it the ground is a kind of hazardous substance like lava. They terrorize the house and remove every couch cushion they can find, laying pathways on the ground as they move from their starting place to their destiny.

For lack of material, they've long learned to collect the cushions they've just trodden, laying them again ahead and leaving no bridge back to their beginning. My kids arrive in a new location, a new room, ready for new endeavors. But you'll find barely a trace of the route they travailed to arrive there.

This reminds me of Katy's work. She has borne Bible translation forward so thoroughly that it's scarcely possible to retread her path. Much remains to be done, but the global church stands far ahead now. The old trodden paths are long gone. The global church is laying highways now—on cushions still warm from her hands.

New Year's Eve 2023
Goring-on-Thames,
Southern Oxfordshire
UK

Jordan K. Monson

Chapter 1

BIBLES AND
BULLET HOLES

In July 2007, Bible translators from a dozen Nigerian languages gathered under a steel-roofed school shelter in the town of Bayara, Nigeria. For the next three weeks, the translators and a few Nigerian, American, and British consultants would work around the clock to begin translating the Gospel of Luke.

On Friday, July 27, they had wrapped their first week of work and made plans to unwind. Multilingual collaboration is exhausting, and everyone was eager to eat dinner and watch a film together.

The translators gathered their papers and books into bags. Some slung laptops over their shoulders. One of them grabbed a USB thumb drive attached to a purple lanyard, which they used to pass files back and forth and store backups of their work.

They walked half a kilometer through the warm evening air to the guesthouse where they were staying. The cooler rainy season had just begun, but this day had been neither cool nor rainy.

And as they walked, about a dozen of them in all, they were eager to get back and enjoy a night of fellowship together.

The group finished eating around 7:30, and Veronica Gambo, the wife of one of the translation consultants, made popcorn. She began filling a large bowl, readying to carry it out to the others in the living room who were setting up the film.

But as she picked up the bowl, the kitchen door burst open, and men with automatic rifles poured in.

Veronica stood frozen. The lead gunman pushed his barrel between her shoulder blades and marched her, still bearing the popcorn, into the living room.

"Get down!" The men yelled.

"They were shooting inside the room."[1] Said Danjuma Gambo, a Nigerian translation consultant—and husband to Veronica who carried the popcorn.

The men fired into the walls and ceiling. They forced everybody to the ground, including the translation project's leader, a silver-haired British woman in her late sixties.

Andy Kellogg, an American working as a Bible translation consultant, remembers lying on the floor. Would the men rob them and leave quickly, or something worse? "If you're in a remote place, and it doesn't seem like help will be coming quickly, you can take your time as a robber. And we were in a remote place." Kellogg said.[2]

Andy considered that he may never see his wife again. His children. Then he remembered his colleague in the adjacent room. She was young. Female. The men hadn't searched that room. Not yet.

Unarmed and lying prostrate, Andy wondered, if the men go into that room—if something happens to her, *What are my next steps?*

Fortunately for the translators, the men were not religious terrorists. The brigands had spotted the laptops as the team made their commute on foot. That's what they came for. They stole nine in all, along with personal belongings, passports, and credit cards.

And somehow, by the grace of God, the robbers never checked that adjacent room with the young woman. It was as if they were blinded to it. The young woman inside was left alone.

All the translation work they'd done was on those laptops. And when there are nine different copies out there of a file, the pressure to keep great backups diminishes. They had one backup—a USB thumb drive hanging by the purple lanyard on a nail on the wall. In those days, passing around the stick was the easiest way to keep the project synced across devices.

The raiders took everything of value they could find. "But by God's grace, they left the lanyard with our backups hanging there on the wall," Kellogg said. "Had God opened their eyes to it, they would have taken that also. But in his providence, they didn't."[3]

When the thieves left, the elderly project leader arose from the ground. She dusted her clothing. After checking with each translator to make sure they were okay, she spoke in that most British way.

"Right. . . . Well, we're not going to let this stop us."[4]

Her name is Dr. Katharine Barnwell. By any account, she's one of the most influential missionaries in the history of Christianity. Some call her Katy. Most call her *Mother*.

Fear could have taken over that night. The projects could have halted, the spread of God's Word slowed. But Katy was there. And the armed criminals were about to become a footnote in the story of a great life.

After half a century in missions, Katharine Barnwell was no stranger to peril. Six times she was robbed at gunpoint, twice stormed by armed robbers. She fled a civil war on foot and upriver without documentation. She endured constant threat from terrorists and constant danger from malaria. She was known to forego food and sleep so that others might eat and have a warm bed.

She wanted to press forward, but she knew that not all had her constitution for the work. So Katy spoke individually with each translator, shepherding and counseling.

Under her leadership, every last Bible translation worker decided to stay on and continue the work. They would not even postpone the workshop. God's Word would not be stopped.

Within a few minutes, Danjuma Gambo said, the group burst into song, praising God and praying for a way to finish God's work. There was one problem: *We have no computers*, Kellogg thought. *This is going to be really hard on Monday.*

But on Monday, when they returned to work, they found that every computer had been replaced. Formerly, this would have taken weeks or even months. It would have meant letters, emails, funding requests, meetings, forms, and petitions to Western agencies. But that never happened.

News of the robbery spread quickly, and before the weekend was done, "computers were provided . . . by groups in the area. There were some influential people in churches nearby who donated." Kellogg said.[5]

It was not the Western agencies who replaced the computers so they could meet their goals; it was the local Nigerian believers and churches. These homegrown congregations and benefactors wanted that work done. They believed in it. And they were driving it.

The projects would have been lost along with those nine hard drives. But still dangling on the nail, not far from a bullet hole, was that lanyard. Securely resting inside, in zeros and ones, were the backups to all the translation projects. From that thumb drive, the translation teams restored everything, and each project went on to finish the Gospel of Luke and then *The Jesus Film*, whose script comes almost entirely from Luke. Many of those projects now have full New Testaments, Kellogg said, and some have moved on to the Old Testament.[6]

Well over a million people from those languages now have access to the good news of Jesus and his Scripture in their first language. If Katy's group had given up that day—if they had given up under the threat of violence or worse—those million-plus people would not have the gospel.

This incident in northeast Nigeria is a freeze-frame from the great missiological shift that has been playing out over the past sixty years: the transfer of ownership from Western individuals and institutions to leaders and churches in the Global South. After hundreds of years, Americans and Europeans are no longer in the pilot's seat of global mission work. They have been rapidly replaced by Christians in the majority world.

Nigerian ownership is what saved the projects born from Barnwell's workshop—or at least what helped them quickly get back on their feet. And it was perhaps poetic: Barnwell, a Westerner, was one of the earliest champions of empowering Nigerians to take over translation work in their country.

In fact, no living person has likely had a greater influence on the world of Bible translation than Barnwell.[7] But unless you've worked in Bible translation, you've probably never heard of her.

Chapter 2

BOMBS AND
TEDDY BEARS

Katharine Barnwell was born in London on August 9, 1938, to Frederick Reginald Lowry Barnwell and Norah Manning Powell. Katy's father "Reggie" was a Civil engineer who worked on railway infrastructure. When World War II began with Nazi Germany, Britain quickly scooped him up to serve in the war effort. Many wars are won and lost not on man power but brainpower. The British knew this and called up their engineers immediately.[1]

Reginald Barnwell served in North Africa, Italy, and in France. And though he never spoke about it with family, he was of great service to the Allies.[2] He would be promoted to colonel during the war and was awarded an OBE, or Order of the British Empire, for his service. His community would call him Colonel Barnwell until he died on December 29, 1984.[3]

Her father's service meant that for most of Katy's first decade of life, her father was not present. And those years were not easy.

Katy's first memory is of the air raids, the sirens. When the British spotted Nazi bombers, they sounded the alarm. When the sirens sounded, Londoners never knew how much time they had before the first bomb fell. Had the best radar stations picked up the bombers over the English Channel? They may have some time. But radar in those days was young and far less capable. If the bombers escaped detection, they may only be spotted by human observers on the coast of England. In that case, there may be only minutes to find shelter.

Starting September 7, 1940, during what is known as The Blitz, the sirens would sound 350 times in eight weeks. For fifty-seven consecutive nights, Nazi bombers descended on Britain, dropping thousands of metric tons of bombs on military and civilian areas alike. In some areas, bomb shelters were too scarce and 150,000 took refuge overnight in the tube stations.[4]

Katy's family was assigned a local bomb shelter in the crypt of a church, an underground burial place with access to tombs and coffins. Katy remembers the sirens, the always-packed emergency bag, and her mother hurrying them to the crypt. Bombs above ground and corpses below.

When I traveled to England to interview her, I asked her if she was afraid. "Not at all," she said. "We weren't old enough to be frightened."

She *was* old enough to be frightened, but children often take cues from those around them. And in Katy's mother Norah, the only emotions young Katy detected were adventure and resolve. Any parent knows the anxiety her mother must have felt, but her acting skills were strong.

In the crypt, there were new people, snacks, and other children. Katy's mother made it all seem fun. She kept a bag ready with a special selection of toys saved particularly for those occasions.

Katy remembers the special pink blanket her mother saved for those nights in the crypt. She also had a special teddy bear. It was big, almost as big as her, and it served as a sort of companion during those bombing raids in the crypt. Katy has held on to that teddy bear her entire life.

"My mother was remarkable, really," Katy said. She was raising two and then three children mostly alone while Katy's father served overseas in the war. Food was intensely rationed. Fruit and other major staples disappeared overnight. Due to the sudden Vitamin C shortage in the UK, the government rallied many volunteer groups to forage. One of Katy's early memories is of foraging for rose hips, many times richer in Vitamin C than even oranges.

England went from one of the most peaceful and wealthy nations on earth to, nearly overnight, enduring constant bombing and not having enough fruits and vegetables for adequate nutrition. And for nearly a year, they stood alone as the only major force fighting the Nazis in Europe.[5]

To escape the dangers of war, Barnwell and her siblings were sent away to live with family in the countryside, much in the way *The Lion, the Witch and the Wardrobe* opens. Like the fictional Pevensie children, Katy remembers filling her days in similar ways and getting in nonfictional trouble.

Moving away from the London bombings would mark a life of dozens of moves. Later in life, entire years passed in which Katy never lived anywhere. Three weeks in this country, five weeks in that, and on and on, helping innumerable Bible translators in every inhabited continent. But that would come later.

She remembers playing and that scolding so common to children after arriving at grandparents' homes—a house not ready for children and grandparents not ready for children's play. Her grandparents had a nice garden. And though the children were allowed in the garden, there were a few trees they were not allowed to climb. In a great irony for the future Bible translator and writer of exegetical commentaries on Genesis, Katy could not avoid the apple trees.

We don't want to commit the biographer's original sin of snatching a scene from childhood and interpreting too much through it, but it's hard not to see this boundary testing continue throughout her entire career. Katy was not a disobedient child. Nor was she difficult as an adult. But if you gave her what she considered a foolish rule, she would not follow it.

The war dictated Katy's childhood. Not only was her father mostly away for her first seven years of life, but Katy knew little of stability or community beyond her mother and siblings. And it wouldn't end there.

Chapter 3

GROWING PAINS
AND GIRL GUIDES

After the war, Colonel Barnwell continued his work in civil engineering for the railways. Every eighteen to thirty-six months, the next letter would arrive. A reassignment. If the new post was close enough, Katy and the family could stay put, but Katy's father would commute for the week, returning home only on weekends. More often, the new position was far enough away that the family was required to move. They would have to begin all over again. Katy couldn't decide which was harder on the family.

Michael, Katy's younger brother, remembers Reggie Barnwell moving ahead of the family in these cases, with the rest of the family staying for a few months, always trying to tie up loose ends. Eventually, they'd follow the Colonel. Eighteen months later, they'd do it all over again.[1]

"I looked up to him tremendously, but at the same time, I think I was probably a little bit afraid of him." Michael told me. "My mother, I adored, all her life. She was the one who came out to [visit me in] South Africa and that sort of thing. I think I knew her better."

Michael described his father as a good provider but emotionally distant. During our interview, it didn't take me long to note that Michael shared Katy's gift for eloquence. He studied at Cambridge and never struggled to express himself during our interview. Except once.

While trying to describe his father's emotional distance, he stumbled, tripping over the words, stopping and starting again. "I've had the same [difficulty] most of my life, in expressing emotion. And I think, this is perhaps, from the upbringing I had as a child."[2] Though Katy was cautious in what she told me on record, it was clear her experience was similar. She adored her mother, but, according to Katy, she and her father "never really understood each other."

Katy's maternal grandfather had been a professional pianist with a storied career. He died December 23, 1931, six and a half years before Katy was born.

The day after he died, the *New York Times* and many newspapers of record around the English-speaking world reported his death.

> Wireless to the *New York Times*.
> LONDON, Dec 23.—Lionel Powell, famous impresario, died here today at the age of 54. A month ago he contracted a chill while on tour with Ignaz Jan Padarewski,[3] the pianist, and pneumonia followed. After a partial recovery he underwent an operation for a gastric ulcer.[4]

He "probably was the world's most traveled impresario, having circled the globe twice and having made forty trips to the United States." He gave more than fifteen thousand concerts, controlled Albert Hall and Queen's Hall in London,[5] and "in the course of his long career he had met most of the members of the royal houses of Europe."[6]

This was the early twentieth century. He was not traveling on passenger jets. He made those trips by ship and by train. He'd spent years of his life at sea going to and from the United States, let alone around the globe.

Katy's mother, it seems, had a childhood much like Katy's. A remarkably industrial father who was gone most of the time.

When Katy was a child, they still had his grand piano. Katy remembers it as the source of much of her quarreling with her sister. Katy endured the small trials that many middle children must bear. She fell constantly into unfair competition with her sister Ann, nearly three years older than Katy and three years ahead in piano practice. Ann didn't want to listen to Katy practicing. "She's only playing scales and five-finger exercises," Katy remembers her protesting.

Why take up valuable piano time with Katy's fingers when she wasn't as good? When Ann sat down, she would outdo Katy. When Katy practiced, Ann didn't want to hear the noise.[7]

Katy thought she must not be any good. She wasn't old enough to understand that it wasn't necessarily about her talent but the fact that she was years behind. And though parents can often muster the patience to put up with early piano lessons, it's hard not to sympathize with the young child Ann for finding it annoying.

Thinking the piano was not her instrument, Katy moved on to ballet. But she did not particularly excel at that, either. One thing she did excel in was writing essays and poems. Katy was first published around age twelve in her school magazine.

It's early, oh it's early as in bed I lie,
Strange, sweet sounds float out across the sky,
Now at the break of dawn no one stirs,
But yet the sky is filled with friendly airs.

What is it, oh what is it, that wakes the sun at
    morn,
So that these sweet melodies across the air are
    born,

Now at the break of dawn the tuneful choir
    rings out,
Through the woods and valleys, it echoes all
    about.

Only I am listening, through the window
    peeping,
All the rest so silently in their beds are sleeping,
A concert for my benefit, that is what I heard,
For who could have sung so sweetly, but a bird![8]

Though not destined to be a poet, it's clear that Katy had a way with words and a maturity of thought beyond her peers. While others were sleeping, or sleeping their way through a noncontemplative life, Katy saw beauty all around. She saw enchantment. She saw the charm of nature. For children who feel the need to describe this beauty, some find poetry, and others find the natural sciences. Katy insisted on an intersection, a place where the sciences and poetry meet. At university, when she stumbled into linguistics by accident, she found what she'd been seeking.

Because of her father's work, Katy's family rarely stayed long in one place. Tewin Wood, Somerset, Rotherham, Inverness, Usk, to name only a few. Katy made friends, but a child learns quickly when every friend she makes disappears in two to three years. Eventually, she preferred acquaintances to friends. They were easier to turn over. Easier to say goodbye to. She has no deeply abiding friends from childhood for this reason.

But four things Katy had. Her books, her mother, the church, in which she was growing. And she had the Girl Guides.

Her grandfather was extremely well read, and Katy benefitted from his books, in time, reading all of them.

The far more important companion was her mother. Growing up under constant threat of war and aerial bombing, endless moves, and losing community after community, Katy saw a strong woman, alone, doing what needed to be done against remarkable odds. This singular attitude would become Katy's for the rest of her life.

And just as a church or school provides a faster on-ramp to community, so do organizations like the Girl Guides (which would birth Girl Scouts and similar programs around the world). Katy's aunts—her godmothers—were leaders in Girl Guides. Under their guidance Katy took a keen interest. She joined as a Brownie at age six and continued all the way through, graduating as a Queen's Guide, the highest level awarded.

The premise of the Girl Guides was to socialize young girls into the roles they'd face in society.[9] Just as the twentieth century asked women to balance traditional and domestic life with increasing independence, so Girl Guides would prepare young girls on both fronts for what lay ahead.[10]

Against contemporary social expectations, Girl Guides was a revolution in teaching young girls the kind of independence, ingenuity, and grit that was normally associated with boys and men at the time. Before Girl Guides, there was hardly an organization on earth training young girls in "physical fitness, survival skills, camping, citizenship training, and career preparation."[11]

Katy loved every minute of it. And based on its worldwide success, it's safe to say she was not the only one.

From a young age, the Guides pursued various honors, tasks, and badges, indicating they had reached certain technical or character mastery. As the Guides aged, they took on increasingly difficult endeavors. The greatest challenges for Guides near graduation were, for example, living in the woods for a week, sheltering in a tent, and cooking meals at campfires they themselves had kindled. It's not the stuff of survival television, but compared to the social expectations of women just a generation earlier, it was a revolution.

Over the years, Katy learned to camp, fish, build shelter, signal for help, start fires, and cook by fires. She learned to use knives, hunting weapons, traps, tools, maps, compasses, and ultimately, she learned how to survive.

Teaching these skills is not always meant as literal preparation. Most in the developed world may never need these skills. But the kind of confidence, autonomy, and preparedness of mind these skills create is invaluable preparation for all. We will all face obstacles that stretch us. We all face difficulties requiring a well-trained capacity for problem-solving. Training in these skills enabled the Girl Guides to train for the uncertainties of life and their future careers.

Little did Katy know, much of the preparation was *literal*.

Girl Guides might seem traditional today, but in an era when women married and were not encouraged to camp, throw, hit, survive, or otherwise thrive in dangerous environments, Girl Guides represented a fierce kind of strength and independence. *Leave It to Beaver*, eat your heart out. These girls could live off the land.

And during every meeting, often toward the end as a liturgical closing, they repeated their motto: "Be prepared." No matter the obstacle, whatever challenges might confront them, *be prepared*.

Years later as Katy escaped a civil war, navigating upriver for five days in dense malarial hotbeds—no roads, no bridges, no communication—we see just how well prepared she was.

Chapter 4

WOMEN MARRY

Born a middle child of three, Katy always felt she was the odd one out. Her older sister Ann was everything Katy was not. Ann's natural demeanor fit well with the times—pretty, average height, and adept in society's contemporary expectations for women. At first the boys noticed and then the young men. Her parents noticed as well. When Ann was a late teenager, their parents arranged an introduction to a family friend, a young Irishman. They were soon married and remained so until Ann's passing in March of 2024.

Every age produces children ideally suited to the social expectations of the time. Katy's sister was one of them. Katy was not. And in the eyes of their father, the Colonel, this distinction was clear.

"Ann was quite sporting, and so was I," her brother Michael told me. "But Katy was not. . . . She was sort of separate from us as a result."[1] Michael went to Cambridge, was captain of the football (soccer) team there, and went on to be a first-class cricketer for Somerset and Eastern Province. But he describes his older sister Ann as the true athletic star of their household when they were growing up. "She excelled at sport, and my father loved his sport as well."[2] Michael describes Katy and himself as children of their mother, while Ann was a child of their father.[3]

Katy loved to think, to read, and to study deeply. She wrote poetry for fun. She claims she was socially awkward.

Katy's parents did not work to find a suitable partner for Katy as they had for her sister. It may have been because of her supposed awkwardness, and it may have been that they knew it wasn't of interest to her. Not then.

She was not a natural with the boys. It did not help that she was tall. Even today, short men and tall women often find dating challenging. Katy was taller than the average man in her day, which left fewer potential partners than if she were of average female height. Then even more than now, men rarely dated women taller than themselves.

Katy's teenage passport records that she was 5' 9 4/5". The fact that she did not put 5'10" tells volumes about how she felt about her height. Given the increase in average height since then, a comparison today might be a young Englishwoman who's 6 feet tall or just a hair shy of it.

But despite the fact that there were no romances (or maybe because of it), Katy's mind was relentless, and her early years in school only whet her appetite. She puts the term *lifelong learner* to shame. Even late in life, on her table next to her sit not only great literature and biographies, but biblical Hebrew textbooks, long worked over, crumpled, dog-eared, and underlined.

Hang around Katy for a while, and you'll hear her say, "I need to improve my Hebrew." Whenever she says this, the people around her laugh. And I can tell that though she's learned people find this amusing, she's never understood why.

Here she sits, eighty-six-years-old, possibly the most influential Bible translator of all time, and she sees only how she can improve. The rest of us see the mountain she's climbed, the rarified air she breathes. She sees only the next summit.

She knew even as a child she wanted to learn. But could she learn as a vocation? Could she study like the boys got to?

Typical for families of that time, little to no money was spent on the girls' education. Katy's brother Michael was sent to what was called "public school." Americans would call her brother's school a boarding school. Michael was sent away at age nine to live and study in a pristine and well-regarded institution with a pipeline relationship to the greatest British universities like Cambridge, Oxford, and St. Andrews.

Her brother was worth the money. But for Katy, the local free school would have to suffice. Those were the times and Katy did not see any partiality in the decision. It's simply how it was in those days. It is ironic then that while her brother would go on to just an undergraduate degree, Katy would go on from an undergraduate degree, a master's degree, and a PhD, to academic journal editor and author of research books by the dozens, never ceasing her endless education.

When she told her father that she'd like to go to university, she received a frank reply. "Women marry." Few kinds of statements age as poorly as this. But judging historical figures by modern standards is poor historiography. They were products of their culture just as we are of ours. We must attempt to read them charitably.

We must remember that almost no women went to university at that time. In 1950, only 3.4 percent of English youth went to university at all, a great majority of them men.[4] Cambridge University did not even award degrees to women until 1948, only nine years before Katy herself would attend university.[5]

If only 1 to 2 percent of women attended university, and Barnwell's parents were not academics themselves, it may have seemed strange and expensive for her to pursue that track. Especially if she were just going to marry soon and live a life of domesticity. Why pay? But against the attitude of the time, Katy's headmistress sat down with her father and made the case. We don't know what she said, but she was able to swim against the gender expectations of the day. She convinced Colonel Barnwell not only to allow it but to pay Katy's way.

May the world be ever grateful for that headmistress and a father who relented. Despite his "women marry" response, Colonel Barnwell went against a mountain of social custom surrounding the education of women and at great cost to himself.

Katy applied to what were regarded as the three top schools in the UK. Katy's first choice was to study English at St. Andrews University in Scotland. It first began admitting degree-seeking female students as early as 1892. Because of this, St. Andrews enjoyed a stronger culture and acceptance of female scholarship than Oxford or Cambridge. She no longer remembers the decisions of those other two schools, but it was never a question for Katy. St. Andrews sent a letter of acceptance, and she needed no further deliberation. In the fall of 1957, she set off to the university.

Chapter 5

FAITH AND CALLING

Katy's great grandfather was a country pastor[1] in one parish for nearly fifty years. Persevering in ministry for more
than a half century seems to run in the blood.

This country pastor's daughters helped run the local Girl
Guides chapter and also served as Katy's godmothers. "They
told me later in life that they had prayed for me every day since
I was baptized as a child. I think I have a lot to owe them for,"
Katy reminisced about her aunts.

Katy attended confirmation classes at her Anglican church
and was happy to make a commitment at age fourteen. She
would later say, "I made a commitment at that point as much as
I understood. But I don't think I understood a lot."

When Katy thinks about her spiritual awakening, she looks
not to her confirmation but to her early days at university. At the
University of St. Andrews, they had a thriving Christian organization called the Christian Union.[2] During Katy's first week,
members of the Christian Union visited every dorm and residence on campus, inviting new students to join them in worship.

"I went along because these friendly people came, and I
couldn't think of any reason not to go." So Katy joined. The
names of the students who invited her are lost to history. But
because they pushed against the discomfort and stepped out in
faith, Katy Barnwell became serious about following Jesus. And
because of this, hundreds of millions of people heard the good
news of Jesus in their first language much sooner than they

would have—if at all. Countless millions would have died before the message ever arrived were it not for Katy's work. Never underestimate the power of an invitation.

Barnwell arrived at university already a believer. She meant what she said in her confirmation ceremony at age fourteen. But when she moved to university and became involved in the Christian Union, she realized, "There was a lot more to it than that. It wasn't just about professing your belief but counting the cost, taking up your cross, and changing your life."

"If you're going to be a Christian," she said, "It's got to be everything. It's got to be everything or nothing."[3]

She does not remember a particular moment, a particular teaching as her turning point. Instead, it was the overall posture of the group. The general camaraderie and fellowship made the difference. This was the first community Katy knew that modeled a vibrant and active life of faith daily seeking God in prayer and in the Scriptures.

With these friends, she came to "value the Bible, the reading of the Bible." She came to "realize the power of the Bible, the power of the Word of God."

In this group Katy's faith shifted from a creed, a Sunday morning liturgy, to the matter at the front and center of her life.

While studying, she enjoyed spiritual encouragement from not just the Christian Union. Having been raised in an Anglican church and receiving Anglican confirmation, Katy decided to continue attending an Anglican church even while in Scotland, which was a country dominated by the Presbyterian tradition. Dr. Patterson, a professor of geography at St. Andrews, also opened his home to students on Sunday evenings for Bible study.

One of Katy's fondest memories of university was the pier walk. Every Sunday after church, the students donned their red graduation regalia and walked down to the end of the pier, climbing the ladder to the top of the pier wall, and then walked back. It's a weekly tradition stretching back more than two hundred years and continuing to this day. While outsiders scratch their heads at such a spectacle, the students and locals know exactly why this act of commemoration eventually became a tradition unto itself. The local newspaper *The Herald* reports that in the year 1800 on a cold January day, a nineteen-year-old student named John Honey saved the lives of five men offshore: "It was from a service at St. Salvator's Chapel that he set out on January 5, 1800, after word had reached the town that a ship, the Janet, was in trouble off the East Sands with a crew of five men on board. Honey tied a rope round his waist, swam out and saved all of them, one by one."[4]

LINGUISTICS AND CALLING

Studying English language and literature was not all classics and writing. Katy also had to take a few technical courses in philology and linguistics. Speaking a second language well might be compared to driving a car. You can wield it. But it doesn't mean you understand the internal combustion of the engine. No, it's the budding mechanical engineer who wants to take the whole thing apart into a thousand pieces and see how it works down to its bones.

This is what linguistics is to language. And as a part of Katy's study, she was introduced to the field. For most students of English, it was simply a course they had to push through to move on to further literature. But for Katy, the lights turned on. She loved it.

She was growing in faith by the day. She read Scripture constantly—in her student groups, Bible studies, and individually. She found it an inexhaustible well. Then in class, she learned linguistics, which would become her lifelong scholarly pursuit.

Precisely at this time Katy got word that a visitor was coming to campus to address the Christian Union directly. His name was George Cowan, and he was the president of a fairly young missions organization in America—Wycliffe Bible Translators.

George Cowan had served in a Mazatec language in the Oaxacan highlands of Mexico, the Huautla language. He worked together with the people to translate the New Testament and went on to serve as Wycliffe's president for decades. In the linguistics community, his claim to fame is that he's one of the earlier linguists to formally describe and annotate whistled tones in Mazatecan languages.[5]

Indigenous tonal languages in remote areas in Mexico are known to be some of the most difficult in the world, making Mandarin Chinese and Cantonese look easy by comparison. If you search the most difficult languages in the world, you'll see a much copied and pasted list across the Internet from the US State Department. This list ranks languages according to how many hundreds or thousands of hours are required for native English speakers to become proficient in them. On these lists, Mandarin, Cantonese, Arabic, Japanese, and Korean often come out on top.[6] But this is only a scale for major institutional languages, which by their nature of covering vast territories and assimilating multiple people groups tend to simplify grammatically. In the era of Beowulf, English was remarkably more grammatically complex than it is today.

The most difficult languages in the world are often isolated and may only be spoken by a few hundred or a few thousand people.

Because many indigenous Mexican languages are tonal as well, like many East Asian languages, they are remarkably difficult. But not for Cowan. He learned not only the local language but also the whistle speech common to the men. After centuries in the highlands and windswept fields, the men could whistle entire conversations back and forth. Given they knew the shared context, they would whistle the tones of the words in mind, and the hearer fully and fluently understood.[7]

Cowan even observed an entire bartering conversation take place solely in whistles. Greetings, discussion, haggling over price, and purchase—all in whistles.[8]

Cowan was a gifted speaker with a "strong, clear voice," his SIL obituary reads.[9] Though there's no record of what he said that day in front of the Christian Union, we do have video from later in his life when he spoke in similar meetings. It's not hard to imagine him before the Christian Union that day saying something similar.

"I can't go before God, honestly, and ask him, 'Lord, you've given me the whole Bible. . . . I've got more versions than I know what to do with. But what about that poor guy out there? He's one of a little group of three hundred. And he's got nothing. What should I pray for him? Lord, give him some crumbs, please—and I'm stuffed with a gourmet meal. Give him some crumbs? I can't pray that.'"

Then, tearing up, he says, "It chokes in my throat. . . . I can only ask that God give him the same as he's given me. How can I ask for any less than what God's given me for every other man? I'm no better than they. And I just hope that no one will ever be able to say, in heaven, that they stopped before they'd come to my language."[10]

That day at St. Andrews, he no doubt spoke of similar stories and adventures. He likely demonstrated this whistle speech. And he told of the work of applied linguistics and Bible translation.

With good linguistics training, a linguist could enter a monolingual and illiterate group, begin to learn the language, and eventually describe it through a technical grammar and dictionary. Together with native speakers, they could then work to translate Scripture.

The work of Bible translation is a marriage of scientific linguistics, translation theory, and exegesis, not to mention one of the primary ways to answer God's call: "Go, therefore, and make disciples of all nations, baptizing them in the name of the Father and of the Son and of the Holy Spirit, teaching them to observe everything I have commanded you. And remember, I am with you always, to the end of the age."[11]

Jesus commands his followers to make disciples of all nations. Part of this call is to teach them everything he's commanded. How can the nations learn of a Savior if his good news is not communicated in their language?[12]

Two millennia ago, the apostle Paul wrote about those who had not heard the good news of Jesus. "How, then, can they call on him they have not believed in? And how can they believe without hearing about him? And how can they hear without a preacher?"[13] How are the nations to hear the good news of a Savior if that news is not in their language?

There are about seven thousand spoken languages in the world. How can the nations believe if the good news is hoarded in only a few hundred of the largest global languages?

"That was it for me." Katy said.

Cowan stayed after to talk with the students. Though shy, Katy knew she would not get this chance again. After a few students received answers to their questions, Katy spoke with Cowan.

"What would it mean if I did join?" she asked.

Cowan described the next steps to her. He mentioned the training courses SIL ran during the summer session. He also mentioned a name to Katy: John Bendor-Samuel.

Chapter 6

JOHN BENDOR-SAMUEL AND SIL

The second leader Katy met in Bible translation would become something of a lifelong mentor. Arguably, John Bendor-Samuel (lovingly referred to as JBS) was the reason Katy became what she became. More than anybody else, JBS saw the potential in Katy and fostered it, encouraging PhD study for her at a time when almost no women attended university, much less earned a doctorate.

John Bendor-Samuel was nine years older than Katy. Raised by two ministers, he would develop a sharp mind and a vibrant faith. Given the times, JBS was required to serve "two years in the army as his national service."[1]

John felt a calling to serve as a missionary and requested that the military station him overseas for this purpose. However, his talent would be his downfall. His ability to teach others was deemed too good to let go. The army kept him in England as an instructor. They recognized something in John that many others would recognize soon after. He had an uncanny ability to steward and shepherd others in difficult endeavors. But despite his talent, the young man wanted out. He wanted adventure, to explore the world.

Finally, in order to "[force] his commander's hand," he resigned his rank. This meant he "could no longer serve as an instructor." The British government relented and sent him to

"Egypt, Libya, and Malta, where he learned first-hand of the need for Muslim peoples to come to understand the Gospel."[2]

Upon returning, he studied history at Oxford. Given the way languages were taught in his childhood, he was nervous about his ability to learn foreign languages. Could he be an effective missionary if he was not strong in language? Little did he know, the way classical languages were taught had little to do with spoken and modern language learning. In fact, the methods were uniquely counterproductive.

In 1953, he stumbled across a flyer for the inaugural Summer Institute of Linguistics (later known simply as SIL) in England, to be held at London Bible College. Its purpose? To "help missionaries learn non-Indo-European languages."[3] It was as if God was directly answering his prayer.

Not having the money to stay on campus, he rode his bicycle forty minutes each way every day to make the courses. There he studied under Kenneth Pike, the president of SIL and one of the most respected linguists in the world. The course was a success, and plans were made to repeat it yearly, as well as to add a second year of courses. Young linguists were interested in using their skills in Bible translation, but there was no missions organization through which they could be employed.

SIL leaders saw in John the same thing the military had. He was a strong self-starter, leader, and educator. Only weeks later, Wycliffe UK was born in John Bendor-Samuel's parents' attic. He had a typewriter, a donated filing cabinet, a heart full of zeal, and a head full of knowledge.

He bought a motorcycle with a sidecar and tramped all around the UK to raise awareness and call churches to join in the work. He also found a more permanent home for the Summer Institute of Linguistics courses—a former army base at Chigwell, Essex.

Because of his visionary leadership and campaigning, SIL and Wycliffe now had a consistent home in the UK, which continues today. Bendor-Samuel soon left for Peru to begin working with an indigenous people group, but SIL did not forget his talent for starting great endeavors from nothing.

Until the late 1950s, most of Wycliffe and SIL's work was in Central and South America. This was not necessarily on purpose but a simple accident of circumstance. William Cameron Townsend (Uncle Cam) lived among Indigenous people in Guatemala when he first began to translate the Bible. After founding SIL and Wycliffe, it was natural that he would want to continue in a familiar area. The US and Canada are also much closer to those parts of the world. In an era before mass aviation, proximity mattered.

Some of the people groups where Bible translators worked in Central and South America were large, but many were famously small, numbering in only hundreds of speakers. Though people from small people groups needed the good news of Jesus just as much as those from large people groups, the number of human hours required to translate Scripture in each was essentially equal.

Missiologically, the Bible translation movement became increasingly aware that there were continents with hundreds, even thousands of indigenous languages that were much larger, their number of speakers well into the millions. Much of Africa and parts of Asia had indigenous languages never before written with tens of millions of native speakers. And with the growing affordability of the passenger jet, Bible translation began to look beyond the Americas.

But proximity still mattered. Many missionaries still had to travel by ship in those years, as Katy would when she first traveled to Nigeria. Reaching Africa from a base in North America didn't make good logistical sense. They needed something much closer.

It had been a long time since SIL began something from a blank page, especially in an area where nobody knew who SIL was or what they were doing. And they wouldn't have Uncle Cam's ingenuity this time since he was busy running the organization Stateside.[4] So, when the time came to strategically open doors in Africa, they remembered the ingenuity of that young man who began Wycliffe's operations in the UK—the upstart with a vision and a motorcycle.

They asked John Bendor-Samuel to begin the work in Africa. And with the same feverish productivity he demonstrated in beginning Wycliffe UK, he set off. In his decade and a half in Africa, he was responsible for beginning translation work in Ghana, Nigeria, Togo, Cameroon, Ivory Coast, Ethiopia, Sudan, Kenya, Burkina Faso, Senegal, Mali, Niger, Chad, Zaire (Democratic Republic of the Congo), Morocco, Republic of the Congo, Central African Republic, and Mozambique.[5]

To imagine beginning from scratch, cold calling government officials, churches, and universities, in these many places where you don't speak the local language, is staggering. And it's not as if just one team or project began in those places.

In each country, often dozens of teams and projects began. In many of these countries today, you'll find hundreds of translation projects all carried out not primarily by Western organizations but by African translation organizations. This would be another of Bendor-Samuel's contributions to the world, but this will come later.

Countless people across Africa today have the Bible who didn't even have written language seventy years ago. The institutional influence of John Bendor-Samuel marks him as one of the most influential Bible translation leaders—and missionaries—in world history.

He managed to do all this while still returning to England every summer to help run the linguistics courses. And in the summer of 1960, just as JBS was beginning his work in Africa, a young English literature student from St. Andrews would attend the first-year linguistics course. She came on the recommendation from George Cowan.

Though the course didn't cost much, even small amounts seem large to a university student, and the question arose as to who was going to pay for it. After being accepted to continue at St. Andrews for her master's degree, Katy's father was not keen on Katy spending even more money to study linguistics in the summertime. "You've got to do something and make a proper career." He said. And linguistics "would have no future as a career." Fortunately, for the world, he was wrong.

Katy paid for the course herself.

JBS met Katy that summer and served as her instructor. Her grasp of the material grew so quickly that she began helping her fellow students as if she were a graduate-level TA (teacher's assistant). JBS had a star on his hands, and unlike many middling leaders, he knew exactly how to develop her into the great linguist she'd become.

John Bendor-Samuel enlisted Katy to come back the next summer as an instructor. It may seem strange today to have a new student begin teaching introductory courses immediately after finishing them, but SIL was young and scrappy. Just like many new organizations, they thrived on a loose structure and followed talent where it led. Later it would be necessary to develop guidelines, bureaucracy, pipelines, and so forth. But back then, if you *could* do the work, they asked you to do it.

This no doubt imprinted on Katy the seeds that would come to fruition some thirty years later. As one of her many contributions to the Bible translation world, she rewrote the qualifications for Bible translation consultants from a Western-centered, degree-oriented résumé to a skills and competencies-based CV. That way, like a craftsman, translators were judged not based on years in the academy alone but on their work.

This was a revolution because it allowed gifted and competent translators from around the world a seat at the table.

Katy was a student of linguistics for only months when she became a teacher. "That was the way it was in those days."[6] Katy said. And given what Katy would go on to accomplish, asking her to teach with only a summer's experience seems the right call.

Before returning to St. Andrews for her master's degree, John Bendor-Samuel encouraged Katy to go on for her PhD. He facilitated an introduction to S.O.A.S., the School of Oriental and African Studies in London. He also introduced her to M. A. K. Halliday, an influential linguist there. Katy would eventually write her PhD dissertation on the grammar of the Mbembe language (Adun dialect) within the model Halliday had pioneered.

In the spring of 1961, Katy graduated with her master's degree from St. Andrews. Returning to the Summer Institute of Linguistics, Katy began teaching others what came so naturally to her. And there she would discover a gift for shepherding and teaching others. Though hard to quantify, some make the case that Katy's ability to shepherd and train translators is her greatest achievement. She trained hundreds of translators and translation consultants over the decades, most of whom went on to train dozens more, who went on to train dozens more. If you were to make a family tree of working translation consultants around the world, tracing their mentor back to their mentor and so on, you'd be hard-pressed to find many whose family tree does not trace directly back to Katy Barnwell.

JBS quickly began work in Ghana while Katy was away completing her MA. At first, he tried to follow Uncle Cam's footsteps. He tried to partner with governments on language development, literacy, and education. But he quickly learned that at that time African governments were much less interested in developing those materials for their minority communities.[7]

Though frustrating, JBS didn't have to spin his wheels for long. One community was keen to partner with SIL—universities. The colonial era was just dying, the corpse still warm in the ground, and the energy in Africa was palpable. African institutions and universities led by Africans were popping up across the continent.

After catching interest in Ghana, Bendor-Samuel realized that working together with Africa's universities and their linguistics departments might pave the clearest path forward. This was the strategy he and SIL took in most West African engagements. This second African engagement would go on to become the most influential in Africa and possibly in worldwide Bible translation: Nigeria.

Nigeria is the most populous African country and has more than 520 indigenous living languages.[8] This is more than any country in Africa and more than almost every country on earth. And unlike other countries in which, for example, Mandarin, Swahili, Portuguese, or Arabic was the Lingua Franca, English is the most widely used trade language and even one of the official languages of Nigeria. This meant that not only native English speakers but just about any Westerner, for whom English is often a second language if not a first, could travel and work there, already equipped with the primary language of wider communication.

After completing her master's at St. Andrews, Katy returned to teach at the Summer Institute of Linguistics. Because of JBS's leadership, many of the students in residence were headed not for the Americas but for Africa.

Bendor-Samuel began preparing Katy for her PhD, her long-term service to the summer linguistics courses, and for a life of ministry in Nigeria. But there was one thing Katy lacked. And if she wanted to join Bible translation, she had some catching up to do.

Chapter 7

SERVING THE CHURCH

In the fall of 1961, plans were for Katy to return in the summer of 1962 for the second set of applied linguistics courses. But she'd already finished her master's. What should she do in the meantime? Go to Africa? No. Not yet.

Wycliffe and SIL leadership asked Katy to get real leadership experience in a church. Today, it's unlikely that such a request would be made of a young translator in training, but the times were different. If she were to be engaged in Bible translation, she ought to have more ministry leadership experience.

And so Katy packed her bags and moved to a city in the UK called Gillingham. At the time, it was an industrial area in Kent. Within days she began service in a local church. And there she would have an experience she didn't seek but has longed for ever since.

Arriving in Gillingham, Katy received her job description. She would lead Bible classes, meet and lead women's meetings, and visit the shut-ins and sick in the hospital.

Katy served in an Evangelical Anglican church. And though the church was not Pentecostal or charismatic, the Holy Spirit has a way of refusing to be bound by our expectations.

The church broke out in revival. According to Katy, regular people who'd never thought much about the gifts of the Spirit suddenly broke out in them, speaking in tongues they did not understand, prophesying, and having truths and secrets revealed to them that had never been shared with anybody. There were healings. The whole community was caught up in it.

Katy was not part of a tradition that even talked about these things. She didn't claim to understand it, but she welcomed it gladly.

One of the criticisms of charismatic revival is that it can tend toward emotivism, a jumbled mass of exultation without much structure or assurance of correct teaching. It's a consistent critique because it's a fair one. This is no different in our day than it was in the apostle Paul's. For this reason, Paul wrote the lines that are often the most ignored in charismatic traditions:

> What then, brothers and sisters? Whenever you come together, each one has a hymn, a teaching, a revelation, a tongue, or an interpretation. Everything is to be done for building up. If anyone speaks in a tongue, there are to be only two, or at the most three, each in turn, and let someone interpret. But if there is no interpreter, that person is to keep silent in the church and speak to himself and God. . . . And the prophets' spirits are subject to the prophets, since God is not a God of disorder but of peace.[1]

Oftentimes, Paul's counsel is ignored, and people pray openly in tongues without interpretation. But it's as if God had marked Katy for language work not only in her vocation but even in her temporary spiritual gift.

Katy found that she was able to interpret these languages. She doesn't know if these were languages on earth somewhere or not, but she simply understood them while others could not. Getting wrapped up in this sort of thing may be the last thing you'd expect of Katy Barnwell, with her scholarly demeanor. But there she was. A revival broke out around her, and much to her surprise, she said, she was one of the only ones who understood what people were saying.

As a testament to her character and even-keeled nature, she told me that her ability to pray in tongues and interpret served the church only during that time. There have been two other occasions in her life when she was able to pray in tongues (briefly and alone in her study), but it was not a permanent or long-term gift. It seems God gave an unsuspecting and noncharismatic scholar the gift of interpretation for a time, for the building up of the church, and did not continue to pour out this gift.

But a different kind of interpretation still lay ahead.

Katy became beloved by that community. That church. And when it was time for her to depart, they shared many tearful goodbyes.

As summer arrived, Katy boarded a train once again for the Summer Institute of Linguistics, now held at a former military base looking for a second life after the war. The place John Bendor-Samuel found on his cross-country motorcycle campaign.

In the summer of 1963, Katy studied the second year of linguistic courses. These were more advanced and continued to prepare her for PhD Study. But more importantly, they readied her for the descriptive work of cataloging and describing the language she'd be working in.

Her first summer at SIL was no fluke. In her second summer she taught brilliantly. And in her third summer, twenty-four-years-old and a student once again, she took the most advanced courses. Once again, she helped the other students. Whether rookies or fellow students presumably at her same level, there she was, night after night, coaching them through the material.

Though a student, she once again was confused for a graduate TA. SIL leaders asked if she would return to help run the courses as often as fieldwork would allow. Katy heeded the request and went on to teach on and off at British SIL for decades. The all-star translators who first studied under her now have gone on to write cutting-edge scholarship, lead organizations, and line the boards of many of the major Bible translation organizations around the world.

Chapter 8

LONDON AND JOHN STOTT

The way SIL students often pursued doctoral study in those days was to first take one to two years of coursework. Then they would move to the field and begin their full-time work with SIL. After a few years on the field, having written hundreds of pages of grammatical notes on the language, they would return to finish their PhD—often a grammatical description of a language that had never before been written. Previously undocumented languages began pouring into the academy with full grammatical descriptions. The secular linguistics community had no numbers or funding to catalog hundreds, let alone thousands of minority languages around the world. The linguistics community owes much to the work of SIL during this time. It's likely that throughout all of human history, SIL may have done more for language preservation than any organization on the earth.

At that time, Katy moved to London to begin her PhD under M. A. K. Halliday. Noam Chomsky was just happening upon the scene then. He would go on to become the most influential linguist of the twentieth century. His grammatical method was much more laser focused on language alone. Though this didn't allow for the fuller anthropological complexity of a model that took in history, culture, body language, and so on, it was effective at analyzing language. His generative grammar also paired well with the advent of computer systems that needed neat binary information trees to process information. Generative grammar allowed for that.

But European linguists weren't as keen on the model. Human language use is not distinct from human culture, history, anthropology, or body language. SIL and most European linguists preferred a more holistic approach.

Katy spent a year learning Halliday's model with the goal of producing a grammatical description of the Mbembe language from Halliday's particular linguistic theory. She also took courses that would aid her work. She remembers lexicography, particularly, the science of compiling dictionaries. This was one of her many goals in the language where she'd be assigned.

Around this time, she was introduced to her team—Ian and Amelia Gardner and Patricia Revill. Together they'd sail to Africa to begin their work.

After living most of her life in smaller cities and villages, Katy now found herself in one of the largest cities in the world.[1] She lived in an apartment and traveled by the tube. She also attended All Souls Langham Place, the church whose pulpit held John Stott, one of the most influential Evangelicals of the twentieth century—and according to *Time Magazine*, one of the most influential people in the world.[2] He and Billy Graham may be called the most influential Evangelicals, even Protestants, of the second half of the twentieth century.[3] Not many years later, they'd go head-to-head. At the Lausanne conference of 1974, arguably the most influential missionary conference of the twentieth century, a momentous division arose.

Because of the particular climate in the United States, there had grown a suspicion of churches and missions organizations that spent a great deal of time and resources helping the least fortunate—as Jesus did. Evangelicals had previously been the first to advocate for the marginalized, the weak, and the oppressed in earlier times in America but not anymore. The abolition movement, the improvement of factory and working conditions, women's suffrage, and even animal rights all owed a great debt to committed Bible-reading Christians.

But because of the Liberal and Fundamentalist divide in the 1920s–1930s, this began to change. Many denominations and Bible-based churches lost their way, departing from the creeds and any recognizable confession of the historic Christian faith. The reality of the virgin birth, the meaning of Christ's cross, the historicity of Jesus's bodily resurrection—all thrown out. In an attempt to syncretize to a modern disenchanted Western society that refused to consider the possibility of miracles, they'd neutered Scripture and turned historical beliefs about the divinity of Jesus into myth.

It would take generations for these churches and denominations to die—though die, they certainly would. No church that stands on water can hold its ground for long.

But it would take time. They still had their people. They still had their funding. Only now, they were much less interested in sharing the good news of Jesus.

If Jesus were only a symbol, a metaphor, a psychology for the good that is in humanity, why bother? Certainly, Hindus, Muslims, atheists, and agnostics have symbols, metaphors, and psychology. If Jesus is not necessary, and if the supernatural world along with its afterlife isn't even real, why take the trouble to send missionaries or evangelize at all?

Many limp-wristed Protestant churches in that era saw a great rechanneling of their resources. Bible study, evangelism, and missions would have to go. Maybe they were offensive, or misguided, or wrong, or flat-out sinful. If Christ weren't the only way, how dare they preach his name to those who don't know him?

All the money and man-hours the wayward churches had been spending on missions and evangelism were now turned toward Jesus's call to love your neighbor and to fulfill his call toward the socially marginalized. This is a real call of Jesus to his followers. But it's not to be divorced from repentance, salvation, the cross, and the resurrection. In fact, adherence to the latter should only enhance the work of the former.

When the theologically wishy-washy churches doubled down on the work of social action with no gospel or cross attached to it, theological conservatives looked across the aisle and came to suspect this social action as somehow misguided, even harmful to the faith. It was as if following the one great command of Jesus to "love your neighbor," somehow kept a Christian from following the other great command of Jesus, "Make disciples."[4]

The good news was split in two. On the one hand, the good news of Jesus was made almost entirely spiritual. When you die, you'll be saved from your sins and live with him forever. What we need to do is share this information with everybody. Let them live their lives as they are, but get this packet of how to get saved into their hands. Anything beyond this is a distraction.

On the other hand, those who overcorrected the opposite direction came to believe that Jesus came not so much for the spiritual but the physical. He came to heal and save us from disease, poverty, oppression, marginalization, and racism. What we needed to do was orphan and widow care, water treatment, education, justice work, and so on.

Of course, biblically, both hands matter. They simply need to be clasped together instead of severed from one another, a posture most of the church throughout time has taken.[5]

The UK never suffered the kind of unhealthy split that North America did. Stott regularly preached that in highlighting the Great Commission in Matthew, to go and make disciples, we are far too quick to forget the other Great Commission in John 20:21: "As the Father has sent me, I also send you."

And one of Jesus's great purpose statements is to fulfill the prophecy of Isaiah regarding the Messiah, the Suffering Servant. Jesus was sent to proclaim good news to the poor, to give sight to the blind and release to the captives, and to liberate the oppressed. John 20:21 is clear. As he was sent, so are we.

Billy Graham tried to make that inaugural Lausanne conference and a follow-up conference in Mexico all about evangelism, at the expense of serving, caring, and loving as Jesus did. Stott wouldn't have it and threatened to resign the committee entirely.[6] Fortunately, John Stott and Billy Graham met, and Graham recognized his error. Billy Graham publicly admitted he'd been swayed by "pressure without thought or prayer."[7]

If it were not for Stott, the global missions movement may have made the same mistake as many American churches, spiritualizing the good news of Jesus to something that concerns only the soul and only matters after this life, not during it, and not in a way that influences or ministers to the surrounding community.

But John Stott held his ground. And Graham recognized his error.

This was Katy's pastor. The kind of man who could stand toe to toe with Billy Graham, calling him out publicly, and be right. And go on to be his friend.

John Stott and Katy Barnwell knew each other by name and saw each other every Sunday. She was simply one of his parishioners then. It's amazing to imagine two of the most influential Christians born in the twentieth century chumming it up at Sunday evening Bible study. She took much from those Bible studies, and she never forgot his teachings.

You cannot divorce the good news of salvation from the good news of the King and his kingdom. And wedding these two ideas is precisely what Katy did with her life's work.

Bible translation proclaims the good news of salvation from sin and also the good news of the kingdom. Jesus is King, and he comes to free us from imposter kings. He saves us from evil spirits, poverty, disease, oppression, and ultimately, death itself. It's only in the good news of Jesus that we can proclaim, "O death, where is thy sting? O grave, where is thy victory?"[8]

Bible translation is powerful precisely for these reasons. It proclaims the King and it proclaims his kingdom. It proclaims the remarkable value of every human being—not just the strong, the healthy, and the intelligent but also the elderly person in the advanced stages of Alzheimer's, the baby in the womb, the marginalized, the disabled. They are all equal in the eyes of God and just as worthy as any senator or king.

This is why, throughout history, the powerful have so feared true Christianity and its holy book. What would become of their power if the poor, the women, the diseased, and the disabled thought they were just as valuable before God as they, the rulers![9]

We in the West are used to this idea because we think this is the stuff of basic human rights. But these were not human rights anywhere before Christianity, and they still are not in most parts of the world where the Old and New Testaments have not deeply infiltrated. What we take for the Universal Declaration of Human Rights, a so-called secular document, is distinctly built on the Jewish and Christian idea of the image of God, the *imago Dei* in all human beings. To many others this is laughable. Many Muslim intellectuals long ago figured this out, and it's why a number of Muslim countries reject the supposedly secular Western idea of human rights. They know how Christian it is.[10]

An old Hindu proverb states, "The tears of a stranger are only water." Jesus says:

> "For I was hungry and you gave me something to eat; I was thirsty and you gave me something to drink; I was a stranger and you took me in; I was naked and you clothed me; I was sick and you took care of me; I was in prison and you visited me."
>
> "Then the righteous will answer him, 'Lord, when did we see you hungry and feed you, or thirsty and give you something to drink? When did we see you a stranger and take you in, or without clothes and clothe you? When did we see you sick, or in prison, and visit you?'

"And the King will answer them, 'Truly I tell you, whatever you did for one of the least of these brothers and sisters of mine, you did for me.'"[11]

The equality of all people, the charge to help the least fortunate as a service unto Jesus himself, is a distinctly Christian idea.

Katy Barnwell could have remained in London. She could have made a career at elite universities and enjoyed financial security, rootedness, and fellowship among peers in her own language and culture.

But she followed Jesus so closely. She so identified with his heart for the least fortunate that she never seemed to consider it. When she was laid up with malaria or slowly starving during the Biafran Civil War, she never even thought to feel sorry for herself.

"Truly I tell you, whatever you did for one of the least of these brothers and sisters of mine, you did for me."[12]

Chapter 9

PREPARING TO DEPART

Though Katy had been working for years at the Summer Institute of Linguistics, she had not yet applied to be a full-time employee of Wycliffe or SIL. In 1963, she applied and was immediately accepted—the application being by that time simply a formality. It was time to begin "raising support," as it's called. In the twentieth century, this fairly novel practice of financing missionaries became the dominant means of mission-sending.

Early missionaries and some today still go as "tentmakers." This is a reference to the apostle Paul largely paying his own way from time to time by his trade of leatherworking, possibly in the area of constructing large tents.[1] In this *tentmaking* model, missionaries go abroad and work in any number of areas to put food on the table, learn the language, and get involved in the community.

Still others finance their missionary work using a *missions organization* model like the IMB—the International Missions Board of the Southern Baptists, one of the largest sending agencies in the world. These missionaries are hired and paid a salary. Though they visit churches and will often have prayer partners, they are paid by the IMB directly.

Lastly, and by far the most common method of financing missionaries today in Evangelical circles is through *support raising*. In this model, each missionary or missionary family communicates with churches, family members, and friends. They share about how God is moving in a particular area and how they plan to serve. Then they ask those churches, families, and friends to financially support them in that work. The missionary and their organization do the math on the cost of living in their particular field, from Zurich to India, and everywhere in between.[2] They build their budget around what they expect to pay to live there. Once they calculate the monthly amount needed, they raise support with that figure as the final goal. All donations—some given as a one-time gift and others as an ongoing monthly donation—are given to the parent organization, which is a nonprofit. Those donations are earmarked for the ministry of the missionary in mind. As churches and individuals pledge to donate regularly, they move toward their goals. Once they reach a certain percentage, say, 90 or 100 percent, they can move to their ministry location. To honor the donors or "supporters" that comprise a missionary's giving team, the missionary keeps these donors informed of the missionary work by means of regular letters or emails.

Thousands of people raised their support through Wycliffe to do Bible translation. Around the world, many tens of thousands have done the same through other organizations.

Though Katy grew into somebody with wonderful social skills, adored by people on all inhabited continents, she was still coming out of her shell at this point.

Getting a PhD? Going to a tribe in a malarial hotbed? These endeavors sounded fun (or at least adventurous). But asking people for money? Even Katy had her limit.

Most missionaries spend eight to eighteen months raising support full-time to reach the level they'll need.[3] But for Katy, God had a different plan.

The curate (or parish priest) who'd invited Katy to serve at the church in Gillingham was diagnosed with cancer. But he was able to see what God was doing through Katy. He'd gone through a revival with her.

As the curate's cancer progressed, he and his loved ones made final arrangements. He told the church that when he passed, he did not want a memorial in his name. He did not want a scholarship, a sculpture, or anything like it. He wanted the Word of God written not on stone but on hearts. He asked that for his memorial the church would instead support the work of Bible translation through Katy's ministry.

When he passed, the church began supporting Katy and so did many of its members. Sixty years later, the church and those members still living today continue to give.

Around the same time, Katy became connected with another church. By this point, her parents had moved to Goring-on-Thames, the village Katy would later come to call home. Katy attended the Anglican church in Goring whenever she visited her parents. The priest there admired her work, but the modern missions model didn't work in the Anglican church. As mentioned previously, the Anglican church employed the model in which the denomination or church body itself would oversee the hiring and sending of missionaries. Instead of raising support, a new missionary would be paid a salary from the church, diocese, or denomination.

In the new era of Bible translation, there were many like the Anglicans who wanted to participate, but the wheels moved too fast for their models. They were well established in the traditional church-sending model. Though a good model, it was a model slow to adapt to new kinds of missions. The systematic, programmatic approach of Wycliffe Bible Translators was new. And since the Anglicans didn't start that kind of mission, they had no bureaucratic means to fund it, at least not easily.

But the priest gave Katy a piece of advice: "Why don't you walk down to the Free Church and ask them?" (The Anglican church and the Free Church sit exactly today where they did in 1963, about a four-minute walk between them.) Katy walked to

Goring Free Church and introduced herself. As it turned out, they had been seeking a missionary to support but didn't know of anyone. God works in mysterious ways.

Goring Free Church began financially supporting Katy then. They made up the majority of her financial support from the beginning and throughout her life. They did so faithfully, having little idea that Katy was set apart from the average missionary. They received her newsletters. And when Katy was in the UK, it was always her home church.

Katy is painfully humble about her talent. "Everything I did, I did in teams," she protests. "I was simply at the right place and right time."

Though her humility is admirable, for six decades, you'd be hard-pressed to find a Bible translation innovation she didn't invent, or at least have her hands on in the beginning stages. But because she was the only Bible translation worker supported by her home church, they had little idea just how influential she was.

Around the 1990s, the hints began to sneak in. A scholar familiar with Katy's work would come through to lecture at one of the nearby universities, like Reading or Oxford. They would stay in town to visit Katy and her church. When her church community met these visiting scholars, they'd think, *Wow, this person is lecturing at Oxford!* And yet the scholar would turn to Katy's fellow church members and say, "Wow, I can't believe you get to attend church with Katy Barnwell!"[4]

To see Oxford scholars starstruck by Katy was a surprise. To her church, she was just Katy. That's the effect she has on those around her.

Because Katy actively avoided the limelight and cared nothing for recognition, little has been written about her. She's not part of the "Evangelical industrial complex," as some American Christians call it (given that it's a particularly American type of ecosystem). She speaks at no conferences outside her profession, markets nothing, and writes only training materials and academic research. And because of her disdain for acknowledging her impact, her church had to get by on newsletters filtered through her humility and these occasional fawning moments from outside visitors.

When my October 2022 cover story was published in *Christianity Today* about her wide-reaching influence, it was the first time Katy's own church got the chance to read the full story. This small church in England had little idea how many hundreds of millions of people around the world met Christ because of their faithful prayers, love, and financial support for Katy these sixty years.

As painfully humble and as serious as Katy can be, she has an acerbic comedic genius that sneaks through from time to time. When I finished asking Katy about her home church and their great support, she got that look in her eye.

"Yes, well, I hope they've gotten their money's worth." She smirked.

Chapter 10

ALL THE SINGLE LADIES

"That's the advantage of being single. You haven't got any ties."
—Katharine Barnwell

*"The unmarried woman or virgin is concerned about
the things of the Lord, so that she may be holy both in body
and in spirit. But the married woman is concerned about the
things of the world—how she may please her husband."*
1 Corinthians 7:34

Because of his training experience at SIL UK, John
Bendor-Samuel had ample opportunity to recruit and
arrange teams. Unless a missionary was incredibly seasoned,
going alone was rarely wise. They went instead in twos. When
one was weak—physically, spiritually, mentally, or emotionally—the other could be strong. They could help each other.
And for Katy, JBS had identified a strong potential assignment
in Southeastern Nigeria. And he suspected he'd found her the
right teammate.

Katy was introduced to a small traveling team who would
become lifelong friends. Ian and Amelia Gardner were married
and a few years older than Katy. Though they did not work in
the same region—they served together in the Nigeria branch of
SIL and would go on to remain friends until today. Their son
Andrew remembers Katy's influence well during his youth. He

and his parents helped contribute to the sourcing of this biography. When we first connected, Andrew wrote, "On a table nearby is a beautiful Nigerian textile that [Katy] gave me when I got married in 1997; somehow she managed to find the time to attend the wedding, which must have been a major challenge for her, given her workload and her travels."[1]

There was one more who Katy would travel to Nigeria with. Patricia Revill, a single woman about Katy's age.

If you visit a few dozen church plants and missionary teams across the globe, you will begin to notice a bizarre trend. At the foundation of almost any expat team, you'll find one or two married couples and a host of single women. There are no single men.

There's an old joke in missions that two out of every three missionaries are married couples. One in three missionaries is a single woman. The rest are single men.

This is not a new problem. Female missionaries have outnumbered male missionaries for a long time. One of the reasons is that women outnumber men in Christianity. Serious believers are more likely to be women, and that's largely always been the case.[2]

One of the early pagan critiques of Christianity came from Celsus, a Greek philosopher writing in the second century. Dripping with the misogyny of pagans at that time, he criticized Christianity as being a religion for women and slaves. True and properly educated men were not led astray by the Christian message, Celsus argued. Only the "silly, and the mean, and the stupid," as well as "women and children."[3]

Not only are there more women than men in Christianity (as well as in most other world religions),[4] but men often have more opportunities for service—especially during Katy's formative years. Gifted male leaders in church were often pegged for pastoral leadership, academia, administrative leadership in Christian organizations, and other ministry positions.

Missions was one of the few areas in the twentieth century where women could serve in nearly an equal capacity. Regardless of someone's theology on women's roles in the church, those differences tended to blur on the field. There's a kind of pragmatic uniformity to much of mission work. Whoever can do the work does the work. That's it. Not to mention that in contrast to preaching in a pulpit on Sundays or overseeing a team of elders or deacons in a weekly meeting about budgets, the lion's share of the ministry work on the field involves building relationships, learning new languages, working a job, keeping a low profile to avoid persecution, and sharing the gospel—all things any Christian can do if they have the spine for it.

Talk to nearly any woman in ministry in the US, and if she's willing, she could talk about the challenges she's faced as a woman in ministry. But in Bible translation, there may not be as many stories to tell. Katy swears that being a woman didn't limit her at all.

I reminded her then that most of her male colleagues who held half a candle to her résumé went on to serve as presidents of Wycliffe, SIL, and similar organizations.

"Yes, but I never *wanted* to do that," she said.

"Many of them didn't either," I said. "But the organizations felt they needed them, appointed them, and they answered the call of leadership. Don't you think if you were a man, the same may have happened to you?"

Her face became troubled, a rare look for Katy. She looked straight ahead but saw only what was in her mind's eye.

"Well, yes," she admitted. "I suppose there may be something to that." From my chair, it seemed she'd never considered the question before.

The troubled look vanished from her face then as quickly as it came. Her eyes brightened and she turned to me. "All the same, I'm glad I was never asked." And she meant it.

Katy's love was for the people, the languages, the shepherding. She was not interested in board meetings or acquiring ever larger donations. People all over the world addressed her as Mama Katy for a reason, and she didn't earn the name in a boardroom.

Chapter 11

SAILING FOR NIGERIA

A few weeks before Christmas in 1964, Katy made use of her father's railway benefits and took the train to Liverpool, one of the busiest ports in England. There, on a cold and bleak day in December, she met her traveling companions and Nigeria branch colleagues Ian and Amelia Gardner and Patricia Revill.

Though air travel was becoming more common in those days, it was still the norm for missionaries to travel to their assignments via ship. Especially the first time when they'd be bringing more luggage. In front of them on the port, there awaited not a large vessel or a relocating cruise ship, but by today's standards, a small cargo boat that took on a dozen passengers. The ship was named the *Tamele*, capable of transporting a gross tonnage of 7,172 pounds, whereas many large cargo ships today carry a gross tonnage of more than 200,000.[1] The journey took two to three weeks, and Katy had little idea how she'd adapt to life at sea. The smaller the boat, the harder the effects of the sea. Fortunately, Katy handled the ocean just fine. Her fellow passengers could not all say the same.

For Katy, the weeks at sea were a gift. It would be a long time until we figured this out as a society, but the human mind takes time to adjust to new circumstances. Having two to three weeks in transit prepares a person for the radical changes ahead. It was discovered later, when so many American soldiers were returning from Vietnam and ending up in a much worse mental state than soldiers returning from WWII, that flying them home was a serious contributing factor.[2] One moment, the soldiers from Vietnam could be dealing and receiving tremendous violence, their lives in the balance. Thirty-six hours later, they're sitting at their kitchen table in middle America with mashed potatoes on their plate. And Auntie can't understand why Tommy doesn't seem thrilled to be home. In contrast, soldiers returning to the US from WWII most often traveled by boat, alongside the men they'd fought shoulder to shoulder with for many months. They had weeks to decompress in community and ready themselves to transition back to homelife.[3]

Missionaries in hard places today struggle with a similar phenomenon. One minute they're keeping quiet, whisper worshipping, watching for terrorists, intelligence agents, or informants. As few as twelve to twenty-four hours later, they're standing before churches, under intense pressure to smile, stay positive, have perfect children, and never say anything negative about their colleagues, their situation, their lack of member care, or their bosses. The pressure to sugarcoat and stay positive is suffocating. Otherwise, they seem too critical, not filled with the Spirit, and less likely to keep their donors. Missionaries often end up feeling homeless—not quite at home abroad in their second or third or fifth language and not quite at home among people who can't understand—and don't really want to.

Missionaries who've returned home for good or on furlough often find a kind of kinship with other missionaries. It's a shared understanding known to few others in the world.

Katy and the other dozen passengers had time to think, prepare, study Scripture, and pray. In one of her early updates to prayer partners and financial supporters, Katy wrote:

Schools of porpoises curving in and out of the waves
. . . small flying fish skimming over the surface. . . .

Even in mid-ocean there were many interesting sights on the voyage out to Africa. Our fellow passengers on the "Tamele" were all West Africans, mostly Nigerian students returning home after courses in Britain, who never tired of telling us about the geography, customs, scenery, and food of Nigeria. We even learnt a few words of Igbo, the main language of the Eastern region.[4]

As the days and weeks went by, the winter air gave way to tropical air. Humidity and salt breeze filled their nostrils. They dined together, and Katy got to know Patricia (Pat), her assigned partner and flatmate in the work to come.

In an email, Pat told me of the fun, youthful shenanigans they'd be up to. "We called at Douala in Cameroun where Ian was drafted in to play football/soccer for the crew against a local team. I'm not sure but I think the local team won!"[5]

Though Patricia would marry a few years later and return to the UK, her friendship was invaluable in those early years. It's doubtful Katy would have remained as long if she didn't have the strong start she did.

Katy thought they may have entered through Lagos, Nigeria's largest city, but she doesn't remember the specific route. Luckily, she kept all of her passports. Following the entry and exit stamps, it's clear that Katy and the team sailed not to Lagos, but to Victoria in West Cameroon.[6] There, the team either caught a different vessel or the ship turned around, eventually docking at Port Harcourt in Nigeria. Today, with the advantage of modern roads and bridges, Port Harcourt sits only seven hours from where Katy wanted to go. But then there were no bridges. There were no roads.

At Port Harcourt, in Southeastern Nigeria, they were met by a colleague named Jack Henderson. Katy and Pat were certainly some of the earliest Wycliffe missionaries in Nigeria, but a handful of teams preceded them by twelve to eighteen months. This eased things for Katy and Pat. The first partnerships had been made. Some infrastructure was already in place. But many moments of culture shock still awaited.

"When we disembarked at Port Harcourt," Pat wrote, "Jack was there to meet us and help us get transport to Enugu. I remember being quite shocked at the change in the pace of life. We waited around outside the docks for what seemed like hours, and Jack showed no sign of impatience or movement to do anything about the situation. At last, a lorry appeared and he negotiated with the driver and we all piled in with our baggage and set off on the three-hour drive to Enugu."[7]

Jack Henderson took them to a house that served as a kind of headquarters for Nigerian operations.[8] Days after their arrival, Katy would experience the first three-week language and linguistics-centered meeting of her career. It's a pattern she'd continue to use until the end of her time abroad.

In those days, SIL's linguists in Africa often partnered with language and anthropology departments at budding African universities. The University at Nsukka provided just such a place. There, most Wycliffe and SIL linguists in the region came together to share notes. Many of these were friends, students who'd gone before or studied under Katy at the Summer Institute of Linguistics in the UK.

In a letter to her ministry supporters, Katy wrote: "Those who have been here a year have now tentatively settled the basis for the orthography of their languages, and after a few more months working on the grammar and learning to speak more fluently, will be looking forward to beginning literacy work and the first tentative Bible translation."[9] Katy couldn't wait. Soon it would be her turn.

This was the first time Katy saw the fruits of such collaboration. Each person brought knowledge, breakthroughs, and questions the whole group could weigh in on. She saw that it greatly accelerated the overall success of each person present. Iron sharpens iron, and getting bright minds together means more creativity per minute. It's a feature of human nature.

Thirty years later, Katy would harness this potential in what we now call the Cluster Model, what some still consider to be the greatest success of her working life.

After three weeks of academic bliss, it was time to get practical. Living in rural, off-grid sub-Saharan Africa is no joke. And any missions organization that sends Westerners in without proper training is begging for failure or even death.

SIL had long been in the business of keeping their people as healthy and prepared as possible. So Katy headed for what was called the "Field Training Course." Pat called this the "West African equivalent of Jungle Camp where new members learnt how to cope with village living." There, they'd live in a village and learn in real time the skills for making a life in a village.

At this point, a missionary could still be sent home. If they were deemed unable or unfit to serve in that capacity, they may have to find a more developed or cushy place to work or return home.

But with Katy's experience in Girl Guides, she found herself more than ready.

Sometimes modern readers can be offended at the idea of a missionary going to live with a tribe. Remembering some of the many evils of colonialism, this can be well-founded. But often, it takes on a kind of racism of its own, discounting the humanity, intelligence, and agency of the people among whom the missionary works.

Rarely is a Westerner offended at a Nigerian missionary or church planter coming to the West to share the gospel. Or of Saudi missionary work in inner cities or Buddhist missionary outreach.[10] And this they do. Many of the largest churches in Europe and the United States are run by Nigerian missionaries and church planters.[11] But the Westerner is not offended by this because Westerners recognize that they have the rights of personal agency and access to information. It's up to us what we choose to believe or follow.

But these same basic rights of agency and access to information are oftentimes not offered to indigenous people. Many Westerners, though they may not realize it, treat non-Western indigenous people groups as if they are somehow less deserving of these rights. As if the ones truly fit to decide what information they should have access to are Western anthropologists. But don't indigenous people deserve literacy and religious freedoms too? Don't they deserve to learn of Buddhism and Islam and Christianity, and so on, and with their own agency decide for themselves? Don't they deserve to learn to read? To keep their own history? To lower their infant mortality? To eradicate leprosy? Why should so few of their young make it past age five? Who are we to withhold their access to information—religious or otherwise—and their agency? Who are we to lock them in a museum exhibit?

There has been a debate around this, but it's largely dying off now. Anthropology as a discipline has come to recognize that its antimissionary expression was often just as patronizing and racist as the policies it replaced. It also helped to humble them that their discipline largely grew out of missionary work and that then and now tribes around the world much prefer missionaries to anthropologists.[12]

Fortunately, those involved in Bible translation are almost always spared the discomfort and the debate. For many years now, Bible translation has been primarily led by locals and for locals, only sometimes with outside help and support from the major Bible translation organizations.[13] Under the Common Framework in place today (see chapter 33), most Western Bible translation organizations won't work with a people unless they are invited.

Native speakers, local leaders, and local churches must decide they want Scripture access, literacy, audio Bibles or oral Bible storytelling, or *The Jesus Film* before entering into an agreement. This agreement is often signed, though paperwork exceptions are made for people groups in areas where Christianity is illegal and persecuted.

These invitations, local leadership, and local agency were codified by the signing of the Common Framework by the most influential Bible translation agencies on the planet, together responsible for 85 percent of Bible translation worldwide.

Katy and Pat would have these same invitations. They did not consider going somewhere uninvited.

"We were very moved to hear a Christian from the Agbo tribe, where one of our teams is working, tell so earnestly and sincerely of what it meant to him and his people to receive the Bible in their own language. Now, he said, they would understand what God said to them; now they would 'see His face.' I praise God for giving me a part in this and thank Him too for all those of you who are partners with me. May He increase our faith and expectation as we continue in prayer to remind Him of His will to 'establish Jerusalem in all the earth.'"[14]

Chapter 12

JUNGLE CAMP

T alk to any old-timer in Bible translation who served in the Americas, and they'll tell you about Jungle Camp. Many a strong translator came prepared to the task of Bible translation with the passion and biblical and linguistic skills to do the work. But moving scholars from one of the most advanced places on earth to a completely off-grid jungle existence is a tall order. No electricity, no running water. It broke many in their first months.

How are you to acquire a bed if there is no furniture store? With no running water, where will you go to the bathroom? Can you depend on a people you've just met to build a hut for you? No, you must be able to do this yourself. In order to train linguists to survive in their assignments, SIL opened a training camp in southern Mexico.

Jungle Camp was a four-month ordeal, and it took place in multiple stages. First, easing the translators in, they met in the Dallas-Fort Worth area. They spent two weeks in a classroom setting. Then, they bused down to Mexico City for another two weeks—learning, acclimating to the culture, and taking culturally enriching day trips. Then the real work started.

They bused down to Chiapas and, at a small airstrip, met a pilot from Missionary Aviation Fellowship. The place they were going was so remote that only the smallest of planes could fly in, landing on dirt runways cleared through the jungle. They flew to a remote area called Yaxoquintela.

While there, they worked through three successive stages, the "main base," "advanced base," and "village living."[1] There, they lived in mud huts, learned how to kill and prepare meat from animals, and how to cook and clean without the conveniences of modern appliances.

They took long hikes, progressing to multiple-day hikes. At night, they rigged hammocks and slept under the tree canopy. Learning to climb into a hammock with a mosquito net and zip yourself inside it made for many self-deprecating stories. But even if mosquitos were taken care of, their nets and repellent did little to ward off fleas, which infested their bodies.[2]

This was only the *main* base experience. At *advanced* base, they had to build their own huts, beds, outhouses, and everything they'd need to survive. As one participant notes, "We built our own bed, chairs, tables, stove, and places to put our kitchen equipment, food, clothing, and whatever else we needed to store. We even built a toilet facility that was several feet from the house itself. It was just a hole in the ground with a seat made of branches of trees cut to just the right size."[3]

They walked with their emergency survival hike gear on them in backpacks at all times. Part of the conceit of Jungle Camp was preparing the missionaries for an immediate departure without forewarning. Civil wars, natural disasters, terrorism, or any number of events can and do bring calamity on missionaries. They needed to be ready. They would not know the day or hour, but when the whistle sounded, they needed to go.

On a simulated emergency hike, each person needed to make their own camp, their own fire, and eat whatever they could gather, hunt, or trap from the land. In a real situation, a strong fire starter could light a fire or trap game for the whole crew, but you never knew when you would be caught alone. Each person needed to be fully equipped.

The final phase of Jungle Camp involved living in a rural village with no Westerners at all. Each trainee was assigned a village and a family SIL already had contact with. Then they were scattered. They needed to use the language skills they'd studied, their survival skills, and whatever else they'd learned to emulate the first five weeks of their future assignment.

SIL's Mexico Jungle Camp was famous, and infamous, for how many people dropped out. *This isn't the life for me,* many thought. But for those who made it, it hardened them and taught them the skills necessary for survival.

Many hundreds if not thousands of linguists went through Jungle Camp over the years, whether working in the Americas or around the world.[4] We're only scratching the surface on the history of Jungle Camp.

But given the distance from the UK and the different needs on the field, John Bendor-Samuel realized quickly that the Mexican Jungle Camp, though helpful, did not teach the same set of skills needed in Africa as were needed in the jungles of Central and South America.

They replaced Jungle Camp with an African variety. Some of the skills were the same, but a few were different. Africa, Nigeria in particular, is different from Central and South America. Nigeria is densely populated compared to the jungles of the Americas. Find a river and you won't be separated from civilization for long. There was also no risk of freezing at night, like in the mountainous highlands of Mexico. In some ways, it may have seemed safer, but it was not.

One cause of death had killed more missionaries than anything since the time of Jesus. Sub-Saharan Africa, including Nigeria, was known as the "white man's graveyard." The four horsemen of tropical disease—yellow fever, dengue, cholera, and the primary horseman, outkilling all the others combined, malaria.

In *Pioneering on the Congo,* William Holman Bentley records in his *Appendix I* a list of missionaries who arrived in the Congo between 1879 and 1886, undergoing the same risks as missionaries in Nigeria. Bentley noted the year they arrived and their current status. What a sobering sight it is. Beginning at missionary 13 and counting to 28, the right column, titled "Remarks" reads:

Died at Wathen

Died at Lukunga

Died at Manyanga

Died at Wathen

Died at Underhill

[No remark, still living]

Died at Underhill

Died at S. Salvador

Returned [home]

Died at Underhill

Died at Arthington

Died at Wathen

Died at Wathen

Died at Underhill

Died at Banana

Died at sea

Only a handful survived. Most died of disease within months or fewer years than you can count with one hand. Others died at sea. Some gave up and returned home.[5]

The risk of death due to disease became so well known that missionaries preparing to embark for West Africa in the nineteenth century would pack their belongings not in suitcases but in coffins.[6] The symbolism was well understood. You will sail to Africa to bring the good news of a Savior. And most likely, in little time, you will meet the same fate as those who've gone before you. When you arrive in the field, you'll remove your belongings. But it may not be long before the coffin is filled again.

The truck pulled up bright yellow, with the words "clear conscience" painted over the front.[7] On this truck, they traveled all the way to Adoru, Nigeria, the village that hosted Jungle Camp.

Katy and the team of new missionaries would sleep in grass shelters, drinking from a cistern filled with rainwater.

The missionaries learned valuable skills for making a life in rural Africa. There Katy learned to "grind guinea corn and local rice, how to butcher an antelope, how to make banana jam. Monday's class is scheduled as killing and preparing chicken. Carpentry—we are making benches and shelves, as well as improvised furniture for our own grass huts."[8]

They prepared local food for the whole group in turns. Midday was hot, so they took to the local custom of a siesta—a midday rest to avoid the direct sunlight and peak heat of the day.

They learned practical and less life-or-death skills too, like how to navigate market day, what to buy, what to avoid, and how to bargain. Katy wrote to her supporters that it was "quite a process as none of the women speak any English and we have only a few words of Igala so far."[9]

Katy went to African church then for the first time, an experience for any Westerner. "It begins at 9:00 African time (which means about 9:15, most of the congregation are there by 9:30). The women in their brightly covered scarves sit on the left, men and boys on the right. . . . They have the Bible in Igala and hymn books too, from which they sing heartily. They respond all through the sermon too, answering questions or agreeing. Occasionally a [stray] dog wanders in and is chased out by a boy with a stick who seems to be on duty for that purpose. After the service, everyone crowds around to greet us and shake hands.

Some of the small children are rather afraid. . . . They have never seen a white face before."[10]

Katy also received medical instruction and tropical hygiene during this course, which may have been some of her most important lessons. Malaria was one of the principal causes of death and long-term sickness, sending missionaries home for years at a time to recuperate. After sixty years, the majority of which were spent in Nigeria and other Malaria hotbeds, Katy contracted Malaria only a handful of times.[11]

Chapter 13

MAKING A LIFE
IN MBEMBE

LETTER FROM PAT

"At the end of the Field Training Course Katy and I were assigned to work together in a language group. We were given a choice—Jack asked each of us separately whether we wanted to work together, but we had a good friendship by that time so I did not find the decision difficult. Jack said to me, 'Katy is very strong,' perhaps thinking that our personalities might clash. But this was not a problem to me, as I needed someone stronger whose judgment I could depend on. Katy did her best to make it an equal partnership but in fact she was the natural leader.

"We were assigned to the Mbembe language group—this was the third language in which Wycliffe work was begun—following extensive language surveys by Jack Henderson and Dick Bergman exploring the many languages spoken in southeastern Nigeria. There were a very few Presbyterian and Catholic churches. The Presbyterian churches were the first churches in the Mbembe area, founded

by members of the Efik community who had trav-
elled up the river from Calabar—the Efik language
was used in Presbyterian churches and schools. In
Catholic churches English was used."[1]

Characteristic of Katy, she painted Pat as the leader of the two. It's hard to tell if this is Katy's way of honoring Pat or the way Katy's mind genuinely interprets things. Throughout her story are supposed leaders, supposed equals. But when you speak with those so-called leaders, they laugh. "No no, Katy was the leader," they say. "Did she actually say that?"

Katy did not lead forcefully but by inspiration. She moved people to great plans and great ideas. And by the nature that the ideas were first hers, she became the de facto leader. But since her ideas were so often the best ideas, it wasn't hard to follow them. And because Katy was so beloved and kind and such a team player, she was easy to follow.

Katy and Pat were assigned to the Mbembe speaking area of Southeastern Nigeria, the third actively engaged language by SIL, if Pat's memory on this is correct. The Mbembe area is about one hundred miles north of Calabar and a few days from the Cameroon border by river.

A small Christian church presence was already there. Mary Slessor had served downriver in Calabar and Akpap Okoyong. She was a missionary hero beloved by the people she ministered to. She left a legacy.

Many became Christians as a direct outcome of her ministry and went on to plant churches up and down the Cross River. This Presbyterian presence was not dominant, but there was often a small church community every second or third village. Slessor may be most famous for helping to end the practice of twin infanticide in West Africa. Before Mary Slessor, many in the region had long believed that when a mother had twins, one of the babies was conceived by an evil spirit. Because you can't know which one was evil and which was good, both were left out to die.[2]

Do missionaries change culture? Even destroy some aspects of it? Certainly, just like any other foreign influence. But you'd be hard-pressed to find a Nigerian twin today who is not happy with that change.

The Roman Catholic missionaries also arrived after the Presbyterians, but they were worshipping in English rather than the local languages. While this practice has changed since the Second Vatican Council in the early to mid 1960s, much of the Catholic world was still worshipping in Latin, or a colonial language like English—not the mother-tongue languages.[3] Only recently has the Roman Catholic Church admitted that this particular distinctive of the Reformation was a correct one. People should hear the Scripture, the liturgy, the blessing of the sacraments, the Eucharist, and hear preaching in the language they know best.[4]

Contrary to the colder relationship Roman Catholics and Protestants had in Western countries during those decades, they got along well in the field. In a climate where you're vastly outnumbered, the differences between the groups don't seem so large anymore.

Just as many non-Muslim Westerners may not know the difference between a Sunni and Shiite Muslim, many from other world religions see Christianity the same way. *I don't really understand the difference between Eastern Orthodox, Catholics, and Protestants,* they may say. *They all believe that Jesus is God, and he was with the Father in the beginning. They believe Jesus was born of a virgin, preached repentance, lived his life in service of the downtrodden, died on the cross for the forgiveness of sins, and rose again bodily on the third day, defeating sin and death. And they believe that those who put their trust in him and follow him will live with him forever.*

From an *etic* or outsider perspective, the branches of Christianity are remarkably consistent in their foundational beliefs. From an *emic* perspective, it may not seem that way.[5]

When surrounded by animism, paganism, or other religions, it was much easier for Roman Catholics and Protestants to see their commonalities over their differences. In fact, many Bible translation committees around the world came to involve representatives from all the local stripes of Christianity, from Roman Catholic, mainline or Evangelical Protestant, charismatic, Orthodox, and so on. With limited time and resources, it didn't make sense to produce four separate Bibles for four different communities. The logic made sense: why not share the labor and produce one great translation all communities could use?

But the strategies of church planters and Bible translators don't always align. Regarding the Presbyterian and Catholic missions, Katy said, "They were particularly in one dialect area, which fortunately or unfortunately, I don't know, was not the one which was linguistically most central or the largest dialect."

A HOME VILLAGE?

Now that Katy and Pat had an assignment as well as an invitation from locals to begin the work in the Mbembe language, they had difficult decisions to make. Which Mbembe dialect? Which village?

In many parts of the world then and even now, it was not known how many languages were spoken in a region, where the boundaries lay, or where languages changed.

Were the different ways people talked merely different dialects but still mutually intelligible to one another? Or were they similar, like Dutch and English, but not the same language? Or were they from the same broader language family, like French and German and Hindi are all from Indo-European (if you can believe it), or from entirely different language families, like Indo-European languages compared against Sino-Tibetan languages that stretch across much of Asia?

The reason we have such good data on how many living languages there are in the world (just over seven thousand), how many speakers they have, where exactly they're spoken, and the vibrancy of the languages in passing themselves on to younger generations is largely the work of SIL's Ethnologue. Walk into just about any research library in the world, and you'll find that they pay to have access to this resource.

One of the many reasons SIL compiles this data is to figure out how many languages, dialects, and variations of a language exist in a given area. Could some dialects be close enough to share a Bible translation? Or are all the languages unique enough to need their own? Even the Nigerian government didn't know how many languages and dialects they had in their own country. SIL and Nigerian linguists did much of that work, and now today, we know Nigeria has something like 520 different living languages.[6]

We don't know exactly why Mbembe was singled out among the twenty or so languages SIL was interested in this region. But we do know they had connections with the Presbyterian church and its pastor in the area. The local churches were led by Efik missionaries and their preaching and teaching were in Efik—not the primary local language. The church leaders heard what had been happening where the Scriptures were translated into the mother tongue, and they wanted it too. They invited Wycliffe to begin work there.

"If a Mbembe man hears God's Word, he hears it in English or Efik, both foreign languages to him,"[7] Katy wrote in 1965.

What the church wanted was the same as what Barnwell wanted. They wanted the Mbembe to hear the Word of God in their own tongue, not a foreign one.

But where should they go? Remarkably little was known about the area even by the Nigerian government. Maps often had little detail beyond a major river or road in this area.

There was little to do but travel to the area and see what they could work out. Katy, Pat, Jack Henderson, and another companion also named Katie made their way to Mbembe country.

They had plans to talk to a local chief as well as the Presbyterian pastor, but both were out of town for a few days. Nobody in the villages spoke English, and Katy had not yet had the chance to learn any Mbembe, so they found themselves discouraged. They decided they would keep on in the direction of Obubra, the district capital. There they would surely find someone who knew English.

Then the strangest thing happened.

"Jack was driving us around the area and we came to an open grass field. In the middle stood a military-looking European gentleman in full Scout uniform as worn by Baden-Powell himself. In front of him, spaced out in neat rows, were about thirty little boys, some in full uniform, some with the top or bottom half only!"[8]

"Suddenly, we came to two tall bamboo constructions and a banner across the road. 'Boy Scouts Jubilee' beside what was obviously a sports field with some major event going on. We could hardly believe our eyes. You just don't see such sights out here!"[9]

"Out of the crowd came a white man, blue and white deer stalker hat, stumpy red Charles I beard, large Scout medallion, thick khaki knee-length socks with scout tabs! We just kept blinking. This proved to be Mr. Huskinson, who is superintendent of a leprosy settlement, working with the British Leprosy Relief Association."[10]

"Thereafter 'Huskie' became a good friend—he kept a kind fatherly eye on us, and we visited him quite often. He had a kerosene refrigerator, (we didn't have one in the early days), from which he produced a delicious blackcurrant drink. Sometimes when we were traveling and extra hot we would long for a drink of 'Huskie's Vimto.' On this occasion when we first met him he allowed us to leave some of our baggage at his house to lighten the load when we moved down from Enugu."[11]

Mr. Huskinson provided much help in those days and, without knowing it, set the course for where Katy and Pat would work. Mr. Huskinson had an assistant named Mr. Arrobo. He was a former leper himself, had lived in the leper colony, and was fully healed. In his time there, he excelled in learning English and already knew several local languages.

As Katy and Pat dove in, they realized just how many dialects and varieties were present in the area.

You can understand the frustration. The feeling of treading water. Imagine encountering highland-Scottish English, inner-city-South-Chicago English,[12] and rural Iowan English only twenty miles apart from one another, and having no data on these varieties. Who speaks them? How many? How localized or widespread are these varieties? How mutually intelligible are these varieties to one another? And even if they do speak some version of English, is there hostility between these dialect groups, or do they generally get along?

It doesn't seem obvious that the rural Iowan speaker's variety may be more intelligible to the other two than vice versa. But it's true. And there are linguistic, historical, racial, and media reasons that some varieties of English are seen as a "standard" while others are not.

Which of the dialects of Mbembe was the standard? Was there a standard? Katy turned to Mr. Arrobo, the only Mbembe speaker she'd met till that point who was comfortable in English.

She asked him countless questions to try to get to the bottom of it. Can X tribe understand Y tribe? Can Y tribe understand X just as well? Does one tribe's dialect get picked on by the others? When Z tribe and N tribe meet to trade, does one side bend their language more to match the other? After much of this, she wasn't getting anywhere.

The man knew what she was up to but couldn't think of a definitive answer for her. Finally, the man's eyes lit up. "We can hear all the dialects, but we sing in Adun."[13]

Adun it was. For some reason, probably long lost to history, Adun was the dialect of Mbembe all the dialects would sing in when they came together. Whether this made it the oldest, the most influential, the one with the most artists, or the loveliest, didn't really matter. What mattered is that if you're going to publish literature like the Bible, much of which is written in the genre of poetry or song, it makes sense to do so in the dialect all its neighbors look to for effectively communicating such genres.

In her 2011 interview with Arthur Lightbody, Katy said, "So after much debating, we settled in the area which was the largest and most central linguistically, rather than the one that had the larger Christian presence."[14]

For church multiplication and missionary outreach, working with a smaller community makes sense if they will be better poised to reach the surrounding area, whether due to geographical or educational advantages. But in linguistics, it often makes the most sense to work with the variant of the language that is the most central or standard. If there are four to ten dialects of a language, there is often a single dialect that is the largest, or most standard, and serves as a kind of trade language between the others.

If reaching as many people with the good news of Jesus as possible is the goal, it's often wise to start with that group, moving on from there to the others.

Chapter 14

ON MISSIONARIES AND CULTURE CHANGE

When Katy and Pat first arrived in the village of Ovonum, where the Adun dialect of Mbembe is spoken, they went by river. A makeshift pontoon was fashioned by linking two canoes with boards stretched across.

There was no tarred road or a road at all in those days. "A timber company would eventually build the first road in," Katy said. "Things are very different now. There's a bridge across the river. There's also a road down to Calabar. There was no road in those days. . . . We saw something of Old Nigeria in those days when we first went."[1]

In Ovonum, Katy and Pat were introduced to a man who, by Mbembe standards, was quite wealthy. His name was Egor Oyama. Though most lived in traditional homes—bamboo sticks, muddied walls, roofs thatched with palm leaves woven together, some were beginning to build concrete houses with zync roofs. This man had not only his own house but was building a second. In Mbembe culture, men with some means could have multiple wives. In order to accommodate multiple wives and families, richer men built not single-family houses but small compounds—a miniature village within the village.

Egor Oyama had three wives and twenty children. But because the house he was building would not be needed for a few years, Katy and Pat began renting it from him.

They were received warmly. The Mbembe were charmed that a *Fadr* wanted to learn their language. They were somewhat accustomed to white foreigners in the Catholic church. And given the Catholic Church's reticence to use local languages at the time, priests were addressed with an attempt at the English word *father* rather than an appropriate equivalent in Mbembe. So, regardless of the gender context, *Fadr* came to mean "white person" whether male or female.[2]

One of the great benefits of their situation is that renting from an important person in the community made them *insiders* more so than if they'd had some kind of missionary base.

The combined family also had many children who helped and showed hospitality in various ways. This included the preparation of meals.[3]

Immediately upon arriving, Katy and Pat began learning the Mbembe language, the Adun dialect, and eating the same foods as the people they lived with.

One thing Katy learned right away is that a woman without earrings was not seen as an adult. A woman was not considered fully dressed without them. Never being one for beautification and accessorizing, Katy made sure to have her ears pierced the first time she could make the trip to a clinic. Blessedly, they would use disinfectant.

Katy began wearing earrings then, and she's worn them twenty-four hours per day ever since. If she takes them out, she feels not fully adult. Not fully dressed.

A normal day began with a breakfast cooked on the fire. Each compound within the village had a firepit. For breakfast, corn was shelled off the cob with a small knife. The corn was crushed and cooked into a kind of porridge. The number of things added to the porridge indicated the level of culinary achievement.

Porridge with "bush honey" or honey acquired in the wild was special. Adding eggs to the corn porridge increased its esteem even more and better prepared the breakfaster against the glycemic high and then the crash of corn.

Porridge with meat was very special. As in most places for most of recorded history, meat was a delicacy for rarer occasions—unless you had means.

Because of their proximity to the river, fish was a staple, and two to three kinds of fish were regularly served.

For lunch, much the same was served again. Corn porridge or yams. Yams are the primary staple carbohydrate and starch. Though not technically part of the same family, yams are often compared to sweet potatoes—though dryer and less sweet. They're native to Africa and likely made up a principal part of the diet for millennia.

Corn, on the other hand, is not native to Africa. Corn grew only in the Americas. The soil of the "Old World" never knew corn until it was brought through trade and increasing globalization after Columbus. Though it is a primary caloric staple now and a pillar of the culinary culture, the Mbembes' ancestors had never eaten it at all.

The merchant and trader class knows languages, business, and travel. They make their lives in cities and are responsible for the trading capabilities of large swaths of the world. And long before their fellow countrymen see a European face, a South Asian face, a South American face, their traders have brought material goods, seeds, livestock, spices, ideas, and art from far-flung places. Those things then begin to take on a life of their own, sometimes centuries before the common person has ever met people from those places.

There is a fiction out there that if only missionaries wouldn't share the gospel, tribal people all over the world could be preserved. The idea is that they exist in a kind of noble perfect

Eden, and missionaries permanently contaminate their pristine environment.

Those who hold this sophomoric view neglect to consider that globalization is coming for indigenous people. And time and time again, logging companies, mining companies, business interests, and exploiters get there first and have their way. The best possible preparation for indigenous exploitation is lack of education, lack of literacy, and ignorance of their lawful rights on their own ancestral land. Ultimately, contrary to the popular opinion that Western or global influence only *follows* contact with people from other continents, globalization often *precedes* contact with outsiders.

The missionary endeavor has certainly committed sins and needs to continually repent and examine itself. But the notion that without missionaries tribes would exist untouched and unharmed is naïve. The tribes who've often been most prepared to defend their culture, language, natural resources, and identity are those who've developed their language, literacy, local education in the mother tongue, and civic pride. They can read the law. And they can stand on it. And no miner, logger, or corrupt politician can pull the wool over their eyes.

Bible translators are human. They're not perfect. But Bible translators did more to champion these causes on a global scale than any other force in human history.

A regular occurrence in the village was the rhythmic thudding of pounding yams. Because of yams' inherent toughness, the locals placed a few at a time in cauldrons, beating them with body-length pestles. Several people would encircle the cauldron and beat the yams, tenderizing them and readying them for cooking.

For lunch, soup was prepared with green leafy vegetables and sometimes fish or whatever was on hand. The pounded yam was then dipped into the soup.

For dinner, the primary staple was yam with stew. And if you were wealthy enough to have multiple wives—or entertain foreign linguists—you occasionally ate meat. This was most often "bush meat," from a hunted wild animal. Wild meat is much tougher, its host carrying minimal body fat compared to its agriculturally primed kin, so meat was rarely served on its own. But served in stew, the liquids had a chance to tenderize what nature did not.

When Katy first moved there, the local economy was mostly a barter economy. Most villagers were fishermen and yam or corn farmers. But paper currency was beginning to be used more every year. This was fortunate for the young missionaries since they had no land or agricultural goods to trade.

Katy and Pat got around on foot. Eventually, they acquired bicycles easing their trips to neighboring villages or the post office a few villages away. After a few years in the village, Katy was given a Honda 50cc motorcycle by a missionary departing from the field.

"Then we were able to travel much more extensively around the area, one of us riding pillion, with a modicum of books or other items on the back carrier. It also enabled us to arrive at places fresh and fit for work instead of hot and tired.

"There was one occasion when this didn't quite happen as planned! We had been invited to a meal with some well-dressed Japanese businessmen who were working temporarily in the area. On the way we slid, Honda and all, into a muddy ditch. Our best clothes were in a sorry state, but there was no alternative but to go on. Our hosts politely took no notice of our disarray!"[4]

The motorcycle also allowed Katy to drive locals to the hospital in Obubra, nearly an hour away.

"Many would . . . ask for medicine. Running a clinic was not meant to be part of our work, but when we had simple remedies

[on] hand we wanted to share these. Iodine was very popular because it stung so much when you applied it and patients would dance around in mock agonies until the pain died down. Of course there was a sad side to this. Sometimes we could do nothing but tell people to go to the hospital in Obubra, and many never reached there. Later, when we had the Honda 50 motorcycle Katy would often do that journey with a sick or injured person riding pillion."[5]

Chapter 15

LEARNING A LANGUAGE FROM SCRATCH

How do you formally learn a second language? For nearly any human being alive today (outside the linguistics or Bible translation community), second-language learning as a teen or adult often means a credentialed teacher giving formal teaching lessons. For hundreds of years, an unbroken chain of textbooks and grammars allow them to stand on the shoulders of giants. They know how the language works and know how to teach it effectively.

But how do you learn a language without any of those materials? How do you learn a language that for all of human history has never been written? And how do you learn from a native speaker who has never taught the language or even thought about it grammatically? Native speakers of any language often share this curious trait. We are able to produce grammatically correct sentences, knowing what's grammatically correct or incorrect, even if we've never learned to read.

Fortunately, learning unwritten languages is a skill SIL had honed over decades, across many hundreds of linguists. They even developed textbooks based on the practice.

One of the first tasks was to work with local leaders and church officials to determine a language partner. Linguists wouldn't expect a teacher since nobody had ever formally taught the language. But they needed a fluent speaker.

Unlike most learning, the direction of the pedagogy was flipped upside down. It was not the teacher who steered the lessons but the learner. Imagine, instead of planning teaching lessons, planning learning lessons, and then having to creatively summon the content you wished to learn for the day. Then the linguist struggles and learns and takes notes as they go.

The first days are the hardest—and funniest. To communicate, the linguist has only their face and body and the world around them. If they share a few words of a trade language like English with their language partner, even better. Some will use drawings, household items, or even small figurines of people and animals. Soon the various items or figurines act out verbs. Or with one's own body, the linguists mime walking, jumping, smiling, laughing, and so on.

The linguist takes notation in the IPA, the International Phonetic Alphabet, since the language has no written form. The IPA has hundreds of symbols which, depending on their combination and use, are meant to convey all of the possible sounds in world languages. You may have noticed these symbols immediately after a dictionary entry.[1]

Katy was paired with a young man named Livinius Odoma who would serve as her language partner.[2] They began with hand signals and pointing. Katy studied for three to four hours each day with Livinius, about the maximum the human mind can focus that diligently at peak capacity.[3] Well, most human minds. Katy then took her notes and studied them, memorizing all the vocabulary, tones, concepts, and verb conjugations she'd taken down during that day's work. As she slept, her mind kept working out the complexity, and she'd arrive at her tutoring session the next day a much better handler of the language than the day before.

Katy described some of the difficulties of learning the language, which belongs to the family of languages linguists call "Semi-Bantu Languages." The Mbembe dialect Katy learned has tones foreign to most Western languages. The tone in which a vowel is pronounced can distinguish between words. In English, a rising tone at the end of an utterance can indicate a question, *can't it?* Apart from this and a few other tonal norms, our use of pitch doesn't get incredibly complex.

In many languages around the world, multiple words use the same vowels and consonants, but only the variation in tones, or vocalic melody, makes the difference in meaning. Thus, as Katy describes in her thesis, the difference between "mother" and "crab," or "dog" and "power" is in the slight variations of tone or pitch contour used in the vowels.[4] It's a mind job to hear tongue twisters in tonal languages. Sometimes one word can be repeated with variations on high tones, low tones, rising tones, or falling tones.

In Mandarin Chinese, there is a well-known tongue twister that plays with the single phoneme "ma." That single phoneme is repeated over and over with varying tones to make an entire tongue-twister question. As a brief example:

"Simplified: 妈妈骂马的麻吗?

. . .

IPA /máma mâ màtə mǎ ma/

Translation: 'Is mom scolding the horse's hemp?'"[5]

If variation in noun meaning were not enough, many of the verb tenses also depend on tone. Where many Western languages depend on conjugated endings and changed endings (think *ed* for past tense or the addition of *s* for a regular third person verb) Mbembe often used a combination of conjugations and tones to mark for tense difference.

Katy had not learned a tonal language before. She had her hands full, but she met the challenge head-on.

"The people were welcoming," Katy said. "We never felt any problem of being accepted there for which we were thankful."

"Happily, the people were very keen on me learning the language," Barnwell said. She remembers a local woman befriending her early on and teaching her new concepts. "The next day, she'd ask me again, and if I couldn't remember, she'd say, 'I told you that yesterday!'"

Those first days and weeks were hard, but soon Katy had built a foundation for basic vocabulary. She began to understand the tenses, how the tones worked, and the ten different noun classes—a terror to many Westerners.[6]

"It used to amaze us, the children just automatically got all these [noun] classes right but it took us a lot of effort to learn." Human language is a gift from God. It's a mystery that PhD-level linguists spend years to document what illiterate children learn with hardly any effort.

Though Katy did not learn the language like a child, she learned it shockingly well for a foreigner. This was difficult for her partner Pat. They spent the same amount of time with their language partners. Why should Katy be so much more adept than Pat?

Pat said this challenge began to compound. People talked to Katy more because they knew she could understand them and reply well, which helped her excel, and so they kept talking to her all the more, but not Pat. Pat fell further behind. Eventually, Pat heard the nickname the local people would call her. "The deaf one." The truth is, she was probably on pace for an average SIL linguist. But it's unfair for just about anybody to have to stand next to Katy Barnwell.

Chapter 16

THE EVE OF BREAKTHROUGH

When you read biographies of great people, one gets the sense they often understood, even early in their lives, that they might lead a consequential life. Many great leaders began keeping a journal or diary as children. When you read the words, you catch uncanny slips through the fourth wall. You catch them explaining something to a future reader other than themselves. They betray themselves in this. They may have written their diaries for themselves, but they clearly write them with an eye to future biographers, admirers, and scholars as well.

Many church leaders and missionaries are the same. Kenneth Pike and William Cameron Townsend hired secretaries who kept a copy of every letter they ever sent, much like you'll find in US presidential libraries. Billy Graham's team did the same.

Katy could not have cared less.

Sometimes she still thinks it is absurd that people want to read her story.[1] Katy's life was a constant blur of moving from one continent to another by plane, bus, train, canoe, and pack animal. Some years, she was entirely transient, spending weeks or months here and weeks or months there, moving through time zones like normal people run errands.

Because of this, she kept little. Even her correspondence was not kept by her. As a single woman, moving from country to country with only a few suitcases, Katy's entire life motto had to be "pack light."

But thanks to Katy's mother, who saved hundreds of personal letters from Katy, and thanks to the SIL archives in Dallas, who saved many of Katy's newsletters and updates to her prayer partners and financial supporters, we still have much of Katy's account in her own hand. And in that account, we see a young missionary blossom.

If there was any social awkwardness left in Katy, it was soon eradicated. Mbembe culture, like many sub-Saharan cultures, is off the charts in friendliness. Every day, dozens of Mbembe people would stop by to visit with them. "Two white women . . . learning our language. . . . Let's see what they are doing today."[2] One day Katy and Pat counted ninety-eight visitors. It's a wonder they accomplished anything at all.

Katy continued to learn the Mbembe language, carefully documenting everything she was learning. Her first goal was to speak the language as close to fluently as possible. Second, to someday write up a formal grammatical analysis of the language for her PhD dissertation. Third, to dive into full-time Bible translation.

In the beginning of 1966, Katy had to leave for the University in Nsukka for three months of linguistic workshops and branch conferences. She and Livinius together decided it was too long to go without daily language lessons. He decided he would come with Katy so they could continue their lessons.

It was not only Katy who felt the pressure to continue learning the language; Livinius felt it too. "If you do not know it well, I will be ashamed. My people will say I have not taught you well!"[3]

Describing Livinius's decision to accompany them, Katy writes, "It is his first journey away from home. He is fascinated by switches you press . . . and a light comes on! And taps you turn . . . and water comes out! The University buildings are indeed a contrast to Mbembe village homes. This is the other side of Nigeria—fast developing and spreading. Here you will meet Nigerians as educated as anyone in Europe or America."[4]

Around this time Katy began to consider ideas that few in missionary Bible translation ever had. If there were Nigerians as educated as any European or American, and many of them also spoke indigenous languages as their mother tongues, why not train *them* to do the work of translation?

It seems obvious now looking back. But it wasn't—not then.[5]

In part, John Bendor-Samuel, Katy Barnwell, and the Nigeria branch of SIL were ahead of their time. But to the credit of SIL in the Americas, Africa was in an entirely different universe than the Americas.

Instead of working among monolingual tribal people in the Amazon who could not read, many Africans were well educated, trilingual, quadrilingual, or even pentalingual, and had advanced degrees. This was not yet the case for Mbembe speakers, but it would be in short order. Katy saw the potential.

What if Bible translation in Africa could be done by Africans, for Africans?

LETTER FROM KATY

"The beginning of the good message of Jesus Christ, the Son of God . . ."[6] It has been a tremendous experience to begin the first, very tentative, translation of the early chapters of Mark's Gospel."

"How do we approach translation? First there is preparation, working through the passage in detail with a variety of English version commentaries and a Greek lexicon. . . . Then we make a tentative version

in Mbembe—there are always lots of gaps and question marks at this stage! Then we go through the passage with Mbembe helpers.[7] One of the teachers, home for the school holidays, has been a great help. Then there is checking, again and again and again, with different people, church members and those right outside the church, to find out their reactions and whether they understand clearly, trying to cut out misunderstandings and misleading words, looking for the most accurate and natural expressions.

Some passages fit readily into Mbembe culture. It would be easy to break a hole through the palm mat roof to lower the paralytic into the house. Men throwing out their nets to fish are a familiar sight on the river. Leprosy is a well-known disease. Tax collectors have a similar social position to that of New Testament times!"[8]

However, there were many cultural problems that didn't translate well.

"For instance, there are many references to the Sea of Galilee in the early chapters of Mark. The only large stretch of water known to the Mbembe is the river, so there is no word for lake or sea. It is clumsy to explain what a sea is each time the word comes! It is hard to find the right balance of accuracy, clarity and emphasis. The parable of the Sower is difficult because there is no crop which is sown by casting seed. To the Mbembe it seems crazy to throw seed wastefully instead of planting each one separately. But the image of throwing must be retained if the parable is not to lose its point. There are other problems too, such as the right word to use for 'baptize,' 'priest' and 'the Son of Man.'"[9]

Katy will no doubt cringe to read some of this. In 1967, she had not yet arrived at her era-breaking transfer of the baton to local translators. But she was making great strides in that direction beyond her peers. It's hard to innovate without first mastering the status quo. And Katy was doing that while also observing.

She was still the one "holding the pen" as it was referred to, but by the time the local teacher, Mr. Oyama, and others had been consulted, the final draft changed so much that it may as well have been the native speakers who drafted it rather than Katy. This prepared the way for her to realize—*Why are we drafting it in the first place? Why are outsiders holding the pen at all?*

What if Mr. Oyama drafted and Katy helped with difficult questions like biblical backgrounds and linguistic issues? What if they then worked together to check it?

In those final lines quoted here, we also see her struggling with what would later be called "key terms." These are extremely important terms, paramount to the Bible as a whole. If you get even one key term wrong, you may twist the message of Scripture. For example, if the way you translate Son of Man throughout the Gospels isn't weighty and Messianic and connected to the eventual translation of Daniel 7, or Ezekiel, or other Old Testament uses of this term, you set your readers on the wrong course. If this translation designates Jesus as fully human but biases against understanding his full divinity, you set the reader and hearer on a course to heresy and a remarkable misunderstanding of the New Testament.

Katy saw the massive importance of getting these terms right. There can be no "building the plane while it's flying." Katy instead compared it to making a cake. If you measure in mistaken ingredients and then bake the cake, there is no return. You cannot walk a baked cake backward into its ingredients again. You cannot fix it. And like ingredients, key terms had to be as strong as possible from an early stage.[10]

Chapter 17

THE BIAFRAN WAR

While Katy was just beginning the revisions on the translation of the Gospel of Mark, a tension hundreds of miles away fomented. It would change Nigeria, and Bible translation, forever.

The British ruled over Nigeria for centuries. But in 1960–1963, they transitioned out of the country. The era of colonization was officially over. It was time to let colonies govern themselves.

In many places around the world, this gave rise to turmoil, power vacuums, and conflicts. Of the many people groups in Nigeria, three were arguably the most powerful—the Hausa in the north, the Yoruba in the southwest, and in the southeast, the Igbo people.[1]

In retrospect, the British colonial era has become particularly infamous for their drawing of boundaries and borders. So often, borders were drawn down the middle of a major people group, as in India and Pakistan, essentially cutting the Punjabi people group off from one another.[2]

In the case of Nigeria, remarkably different peoples were lumped into the same country borders, and when the British left, these people groups beheld one another not as fellow countrymen but as competitors for power.

In the Muslim north, the Hausa and Fulani people made up the strongest military force. The Yoruba in the southwest had the greatest business and banking possibilities with Lagos, the largest city in all of Africa. And in the southeast, there was newly discovered oil among the Igbo people.

The Igbo had resources and their own culture. They weren't much interested in seeing their oil resources poured into the Muslim north or the already wealthy Yoruba in the southwest. They wanted to be their own country.

Though an oversimplification, these elements formed the powder keg that became the Nigerian Civil War. It would become one of the deadliest African conflicts on record. According to some, it was second only to the Rwandan Genocide.[3]

On May 30, 1967, the southeast of Nigeria announced that it was seceding from the rest of Nigeria.[4] They would become a nation called Biafra. But the rest of Nigeria, in control of the government, the power structures, and the business capital, was not on board with Biafra's plan. It was their southeastern coast, and they were not about to let go of that recently discovered oil.

What followed, some say, was "perhaps the most significant event in Nigerian history."[5]

Biafra didn't have the soldiers. It didn't have the navy or the air force. It had few weapons. It was clear to most strategists that they would not win this civil war. But they fought harder than the world expected. They resisted longer.

The Nigerian administration "came to the very reckless conclusion that the only way to break the deadlock would be to trigger its nuclear option. . . . To impose an economic blockade on Biafra that blocked the flow of all food and ammunitions supplies by land, air, and sea. This move would turn out to be perhaps the single most destructive political decision in West African history, as it would ultimately lead to the death by malnourishment of an estimated two million citizens, most of whom were children suffering from the protein deficiency disease known as kwashiorkor."[6]

When starving adults don't get enough protein, their bodies resort to autophagy—metabolizing their own muscle tissue as a last resort. Adults often have a bit of excess fat and muscle to spare, but growing children don't have enough. And once the body eats its own fat and muscle, there's not much left but the organs.

Now in the era of television, this was arguably the first major calamity that played out on the world stage in a relentlessly televised manner.[7] Images of starving Nigerian children flashed across the screens of the entire world.

People were dying and most weren't soldiers. They were children. Soon it began to be described as a genocide, with both sides pointing fingers. The Biafrans blamed Nigeria for causing all this atrocity—blockades and sanctions that starved their people. The Nigerians accused Biafra of not seeing the writing on the wall—that they were killing their own people for a lost cause. They had no chance. They never did. Give up already.

When the signs of civil war first appeared on the horizon, many Wycliffe and SIL employees in the region left for their own safety. Who can blame them?

But Katy and Pat stayed. If their heavenly Father was still working, they would work too. Pat put it this way:

Katy and I were given the choice—we could either go up to Enugu and, with the remaining Wycliffe members there, join the convoy of ex-patriots that was being organized to leave the country, or we could stay quietly in Mbembe and go on with our work. It looked quite possible that the war would never touch the Mbembe area, and we had just returned from Enugu and had at least three months' supply of tinned food and money. So we prayed together about this, and both decided it would be right to stay. The phone line from the Post Office in Obubra to the Group House in Enugu was still open at that point and I remember phoning to let them know of our decision.[8]

It became clear that their home country was supporting not the Biafran cessation but broader Nigeria in the conflict. But "despite the understandable resentment which the British government's attitude in the dispute has aroused, we have experienced only courtesy and helpfulness from the people, and I think this is the general experience of the Europeans who have remained."[9]

Katy and Pat continued to question their decision to stay, and Katy asked her supporters to pray what was almost an omen for what was to come:

Pray that "we won't run away too soon, or stay too late!!"[10]

The intelligence that made it through to the British and the international newspapers was much better than what Katy and Pat had access to locally. And soon, SIL knew what Katy and Pat did not. The war would reach them. And sticking out like sore thumbs, they would be in serious danger.

SIL sent out the call that all of their employees still in the region should leave. And they did. But Katy and Pat never got the message. All communication to Biafra had been cut off. No postal service, no phone lines, no telegrams.

And so they stayed on. And they stayed on. They spent nearly a year without any communication with the wider world. SIL did not know if they were alive. Their families did not know if they were taken hostage.[11]

But the war had not reached them. Not yet. They enjoyed much more peace than their loved ones, who had no idea if they were still living.

This extra year allowed them to accomplish great work. It meant an extra year of language learning. And in God's timing and providence, it allowed them to begin the work of Scripture translation. Katy laughs remembering how little she knew of translation principles in those days.

A local church wanted to begin an evangelistic campaign centering around twelve key verses in Scripture. But English or Efik wouldn't do. They wanted the verses in Mbembe. But they weren't sure how. They were not Bible scholars or linguists, and nobody had trained them. They asked Katy for help.

Together with the local church, Katy and Pat helped them translate those verses into Mbembe. The problem was, many of those verses "came from the epistles," she said laughing, "which is not where you want to start translation."

The letters of the New Testament are notoriously hard to translate, from Paul's tacit debate partners in 1 Corinthians to Jude's rant, the dense theological concepts in Romans and Hebrews, or for the latter, its high prose. It's best saved for later in the translation process. A great genre to begin with is narrative. But Katy would figure that out later.

Despite the difficulty, "there was a good response from early on," Katy remembers.

Quite by accident—or the providence of God—Katy fell into the mold she would use the rest of her life, and one she would pioneer for the rest of the world. The church invited her to begin the work of translation, and when she was ready, the church spearheaded an evangelistic campaign. The church asked Katy and Pat to come alongside them in the work they were carrying out. In essence, the Bible translator was in the copilot's seat, serving the church, helping the church, and ultimately, following the lead of the local churches.

This is not how Bible translation was done.

But it worked, Katy realized. It worked far better than the model she'd been taught. In the model Katy was taught, the pioneering Western linguist blazes in, Indiana Jones style, learns the language of the people, and drafts a full New Testament. Though pieces of it were sometimes made available for the church, the work often lived in file cabinets until it was complete. Then, some fifteen to twenty-five years after starting the work, the New Testament would be published.

In some communities, the outcome was still beautiful. But in many communities, for whom literacy was scarce and the most important things were communicated orally rather than in print, those New Testaments just sat on shelves, collecting dust.

Katy began to see a better model. What if the local churches drove the process, using the translated word in their preaching and teaching as it became available, in the forms most natural to the community? By the time the New Testament was published in that model, many of its books would have already enjoyed decades of engagement in the community.

Katy began meeting with church leaders. Why should she choose which books of the Bible to translate first? Why not let the church choose?

"I remember talking with the church leaders . . . where we should start translation. The place they wanted to start was Psalms. . . . They thought Psalms would be good. And I think they were right, it would've been a good place to start, but we didn't think we were quite ready for the Psalms at the beginning."

Poetry may be one of the hardest genres to translate faithfully, clearly, and accurately from one language to another. But through conversation, they were able to work together so that the church was driving the process of translation and then using the translations produced. Katy began to wonder, *What if all of Bible translation—wherever there was a church at least—worked like this?*

What about one of the Gospels? The Gospels hold a unique importance among canonical books because they tell the story of the birth, life, teaching, miracles, death, and resurrection of Jesus. And given Mark is the shortest, the simplest in its Greek, and was likely penned first and used as a source for Matthew and Luke, why not begin with Mark? It would give them a great head start on Matthew and Luke.[12]

In those early drafting sessions, Katy quickly realized what translators have had to keep relearning for thousands of years, that native speakers will always have an advantage over an outside linguist. Especially when it comes to the natural feel for their language.

But what Katy knew better than her Nigerian colleagues was the linguistics. She found herself offering help with biblical backgrounds, theological concepts, and exegetical and linguistic data. And with those tools at their disposal, the native speakers were translating. Katy, speaking the language well but not natively, understood and was able to prod, ask questions, and help test the work for clarity. But their native fluency produced incredible natural translations that Katy herself could not have uttered after a lifetime of living there.

Could the model used in the Americas possibly be a poor fit for Africa? Given the multilingual and literate church leaders available in much of Africa, could they instead be trained to do the work? Could outside consultants help with precisely the most difficult scholarly questions?

What if Bible translation were to shift to training Africans to translate into their own languages? What if the outsider simply came alongside to help with best practices, tricky biblical and exegetical concepts, and helped ensure the translation was faithful?

What Katy didn't know then is that soon she would not just be afforded time to consider this; she'd be forced to. A major offensive was coming, and it would not be safe for Western women to be there. Katy and Pat needed to leave, likely for years until the Civil War ceased.

But why should Bible translation be contingent upon the presence of Westerners? Couldn't it be led by locals, for locals, the whole time?

Translation is extremely demanding cognitive work. The brain only weighs about 2 percent of our total body weight but uses 20 percent of our calories and oxygen.[13] Anybody who's taken a three-hour standardized test has felt this drain. Or you may have found yourself vampirically searching for sugar while trying to finish a difficult paper in the wee hours of the night. Now imagine doing this on eight hundred daily calories—for months.

"We eked out our three months' supply of tinned food as much as possible, but by the end of about four months these were exhausted," Pat wrote. The missionary women did not have farms, fields, or animals to fall back on. And their money was quickly dwindling. They had one tin of sausages that they did not open. West Africa is such a hospitable culture that it was more important to go without and save something *nice* to share with others, should they have visitors.

Katy often calls Nigeria home. She's more comfortable there than about anywhere. And Africans treat her as one of their own. The Mbembe understood the women's situation, and they stepped in to help. Long after an anthropologist would have abandoned them, these missionary women stayed on, helping the local children, providing medicine, and driving them to the hospital. Some of the most hospitable people on earth would not let Katy and Pat's hospitality go unanswered.

Pat writes, "Local people realized that we couldn't go to Enugu anymore and that we didn't have our own farms as they did, and shared with us—a prized chicken, a yam, bananas, and one day two steaming bowls of yam stew, all ready to eat. I particularly remember that day, because it was my turn to cook the meal, and I had been all round the village looking for someone selling produce and found nothing. Just as I got back the yam stew arrived. Truly the Lord knows our needs. . . . Then on Christmas Day 1967, Lawrence Ebak and his wife invited us to dinner—roast chicken, roast sweet potatoes, green vegetables, all with the warmth of Christian fellowship."[14]

"Our supply of money also dwindled as time went on," Pat said. They couldn't get enough food. They were losing weight. They used to wire money or send for funds every three months.

But with all communication cut off, they were now at six months, seven months, ten months without new funding.

They began selling their possessions. They sold their bicycles. At some point in the previous three years, they'd purchased a kerosene refrigerator, no doubt inspired by Mr. Huskinson's. But this too they sold. They couldn't get much for them in rural Nigeria in wartime, but it was something—a few meals here and a few meals there.

The world watched the Biafran war in horror. And so did the Cameroon branch of SIL, right next door. As the crow flies, many SIL employees lived within fifty to one hundred miles of Katy and Pat just over the border, but they did not know if they were safe. Were they even alive? Did they have anything to eat?

One thing they knew: because Biafra was completely cut off, Katy and Pat had not been able to draw from their bank account in the UK for nearly a year. If they were alive, they would be in desperate need of funds.

But a group of Westerners can't just walk into an African war zone with a bag full of cash. How could they get money to the women without it being confiscated along the way?

Then somebody had a bright idea. What about a Christmas card?

SIL employees in Cameroon paid a young man to hand deliver a Christmas card. They told him to avoid the river but never stray so far that he lost the river's path. He was to walk the bush paths away from the villages. He must have been paid handsomely because it was a multiple-day walk. And there were snakes in the bush.

He must have wondered what all the fuss was about just for a Christmas card. For his own safety should he be stopped by soldiers, they didn't tell him what he carried. As far as he knew, it was simply an important letter. But it was a great offer, so he took it. Once he had walked the correct number of days, he began asking. Where is Ovonum? How much farther? Only when he got there was he to ask for the two Western ladies.

When Katy and Pat received the card, they were touched and a bit confused. Why go to so much trouble for a card? They didn't suspect anything.

But later that evening, at the dinner table, one of the children of the compound picked it up and felt it. She squeezed it and ran her hands over it.

"It's thick." She said in Mbembe.

Katy approached the child and curiously took the card. Yes, it was thick. Quite thick.

But there was nothing in it, not in the way you'd normally expect a gift in a card. Where did the thickness come from?

Katy realized that the cardboard backing of the card was double-paned. There was something inside. Prying it open, Katy beheld many months' wages in crisp large bills.

Food was still scarce, and Katy and Pat had lost a shocking percentage of their body weight. But the cash was enough to back-pay their rent and keep them fed—at least enough to not lose more of what little body weight remained. When Amelia Gardner saw them later, she would describe them as "emaciated."[15]

"In January we began to hear distant sounds of warfare as Nigerian troops landed in Calabar and began to fight their way up the East side of the Cross River,"[16] Pat wrote. They *lived* on the Cross River.

In February, they began to hear the first sound Katy remembers in this world. In the distance, bombs pummeled Biafran strongholds.

"By March the guns were loud," Pat said. "I remember a helicopter flying low over the village and a child running and screaming—she had never encountered such a monster!"[17]

"We should leave tomorrow." Katy said.[18] But it was long past time to leave.

They'd stayed on in a war zone. Had they left earlier, they could have driven through the Nigerian forces to get into territory well beyond the war. But now a great offensive was sweeping through their region. To drive toward the approaching troops was less than wise.

As she had as a child, Katy packed a go bag. This time, it wasn't Nazi bombs that threatened but soldiers across the bloodlines of a civil war. They weren't looking for British people, but if you know anything about war, you know it's best not to find yourself in a freshly conquered village, especially if you're a woman or a child.

They had trained for this. They knew how to make it on their own. But they couldn't go toward central Nigeria or the coast. They would have to escape in another direction. Fortunately, they spoke Mbembe now. And Katy also spoke French.

Chapter 18

FLIGHT OUT OF BIAFRA

Katy and Pat knew southern Nigeria well. They'd taken many trips to Enugu, Nsuka, Lagos, Obubra, and Port Harcourt. They thought that when it came to fleeing, they could take the river to the district capital and hop on a bus to any one of these important centers in Nigeria.

But with soldiers descending into the seceded Biafran territory, it wasn't safe. They would have to go by river in the other direction—to Cameroon.

All Katy's time in Girl Guides and Jungle Camp came to bear now. It was a five-day trip on foot and by river to Cameroon. They had only what they could carry.

They set out early to beat the morning heat. They were fortunate it was still dry season should they have to make camp in the bush overnight.

They knew if they followed the Cross River upstream toward its source in the Cameroonian highlands forests, they would eventually cross the Cameroonian border. Among the many problems they had already (two white women traveling alone during a civil war, on foot, with one bag), they had no papers to enter Cameroon. And they didn't have time to travel to an embassy to get them. They set out, hoping against hope that they would be admitted entry even without a visa.

They began walking in the morning, catching an upriver canoe transport whenever the timing allowed. Even with her star status as a Girl Guide, Katy remembers Pat as the stronger of the two. Pat, who's also still living at the time of this writing, remembers the opposite. Either way, they made a great pair.[1]

When the heat of the day arrived, they rested in the shade. It was too hot to walk that many miles on foot. They'd lose too many fluids, and after lack of proper nutrition and little access to water purification, they had little hydration to spare.

Once evening came, they walked more, always staying close to the river. Rivers are the highways of humanity, and to this day, one of your surest bets for finding civilization anywhere on earth is to walk downward toward a river and then walk along it until you find people.

By walking the river, they knew they could not get lost. And they knew that with their Mbembe, English, and some French, they could get help.

As it turned out, help they would get.

News of the *Fadrs* who spoke Mbembe had reached far and wide. Many church workers and missionaries before them had never bothered to learn the language, ministering instead in Efik or English. Katy and Pat may have been the first Europeans to ever speak the language.

The fact that all around the world, thousands of scholars from Western countries learned peoples' indigenous languages was one of the great witnesses to the good news of Jesus.

If God would empty himself,[2] translating himself into human existence, that we might behold him without a veil and speak to him in our language, then the good news of Jesus can and should be translated to every other person on earth that they might see and hear him in their own tongue. This is one of the principal differences between the missionary expression of Christianity and Islam.

The Orang Asli people in Malaysia understand this well. The Malaysian government puts many resources into the Islamization of indigenous groups. To make them Muslim is to make them Malay. Once they're Malay, they can be assimilated and culturally erased.[3]

As Eliza Griswold writes,

Since the 1970s, as part of a controversial, long-secret program, the Malaysian government has sponsored Islamic teachers to go live in Orang Asli villages, has built almost three hundred prayer halls (some in villages with few or no Muslims), and has paid Malay Muslims (up to $3,000) to marry Orang Asli women. All of these efforts to do *da'wa*—to proselytize—are intended to ensure the aborigines' conversion to Islam and introduce them to life as modern Malays. The government also grants Orang Asli who convert to Islam better health care, education, housing, and jobs than those who do not. Despite these incentives, the government has had only negligible success among the Orang Asli, who have resisted Islamization for centuries.[4]

"Much to the government's dismay," she writes, "Christian missionaries—ranging from local Catholics and Methodists to South Korean Presbyterians—also evangelize the Orang Asli. Many argue that, unlike Islam, which transforms the Orang Asli into Malays, and thus erases their identity, Christianity allows the indigenous people to retain their way of life—to eat what they wish, pray as they like, and marry whom they want."[5]

Christianity contextualizes far better than any other world religion. It's in the DNA of the faith.

Christianity is the only world religion whose Scriptures are not written in the teaching language of its founder.[6] The New Testament is written in Koine Greek, the wider trade language at the time, but Jesus taught almost exclusively in Aramaic. Not only is God the Father translated to us in the person of the Word, Jesus of Nazareth, but his good news comes to us already in translation. We don't have the Aramaic original.

You could say the doctrine of the incarnation is the doctrine of translation. God made himself man and humbled himself. He took on flesh and lived under all the predicaments of a human man. If God translates himself to us, then we translate his Word to all the peoples, tribes, tongues, and nations who will be standing before him in heaven, shouting: "Salvation belongs to our God, who is seated on the throne, and to the Lamb!"[7]

This incarnational approach to ministry did not end with Jesus. The apostle Paul, the church's greatest theologian, adopted it too. He writes:

> Though I am free and belong to no one, I have made myself a slave to everyone, to win as many as possible. To the Jews I became like a Jew, to win the Jews. To those under the law I became like one under the law (though I myself am not under the law), so as to win those under the law. To those not having the law I became like one not having the law (though I am not free from God's law but am under Christ's law), so as to win those not having the law. To the weak I became weak, to win the weak. I have become all things to all people so that by all possible means I might save some.[8]

That Europeans would not only bother to learn Mbembe but relish it and write primers and grammars and dissertations on it doesn't make much earthly sense. That is, not without the incarnation. Not without the charge to become all things to all people, that by all means they might hear of the Savior in their own language. Just as Katy first heard of a Savior in her language.

Katy's and Pat's fame had stretched far and wide within Mbembe society. They did not visit a single village where the people did not know who they were.

Katy wanted to walk at night, but they could not. There are many venomous snakes in the bush, and they're most active at night. One minute, you could be walking, and the next, you step on a venomous snake. What will you do with your twenty-seven agonizing minutes to live? It wasn't worth it.

But they'd learned enough about Africa to know that they could depend on hospitality wherever they could find a village.

Unlike in the West, much of the world holds hospitality in high regard. This is why ancient travelers would often arrive in a town and knock on an unknown person's door rather than find an inn. In the pages of Scripture, we see this scenario again and again, and it's often confusing to modern Westerners. But in West Africa, hospitality is bound up with the culture.

And news of these white ladies who spoke Mbembe preceded them. Every village they stopped in wanted to host them. Often, the chief won the honor, serving them dried fish or hot pepper directly from his bowl—a particular honor. The chief was also likely to have the largest compound, making it easier to accommodate guests.

There, though Katy and Patricia hoped to rest, boil water for the morrow's journey, and get good sleep for the day ahead, they were instead entertained by the important people of the village. They were grateful, and they were often sent on their way with more than they'd asked for.

Finally, after five days, they approached the Cameroonian border by river. Not many things make Katy nervous, but fleeing a civil war on foot without documents was one of them.

They said a prayer together that the border guards would understand. A war zone is no place for two unmarried foreign women.

Katy stepped forward, ready to use her rusty French she hadn't actively used since university days. She explained their situation. That they'd fled the civil war. It wasn't safe for them. They weren't able to visit an embassy to acquire visas because that's where the fighting was.

They held their breath.

What was their plan? He asked.

To go to Yaoundé, where they had colleagues, and catch the first flight back to Europe. The border guard nodded. They exhaled. It was a plan.

The border agent allowed them entry. And with the little they had, they arranged for a fifteen-hour bus ride to Yaoundé, the capital of Cameroon. Wycliffe had a number of employees there.

Because of the civil war, Katy and Pat had not communicated with anybody in almost a year. When they arrived in Yaoundé, it was a surprise to Wycliffe members there. "You're the two women from the prayer request telegrams? What are you doing all the way over here?"

Katy and Pat didn't have enough money to get back to the UK without visiting their bank connection or without a wire transfer from the home office. Travel was a lot more complicated before the Internet and consistent phone lines.

Once they'd arrived at the Wycliffe center in Yaoundé, the members there lent them whatever they needed to get back home. Katy and Pat would make sure to return that money once they were settled and safe in a place where they had access to their accounts.

There were no flights to the UK, but they could get close. A flight was planned for Lisbon, Portugal. They booked it and arrived in Lisbon on March 21, 1968. They immediately connected and caught the famous overnight train from Lisbon to Paris, the Sudexpress. From Paris, they took the train to Lile and then up to the coast at Calais.

There was no Chanel Tunnel then (lovingly referred to as the "Chunnel"). That would be constructed some three decades later. In Calais, in the northern French climate in late winter, they had to board a ferry to cross the English Channel.

Forty-eight hours after fleeing the bombs, the civil war, and trekking through the jungle without papers, the women sat shivering on a ferry north of France, aware how out of place they were among their own people. "We shivered in our cotton dresses (our warm clothes had been left in Enugu long ago) and felt very shabby and out-of-place amongst a fully equipped skiing party crossing at the same time."[9] Of course, those skiers would never know the real story. Even if they'd told them, they could never understand. This is the absurdity of missionary life.

Finally, they arrived in central London at Paddington Station. They walked to the English pay phones they hadn't had occasion to use in half a decade. But you never forget your home phone number. Their families hadn't heard from them in a year.

Family members burst out in tears at hearing their voices. Finally knowing they were alive. And in London! They would be home that night. Katy and Pat parted ways then, each to her respective hometown. They each received an impromptu celebration and reunion.

You never know when you're in the good old days. Not until they're gone. Katy and Pat were colleagues, roommates, and best friends.

It's rare to find a friend you can spend the whole day with and never tire of. One with similar interests, similar humor. Katy and Pat had that kind of friendship. But like so many good things—especially in a missionary career—it wouldn't last forever.

And so, four years after arriving in Nigeria, Katy was back in the UK. It was earlier than she'd planned, but not by more than a year or two. SIL linguists often spent four to five years gathering data, becoming as fluent as possible in the language, and then taking a furlough to write up their PhD dissertation on the language. Once finished, they would return to continue Bible translation.

By this account, the Biafran war hadn't put Katy behind. She left a bit earlier than she wanted, but she was a stronger speaker and had better data than most ever managed.

Despite the need to pack light, Katy took as many notebooks as she could of her linguistic description. She returned to her parents' home in Goring-on-Thames, a village about an hour west of London by train or car. The house on the hill, she called it.

From 1968 through 1969, while the Biafran war made returning to Nigeria all but impossible, she would make a home office there in Goring. Besides sporadic trips into London to meet with her doctoral supervisor, or Horsley's Green, Wycliffe's UK headquarters, you could find Katy working at her desk in Goring.

It was a strange thing for Katy to be home, but it was stranger for her parents. If Katy had always seemed to be a bit shy, a bit socially awkward, suddenly a confident young woman who knew exactly why she was on this earth returned from Nigeria.

Katy taught at the summer linguistics courses, she spoke at universities, she spoke at churches. She was sought after. Wycliffe HQ asked for her to give speaking engagements. She led programs, groups, clubs. Who was this person?

Here, the doctoral candidate at a prestigious university worked on her PhD dissertation, a grammatical and linguistic description of a language that had never before been written down.

Few of her family had even gone to university.

Letters began to arrive at the house on the hill for a "Dr. Barnwell." Katy remembers her father starting, almost incredulous. "Are you a doctor?"

It's a strange thing for parents when the child who was bragged on the least in childhood becomes the shining star among their siblings—or of an entire generation.

It took Katy less than one year to write her thesis. This is lightning fast for a 314-page grammatical description of a previously unwritten language. And this, after being out of academia's official rhythms for years. Of course, for those who came to know Katy's ability to focus, this was only the beginning.

Katy knew exactly who she was. And as soon as she could get back to her chosen life, she would. In the early days of 1970, the Nigerian Civil War finally ended. In a matter of only days, her passport shows she visited the Nigerian embassy and received her visa to return.

It was time to get back to the field.

Chapter 19

RETURNING TO NIGERIA

Dear Friends,
    OVONUM. We drove into the village quite
late one evening. It was dark, but everything looked
just as usual: thatched houses, palm trees, low fires,
and here and there a shadowy figure with a lantern
returning late from farm. Quite suddenly, the car
was surrounded by people shouting and hugging us.
It was some time before we could even get out.
    Pat and I were quite overwhelmed by the wel-
come we received. So many familiar faces—and
people haven't changed much in the two years we
have been away. There is the sadness of a few faces
missing.[1]
    We were much moved by some of the sights we
saw on the journey down and by the accounts of ref-
ugees from the inner part of former Biafra. But some
of this doesn't bear telling and the rest is better not
told. Everyone is thankful that the war is over and
that life is beginning to return to normal.[2]

The missionary life is hard. Some figures calculate the total duration of an average missionary tenure as low as twenty-four months.[3] One of the reasons Katy made it so long on the field is her incredible positivity. Compared to so many missionaries who utterly burn out, Katy was spiritually, emotionally, and mentally healthy. Even thriving.

Katy is, I joke, pathologically humble and positive. Though she's relentless when it comes to the quality of a translation, she has no time for criticism of people. She thinks the best, sees the best, and doesn't seem to have a skeptical bone in her body. To imagine another person may have an evil or less-than-righteous motive for anything is beyond the pale of her thinking.

It's one thing to be cheerful as far as Westerners are concerned. Most Africans will put up with much more than Westerners. But Katy put even Africans to shame in her acceptance of humble circumstances.

"I remember a time we went to Nasarawa state," Danjuma Gambo told me. "That was, I think, 1983. We went there to run a workshop on literacy, preparing them for their New Testament dedication. So Dr. Katy, Steven Young, and myself, we went. The three of us.

"When we got there, there was no food for us. So we had to travel back to the village on the road to buy food to eat. And of course, just on the roadside, there wasn't any good food but Katy would say 'It's good! It's good! Eat!' With Katy, anything was good.

"We went back in the evening, and there was no accommodation for us. So the three of us had to sleep in the sitting room. We put mats on the floor, and lied down, everyone taking a corner."

"It was really hard. But for Katy, 'That's fine! That's good! That's okay!'

"When we came back to Jos, all three of us had malaria at the same time. . . . Steven Young couldn't go to the office. I was drowsing. But Katy, you know, she is an extra strong woman. I don't understand. Even when some of us are feeling very weak, she's still strong."[4]

Katy is remarkably optimistic. Her spirits are constantly high. God is in control, and he holds the world in his hands.

This is why, her face on the floor, held hostage, automatic weapons fired above her head, she can arise. She can shake the dust from her garments. She can pray. She can comfort. She can smile.

"For God has not given us a spirit of fear, but one of power, love, and sound judgment." (2 Tim. 1:7)

It's precisely this quality that makes her such an era-defining missionary. Coincidentally, this also makes it challenging to write her biography. Katy regards the trials of her life as insignificant.

More than anybody I've ever met or, I suspect, will meet, Katy embodies this command from the apostle Paul:

Don't worry about anything, but in everything, through prayer and petition with thanksgiving, present your requests to God. And the peace of God, which surpasses all understanding, will guard your hearts and minds in Christ Jesus.

Finally brothers and sisters, whatever is true, whatever is honorable, whatever is just, whatever is pure, whatever is lovely, whatever is commendable—if there is any moral excellence and if there is anything praiseworthy—dwell on these things. (Phil. 4:6–8)

Because Katy is so relentlessly anxiety-free, handing up everything to God, and because she focuses so purely on the true, the just, and the beautiful, she's forgotten the pain. The memories in a minor key don't get much airtime in her mind. And unlike a file system, our memory is "much more dynamic," according to Texas A&M University.[5] The more frequently certain neurons interact and fire together, the stronger those pathways become. Memories that are often rehearsed, or that replay against your will due to trauma, are more likely to remain.

Just like a song played more often on the radio will have more staying power than a song you heard only once.

But the "brain is a plastic organ," they report. If you don't use certain neuro pathways or memories, you lose them.[6] Katy wrote regarding the atrocities of the war, "But some of this doesn't bear telling and the rest is better not told." She takes this posture on almost anything you could count as bad news. This habit of flushing out the bad and rehearsing the good is what allowed—and allows—her to forever push ahead, forgetting what lies behind.[7] Fortunately, she wrote about some of it and hinted at other parts before her mind off-loaded the memory.

In 1970 when she returned to Nigeria, Katy was anxious to get back to Bible translation. This was her life's calling. As important as the linguistics, literacy, and grammar work were, they were preparatory work for Bible translation, of which she'd give more and more of her time throughout her career.

One difficulty with getting back to translation is that the star local Mr. Oyama,[8] the most helpful Mbembe speaker in drafting Bible translation, had since been hired away as a teacher in Calabar. This is a perennial problem in Bible translation. Those most suited to the work can almost always make money, or more money, by employing their education in other fields.[9]

But from time to time he received leave. He would travel home and spend much of that time working with Katy to draft the book of Acts and work on a final revision of the Gospel of Mark.

The global church owes much more to Mr. Oyama than is recognized. While he was busy carrying out his responsibilities to take care of his family and seek gainful employment, Katy was beginning to realize that he was the true star of translation work in Mbembe. Having his help for only a month here or there was not an ideal arrangement.

What if a whole team of educated Africans were to own this project? And later on, what if they could exercise these gifts not only on a volunteer basis in spare days or weeks but as their primary vocation? But she would have to wait until the 1990s before she got to fully test that idea.

Pat and Katy settled back into village life. Their former language tutor jumped right back into his former role, also helping them with small tasks around the village.

Teryl Gonzalez, one of Katy's mentees and the head of Wycliffe's quality assurance and consultant training pipeline, often wonders not just how Katy got so much done but how she did it in the midst of all the visitors she entertained.[10]

Gonzalez, a few decades younger than Katy, describes a scene from the early 2000s as an example of her hospitality, her busyness.

In a typical month in Nigeria, Gonzalez explained, eighty translators from twenty-five different languages converged upon Jos for one of Katy's famous "one-book workshops." (In a one-book workshop, dedicated attention was given to one book or letter of the Bible. Katy would lead participants through genre considerations, tricky cultural background issues, discourse analysis, exegesis, theological concepts, key terms, and translation guidance.)

And "every one of those people saw her as a mentor, a mother, a benefactor in some way," Gonzalez said. And the cultural desire to honor her meant paying her an individual visit. "Every time you turned around, somebody was knocking on her door. Coming to greet. To express their affection."[11]

One night in Nigeria, Gonzalez left her lodging later than she'd normally go out—about 10:00 or 11:00 p.m. One of the translators was leaving Katy's home. The next morning, Teryl had to be up early. And at 6:00 a.m., as Gonzalez walked out, she saw another translator leaving Katy's home after having already visited and shared tea.

That's how it happens in Nigeria, Gonzalez said. The schedule is truly around the clock. And somehow, Katy ran these workshops all day, entertained scores of individual visitors at all hours, checked Scripture from other projects in between, and did the work of an entire platoon.

Newsletter from Katy, 1970:

> *The first rush of visitors, which filled our house with people all day and every day (or so it seemed) has lessened, but there are plenty of people in and out and constant crises to prevent any danger of falling into a dull routine. Many people come to ask for medicine, and this can be a problem. You can hardly refuse to help when a man is brought in from the farm with a deep machete cut on his leg, or a child who has fallen into the fire, and yet sometimes we feel as though we are becoming a full-time clinic!*[12]

Though Katy was already distinguished as a young scholar, these years marked a separation for her. She was one of only twenty to thirty women in SIL who'd ever received a PhD.[13] She was publishing papers and presenting them alongside Kenneth Pike and Eugene Nida (giants in the translation world). She wrote her dissertation in blinding speed and continued to write and teach, showing a tremendous gift for teaching and shepherding others into the work.

These things did not go unnoticed. Pat recounts:

> *In early 1966 Katy and I went to a 10-week workshop run by Dr. Kenneth Pike at the university in Nsukka. The workshop was attended by some others from different missions and we enjoyed making new friends amongst them. I believe it was during this period that*

Katy's skills as a linguistic consultant showed themselves. Dr Pike had been unable to bring an assistant with him and Katy stepped in to help him in various ways. Dr. Pike's linguistic concepts didn't come easily to lesser minds! He did realize this himself, and sometimes called on Katy to sit in with him on a tutorial where a student was struggling (she sat in on one of mine). She has an ability to put things clearly and simply, and to encourage and get alongside those finding things hard. I was rooming with her at the time and know that she sometimes found these sessions exhausting. Each student at the workshop was expected, with Dr. Pike's help, to produce a paper on some aspect of the language they were learning, and these were to be published as a collection of linguistic papers after the workshop. So there was a certain amount of pressure to produce! Katy made good progress on an early description of the grammar of Mbembe during that time.[14]

SIL began asking more and more of Katy. It seemed whatever she touched turned to gold. But Katy did not allow all of her time to be filled with the projects of others. She had an inkling, an itch to try something. Time away during the Nigerian civil war had given her plenty of time to think on it.

Much of the best work on Mbembe had not come from her but from Mr. Oyama and others. Surely this was not unreproducible in other places. What if educated mother-tongue speakers of indigenous African languages could be trained in Bible translation all over Nigeria? All over the world?

John Bendor-Samuel had been thinking the same thing. And in a show of just how high Katy had risen, it was decided that in a country filled with older male PhD linguists, Katy Barnwell, at the ripe age of thirty-two, the ink on her PhD dissertation still smudging, would take on the challenge.

Chapter 20

THE BOOK

"The greatest missionary is the Bible in the mother tongue.
It needs no furlough and is never considered a foreigner."
—William Cameron Townsend

Katy was not the only person working in Nigeria. And even if she may be the easiest person to point to, she did not come to her conclusions in a vacuum. Many times she engendered the ideas. Other times it was John Bendor-Samuel, Ron Stanford, the Gardners, Mona Perrin, Elaine Thomas, or Hans-Juergen Scholz.[1] Katy stressed, "All of it was dreamed up in collaboration. In teams."

In 1971, we see just how remarkably ahead of their time the Nigerian branch was. Reading Nigeria branch minutes and letters in the mid to late 1960s, and then jumping forward to 1970 and 1971 is like crossing a great chasm. Like traveling through a wormhole. The kinds of missiological changes that normally take lifetimes happened in only months.

This was no doubt partly due to the Nigerian Civil War and the removal of almost all foreign linguists. The late 1960s were also a coming-of-age season for the world, with colonialism officially dead or on its last breath, the Vietnam War, the Cold War, and the sexual revolution. It was a time of great upheaval. And mission work was no exception.

By 1971, in a proposed policy statement, the Nigerian branch director Ron Stanford, after much thought and prayer with Katy and other leaders in Nigeria, drafted what in hindsight is a magnum opus of *twenty-first-century* missiological thinking—four decades before much of the rest of the world got on board.
He writes:

> *1. The ultimate objective of our activity in Bible translation in Nigeria is to see the Scriptures available to as many as possible of the people of Nigeria in a language which they really understand and in which they can make an adequate response, and to see these Scriptures read and used as widely as possible.*

> *2. We believe that this is primarily the responsibility of the Nigerian church itself. One of our principal roles therefore is to serve the church in:*

>> *A. Helping it to see its responsibility to pray, to set aside some of its members for translation and literacy work, and to make financial provision for them;*
>> *B. Providing training for Nigerian translators and literacy workers;*
>> *C. Giving on-the-job encouragement and assistance at all stages of their work.*

> *3. Recognising that, all other things being equal, the best translator is one who is translating into his own language and, further, that a local church has both a special interest in its own area and a special responsibility to meet the needs of that area, we give high priority in our planning to stimulating much greater involvement by Nigerians in Bible translation and literacy work in their own languages and to training, encouraging and assisting such people.*

4. We recognise that there may be cases where Bible translation is needed and where the local church is unable or only partially able to meet the need—or even where there is as yet no local church. In cases such as these, more direct involvement of our own members will be called for. Such cases, however, should be regarded as the exception rather than the rule."[2]

He goes on to argue that they are not the primary leaders or doers. They are not the pilot, so to speak. Instead, they are a *"specialist service organisation, serving the Nigerian church."*[3]

It's hard to believe the date on this document. But it's correct. November 1971. The rest of the Bible translation world was just beginning to debate if it was appropriate to "use" "language helpers" as the actual drafters. Here the Nigeria branch is saying they must hand the baton to the Nigerian church, let them own the process, supply workers, and what financing they could, and the Western Bible translators ought to step out of the driver's seat, instead focusing on teaching, training, equipping, and walking alongside them, serving the Nigerian church as the church carries out the Great Commission among its neighbors.

Perhaps only the work of the Holy Spirit can explain it. Missionary movements take time to change. Decades, centuries. Not mere days and weeks. But it's as if the Nigeria branch returned after the Biafran war and woke up forty years into the future.[4]

KATY'S BOOK

In 1971, the Nigeria Branch of SIL would dip its toe in training Nigerians to do Bible translation. And who better to teach translation than Katy?

So Katy packed her bags and moved to Jos, SIL's headquarters in Nigeria. She continued to travel to the Mbembe whenever she could to continue their New Testament with them, but she could no longer live there. With her increasing responsibility, she needed to be in a central location. Soon, many hundreds of Bible translators in training would travel to her. And she needed a place to house them and feed them. And preferably, they should be able to travel by bus, car, or plane—not by river.

But what would she teach from? The only textbooks that existed on the subject, from authors like Beekman and Callow and Eugene Nida, were extremely technical. They were meant for PhD linguists who at that time were mostly Westerners.

How could she teach nonlinguists basic translation principles? Were there any teaching materials or books on this? There were not.

According to Ernst Wendland, professor of ancient studies at the University of Stellenbosch and one of the world's leading Bible translation scholars, none of the contemporary published training materials were any good—not for nonlinguists.[5] And so, beyond the monumental task of drafting the Mbembe New Testament and beginning consulting work to check Scripture all over Nigeria, Katy had to write her own materials for the course.

Barnwell leaned on the linguistic theory of influential thinkers like Eugene Nida, Charles Taber, John Beekman, and John Callow. But while they published almost exclusively for the academically fluent, Barnwell translated lofty ideas for people who had never studied linguistics.

For instance, where Nida proposed the hugely influential theory of "dynamic equivalence," Barnwell coined the term "meaning-based translation"—a simpler and less intimidating door to the same concept.[6]

She began writing teaching notes, slides, lectures, and scriptural exercises. And when she taught her first cohort, it was as if an electric current passed through the air.

Regular university students were learning how to develop a grammatical understanding of their own languages. They were learning translation principles. Within just a few weeks, they learned to draft strong Scripture translations. Not overly literal, wooden, slavish to English or any other major language text but genuine idiomatic translation, as if Jesus and the writers of the New Testament had spoken African languages all along.

Katy saw it then. She knew what Bible translation could become. Others saw it too. Her teaching materials, handouts, lectures, and slides were requested all around West Africa. Other branches and countries wanted to teach the same course.

Making copies of all that material quickly became tedious. SIL suggested she turn it into a single volume. A book. A book would be relatively easy to publish compared to all those disparate teaching materials. And after printing in bulk, it would be easier to hand it to students and ship them to various branches around the world. That is, should they keep wanting them. And want them they would. For fifty years now.

Over half the work was already complete because of the number of times Katy had run the course. Any tricky spots or errors had been caught by her students or teachers from other West African branches. She sat down to the task and soon had her draft.

She typed it herself, formatted it herself, and had it locally printed in Nigeria in 1975.

Feedback poured in from colleagues around West Africa. They loved it. They only wished it addressed even more issues and concepts in translation. Could she add those too?

As with any quickly produced and more-or-less self-published manual, Katy found many things she wanted to add, tweak, or improve. Word was beginning to get out not just in Africa but all over the world. *You can train mother-tongue speakers now. And there's a book that opens the floodgates.*

If *Bible Translation: An Introductory Course in Translation Principles* was going to go global, Katy needed to revise it.[7]

"I didn't realize it was going to be significant," she said. They were just her handouts and lecture notes at first. But she'd struck a nerve.

Had Katy met a need, or did she create the change by writing the book?

"I hope it was a bit of both," she said. Her hopes came true.

Her first edition convinced the early adopters—the type who stayed sharp and attended global conferences. They were eager to move in this direction. They took as many copies as they could with them, and even if only a few copies made it to a continent, it began to make its mark. The pen was beginning to shift away from the Westerner's hand and toward the local translators.

If the early 1970s saw the moment when Katy began to be distinguished among her peers, the early to mid-80s saw her star rise in the worldwide Bible translation movement. She caught people gesturing to her at conferences and whispering in their neighbors' ears. The temperature of a room changed when she entered it.

But not everyone in the translation world was smitten with the idea of equipping first-language workers to lead projects. William Cameron Townsend, who founded both Wycliffe and SIL, rejected the notion of having "tribesmen" take charge of translation efforts, believing that Westerners had an obligation to lead the work and not "pass the buck [and] let the nationals do it."[8]

Katy rarely paid attention to these things—the criticism or the praise. It was silly. What mattered was the Word of God translated for all people. And you were either for it or against it.

By now, not just translator trainers wanted her book. Not just directors and professors wanted it. Everybody wanted it. National translators trained on the first edition were now senior consultants themselves, training the next generation, and the next. A massive printing was needed. But shipping thousands of books was too expensive. Instead, the files would be digitized so they could be shipped on disks and printed locally.

All of Katy's publications were given as open a copyright as possible—exactly for this purpose. She never made a dime off of any of her work. I doubt she ever thought it could have been a possibility.

In 1986, the third edition was published. This was her magnum opus. She'd perfected her method and honed her craft. The lessons had already spread around the world, but the third edition would stand unaltered for thirty-four years until the fourth and final edition would be released in 2020.[9]

What made Katy's book so influential? Like so much of her work, it was completely different, and much more reader friendly than the texts that had come before.

Katy's training was revolutionary, said Ernst Wendland, one of the leading Bible translation scholars in the world. "In the old days, you'd have a translation workshop where you'd have someone teaching on semantics, someone on lexicology, some on syntax, some on discourse, and then you'd expect the translators to go out and apply that themselves in their actual work."[10] Wendland referred to this as the deductive approach. When they opened the Scriptures, they were lost for how to begin. "That's not the best way to teach translators."[11]

Anybody whose eyes have glossed over while hearing lengthy rules to a board game knows this feeling. Imagine training in advanced linguistic concepts for months with zero hands-on experience. But if you're thrown into the board game with seasoned players helping you and advising as you go, you can learn much faster and more enjoyably.

It seems obvious now—the same reason you wouldn't teach swimming on a chalkboard. Some learning is best grasped by doing. Inductive learning. Katy did this for Bible translation.

In her training, she invited first-language speakers to wade into the pool, getting their feet wet with real translation work and encountering real problems as they went. Rather than learning rules and concepts, they worked through the Bible, becoming skilled in semantics and discourse and all the fancy disciplines along the way—without necessarily knowing the names of those fields. In this way, she discipled her students. She shepherded generations of them.

It might seem obvious in light of today's learning theories, when we just seem to know that you wouldn't teach swimming on a chalkboard. But at the time, Barnwell's training was revolutionary, and it multiplied in ways she couldn't have imagined.

Katy's approach took more effort, but it produced better results.

Scores of her translators went on to become consultants and trainers, and they spent a career doing that work. And their students did the same. Larry Jones, the former CEO of The Seed Company, together with other senior colleagues, estimates that in Asia, Africa, and Latin America, the number of translators trained on her materials numbers in the thousands.

She didn't know it then, but nearly fifty years and four editions later, her book would still be the standard manual for training Bible translators the world over. I used it in my training overseas, and so has every translation consultant I interviewed for this book. One person I interviewed (Danjuma Gambo) even had to step away from teaching Katy's book in order to interview with me via Zoom.

According to Wendland, competing materials were developed by UBS and other organizations, "But none to my knowledge have really succeeded in replacing or in doing something better than [Katy's book]."[12]

SIL doesn't keep reliable sales figures for her book.[13] That's because it's given away for free in Translator's Workplace—the software program Katy and her team created in the 1990s. And in that software program, across the dozens of languages it's translated into, her book is one of the most used. It often sits permanently open, highlighted, dog-eared, and flagged.

Of the approximately three thousand[14] Bible translation projects that have begun since the 1990s, once Katy's methods were well ensconced across the Bible translation world, you'd be hard-pressed to find more than a dozen of them that aren't directly downstream of her book, her teachings, her consultants, or the many consultants and translators trained by her generations of trainees. This means that Katy's book, *Bible Translation: An Introductory Course in Translation Principles,* is one of most influential books not only in missions history but in world history.

Katy and the Nigeria branch were having a decidedly good go of things. In these moments, you wonder, *Can the high last forever?*

That's when the rumors started. The accusations. Were Katy and her colleagues CIA intelligence agents?

Chapter 21

THE CIA

*"It is astonishing how many communities that were
previously consigned to the dust heap of society received
a new lease on life from their encounter with the gospel."*
—Lamin Sanneh

Course after course, Katy had the evidence. Africans can translate their own languages better than outsiders. But like any non-Bible scholar, they need help. With some translation theory and a whole lot of biblical background and exegetical help, Katy saw a future in which Westerners no longer "held the pen."

But old habits die hard.

Already the Nigeria branch was being singled out for criticism. It hadn't gone unnoticed that in 1970 the whole Nigeria branch seemed to wake up in the next century. Everybody else was still happy in their models from the 1930s and 40s. Who were these Nigeria branch folks, and who did they think they were?

How could indigenous people ever hold a candle to the level of work Westerners could do?

In many ways, this way of thinking was racist and colonialist. But in real life, there are rarely such easy straw-men targets. The linguists doing battle with Katy were not monolingual uneducated Americans, unsympathetic or unaware of the ability of non-Westerners. Many of them were trilingual and had spent more of their lives overseas than in the West. It's not as simple *as good guy–bad guy.*

If you think charitably about the situation SIL was in when they began, their methods were appropriate. Had the Bible translation movement begun in Nigeria in the 1960s, it would have taken a different heading. Not because of racism or lack thereof but for the pragmatics of it.

The Nigeria branch was quickly figuring out that in their context the SIL methods used in the Americas simply wouldn't do. But people become attached to their methods. It seemed like the debate would rage on for decades, with a slow sliding scale eventually tipping to Katy's side. But soon a catalyst nobody expected would radically alter the history of worldwide Bible translation.

On February 13, 1976, Lieutenant Colonel Bukar Suwa Dimka and a group of his followers attempted a coup d'état in Lagos, the capital of Nigeria at the time. Though the coup was carried out by Nigerians, suspicion over outsiders exploded.

Did foreign intelligence have anything to do with the coup attempt?

The Nigeria Bible Translation Trust's internal historical documents show that just two weeks after the attempted coup, "two Immigration Officers called on the Officers of the Institute of Linguistics and asked them to go to Lagos on the 18th of March 1976. While in Lagos, the leaders of the Institute were asked to [close down] and produce a specified and clear plan of the turning over by 1st April 1976."[1]

"Politically," Katy said, "some people felt they didn't want to promote the minority languages. Division between the different language groups or tribes was a sensitive issue. Any excuse was a good one to keep the minority languages down. That was the main reason—there were people in authority who didn't want to see that [promotion] happen."

Any outsider was to cease work, transfer their research to the university in Jos, and leave the country—all within just days.

Around this time a dogged rumor, long haunting Bible translation, was transplanted from Latin America into Nigeria. The *Daily Times* of Nigeria reported that "the government felt concerned with the activities of the institute."[2] Rumors had been circulating that the linguists were linked with the US Central Intelligence Agency. The *Daily Times* did not directly allege this since there was and is no evidence. Still, only sentences later, they tie the closing of the Institute to the closing of something else, the "US radio monitoring base at Kaduna."[3] These radio monitoring bases were widely known to be US intelligence gathering operations.[4]

The linguists were not intelligence agents, but rumors are notoriously hard to disprove. Time and time again, this rumor has developed and spread.

Imagine, dozens of Western scholars with PhDs choose to make their lives among tribes, minority people groups in the jungles, contracting malaria—all when they could be sitting in endowed chairs in Western universities. Why would they do this?

I'm sympathetic to the suspicion. Without the motivation of the gospel, it simply doesn't make sense. But with an understanding of the gospel, there could be fewer higher callings. "And everyone who has left houses or brothers or sisters or father or mother or children or fields because of my name will receive a hundred times more and will inherit eternal life. But many who are first will be last, and the last first."[5]

In Colombia, translator linguists were victim to a similar rumor. In 1981, the *Boston Globe* reported that about a decade earlier in Colombia, "speculation arose that a secret US rocket base was being constructed at Lomolinda, perhaps in the lake."[6] The Colombian government began a commission "to investigate the institute. For several months, Colombian soldiers, accompanied by several anthropologists, surveyed the Colombian interior by airplane, made surprise visits to Lomolinda and to several of the tribes with whom the linguists were living. . . . Although scuba divers explored the lake at Lomolinda for three days, they found no rockets or other suspicious materials. Overall . . . the investigation produced no evidence that the institute was engaged in spying or smuggling."[7]

At the height of anticolonial sentiment, every Westerner and Western institution was now viewed with suspicion. Truth blurred with conspiracies and James Bond plots. But it wasn't all conspiracy. The suspicion wasn't entirely without reason.

In 1959, Americans named Thomas Anthony Dooley III one of the most admired men in the world,[8] immediately behind Billy Graham.[9] Dooley was a Navy physician and medical missionary serving in Southeast Asia before the Vietnam War. Many called him the "Jungle Doctor." There was even a strong push to canonize him as a saint within the Roman Catholic Church.[10]

But a few problems emerged. One was that he was caught engaging in homosexual activities, which in that era meant the end of his military career. Fortunately, for him, because he was a hero, the Navy didn't publicly shame him as they normally would have. The other problem is that after leaving the Navy and working as a missionary physician, he was recruited by the CIA. He served as an intelligence informant for years.[11]

For a world waking up from colonialism and the fever pitch of anti-Western sentiment rising to conspiracy theory in every corner of the globe, this true story is the fodder that fed a thousand fires.

It turned out that though there's never been evidence this happened in Bible translation, the CIA had sought intelligence from a variety of religious nonprofits and missionaries working overseas.

The missionaries often meant well, trying to slow the spread of communism or keep religious freedoms. But missionaries informing for the CIA, payment or no payment, was simply unacceptable.

The US government publicly repented of this in 1976. "In 1976, a public policy statement was issued by then-CIA Director George Bush that the agency had terminated its 'paid or contractual' relationship with American clergymen and missionaries and would not renew them. CIA internal guidelines in effect since 1977 state that 'American church groups will not be funded or used as funding cut-outs (fronts) for CIA purposes.'"[12] They also state that the CIA shall establish "no secret, paid or unpaid, contractual relationship with any American clergyman or missionary . . . who is sent out by a mission or church organization to preach, teach, heal or (proselytize)."[13]

But the damage was done. All interviews, research, and journalistic correspondence considered (at least all those passing across my desk), it is likely that far fewer than 1 percent of missionaries overseas between the years of 1950 and 1976 had ever been pursued by an intelligence agent in the first place, and most of them never engaged out of principle. However, a rare instance or two made headlines, and this was enough for the rumors to affect missionaries all over the globe for decades to come and still today.

Politicians and wealthy businessmen who wanted to see Nigeria's tribes lose their land, resources, mineral rights, oil rights, language, and customs, did not want those tribes to become literate. From their point of view, that would be a disaster. They did not want the local language codified, written, or taught through children's primers, dictionaries, Bibles, and liturgical material. They didn't want them to be committed Christians, knowing their equal worth before God. They didn't want them to be able to read the constitution, send local representatives to university, become lawyers, and muck up the long process of exploiting them, robbing them, and running away with their birthright.

And those exploitative politicians had an ace up their sleeves. Accusing missionaries of espionage is a perfect political move. It requires no proof but almost always works.

SIL was not working with the CIA then or ever. Though many journalists and scholars have bet a substantial portion of their careers in trying to find a connection, none have turned up any evidence at all.

As a scholar and journalist myself, a regular hunter of skeletons, the notion that a group of Bible translation organizations with more than ten thousand employees around the world could be working with US intelligence and manage to keep this a complete secret with no evidence is laughable.[14]

There were almost no Americans with SIL in Nigeria. Most Westerners were Brits, Germans, and Swiss. If they were going to endanger their lives, reputations, families, and work by informing on local politics, wouldn't they work with MI6 or the German BND? Does it make sense to give that intelligence to a nation to which they didn't even belong?

I asked Danjuma Gambo about these allegations. "They were just using that as an excuse," he said, "because they knew that the work [we] were doing—the liberation—the development of the local languages, was making people more aware of their rights."[15]

This is a theme across Africa and the world. The development of the local languages, dictionaries, and primary school in the mother tongue is powerful. Not to mention Bible translation. Reading and hearing in your first language that you, too, are made in the image of God, that you, too, are of no less value to God than kings—the cultural power of this cannot be overstated.

"It is astonishing how many communities that were previously consigned to the dust heap of society received a new lease on life from their encounter with the gospel." Wrote the late Lamin Sanneh, professor of world Christianity at Yale.[16]

The good news of the gospel elevates and dignifies the marginalized, the lowly. True Christianity is often a threat to those who hold the keys of power, and those in power have taken note. But politically, accusations of espionage have proven to be one of the most effective ways to rid a country of missionaries.

After these accusations, Nigerian and expatriate leaders hatched a plan. They formed a committee of influential Nigerian leaders, including governors, general secretaries of major organizations, and even Bishop Festus Segun, the Anglican bishop of Lagos, now the largest city in all of Africa. With only days to prepare, this committee traveled to Lagos to plead their case.

They had a bold request. If they transferred full ownership and leadership of the work into Nigerian hands, could the work continue on in the form of a Nigerian organization?

The federal government of Nigeria granted this request. This organization would become the Nigeria Bible Translation Trust, which for decades was one of the leading Bible translation organizations in Africa.

The second request, Gambo told me, was a concession. If they were to lose dozens of Western scholars, they requested to keep four expatriate workers for twenty years in order to fully train and transfer the leadership of the organization. The request was granted but only in part.

Three expats were given temporary visas for only one to two years, and they were only allowed to operate at the University. As for the NBTT, as it grew and took on exclusively Nigerian translators, only one expat could remain to train them.

It's not difficult to guess who they chose.

Chapter 22

THE END OF
SIL NIGERIA

"Why don't we always live life like this,
with the Last Day in mind?"
—Katy Barnwell

June 29, 1976

Dear Everyone,
I wish it was possible to share with you all the
experiences of the last three months. At no other time
in my life have I been made so much aware of God
acting in human affairs, working out His purpose.
Often it has been the events which at first sight
seemed the most disastrous and painful which have
been the very things which He has used for good.
The biggest blessing of all has been the way that the
fact that expatriate members of Wycliffe are having
to leave Nigeria has stirred up Nigerians to take up
the responsibility for Bible translation here.
For a long time we have been praying for more
Nigerian involvement in this work. Now we find
ourselves within three months in a position which
would have taken years to work out without those

*somewhat drastic recent events. From July 1st the
"Nigeria Bible Translation Trust" will be taking over the work begun under Wycliffe Bible
Translators, with a Nigerian administrator in
charge and a completely Nigerian council and executive committee. The strong support which these
men have given has been heart-warming and gives
grounds for great expectations for the future. Many
of them are in important positions, carrying other
responsibilities, and yet they have given much time
and energy during these months.*

*It is entirely due, under God, to their initiative
and persistence that the continuation of the work
begun under Wycliffe will be possible. At one time it
looked as though all the facilities here, built specifically for the furtherance of Bible translation and
literacy work in Nigeria, would be taken over for
other purposes. But now it is officially approved that
the Trust can take over the centre here, including the
printing press, and continue the work.[1]*

*They also secured permission for four of the pres-
ent Wycliffe members to continue to work in Nigeria
under their auspices, functioning as consultants and
assisting in the training programme for Nigerians.
The aim is to train Nigerians to the point where the
work can be completely Nigerianized by the end of
five years. I count it a real privilege to be one of these
four. The others are Mona Perrin, Elaine Thomas,
and Hans-Juergen Scholz, with his wife, Christel.*

*The news that any of us could stay came through
only 7 days ago, and was confirmed only this morning (29th June). There is nothing like an expected
dead-line date for spurring one on to get things
done. There has been maximum output in these
last weeks as everyone has put all their effort into*

preparing manuscripts for production. In more than one area, churches have set aside their leading men to help in checking translated scriptures in the short time available. Three New Testaments have been finalized for publication, and three others are near completion point. And the Printing Department has been working overtime for weeks on end. There has been a great clearing out too, as the dusty redundant papers accumulated over twelve years of work in Nigeria have been thrown out of the files for burning. Trivialities have been swept aside to make time to concentrate on essentials. Why don't we always live life like this, with the Last Day in mind?"

With Western translators removed from the country, Katy dove into training Nigerian translators. They were the laborers God was sending into his harvest. But sometimes your star rises too quickly for you to find your footing.

Katy was no longer just a standout among the Nigerian Branch. She was becoming recognized as one of the most standout individuals in *global* Bible translation. The shift toward mother-tongue translators leading the charge was just beginning, but it carried an inevitable momentum. Even the many who were against it seemed to understand that someday it would be the norm. The question was simply *how long it would take until the world was ready.*

Katy said they were ready *now.*

And the foremost papers, articles, presentations, and training book came from Katy's desk. So, just as she was gaining a firm footing training Nigerians as one of their only Western colleagues, she was promoted.

In 1980, Katy became the translation coordinator for Africa Area. This meant that what she had been doing in Nigeria wouldn't necessarily change. The difference was that instead of leading a single country, she'd be leading a continent.

Africa was ripe for the change Katy was bringing. Under her leadership, many local branches and national Bible translation organizations would spring up. And they all wanted Katy to teach their trainees.

It was as if SIL couldn't promote her fast enough. Though her responsibility was for Africa, the news had gotten out around the world. Katy's second year on the job shows not just African travel but a globe-trotting itinerary. It's hard to point to a single city, a single continent even, and call it Katy's home.

Much later, leading up to her fiftieth anniversary as a Wycliffe member, she was asked for a full timeline of her career. As her memory has begun to fade, this timeline from 2011 has been invaluable in piecing together Katy's wild working life.[2]

Her itinerary for 1981 reads like this:

"Consulting in Sudan (early 1981)."

"To Solomon Islands (three months)" Katy then footnotes "journey from Sudan to the Solomons included a sandstorm in Cairo, an earthquake in Athens and an airline strike in Australia." After three months in the Solomons,

"Papua New Guinea (three weeks),

"then Philippines to lead seminars and explore ways of fostering national leadership and responsibility in Bible translation, also training of translators.

"Consulting and leading Translation Consultant Training Workshop (TCTW) for

Ethiopia (June 14–July 19) and Sudan (July 20–August 31).

Led TCTW in Cameroon for Africa Area teams (Oct 17–Nov 14)."

"Consulting in Togo–Bassari (Nov 21–December 8),"

"in Nigeria–Mumuye, Mwaghavul (Dec 8, 1981–Jan 20, 1982)"

"Visited Mbembe area over Christmas and New Year for checking of Mbembe New Testament."

Her training and consulting trips got so complex, she resorted to scheduling some to fit within the bookends of a longer trip, much as Mark writes stories in his Gospel. She began training in Mwaghavul on December 8, broke to work on some of the final stages of her original project, the Mbembe New Testament, and then returned to Mwaghavul to finish consulting. It's tempting to ask, "In 1981, did Katy have a home address?", and 1981 is no particular anomaly. Every year following this until 1989 showed the same nomadic existence—training, checking Scripture, and consulting around Africa and the globe.

This reminds me of a warning Jesus gave to an optimistic upstart who wanted to follow him: "A scribe approached [Jesus] and said, 'Teacher, I will follow you wherever you go.' Jesus told him, 'Foxes have dens, and birds of the sky have nests, but the Son of Man has no place to lay his head'" (Matt. 8:19–20).

The missionary life is a trying one. And many who serve God in this way follow Jesus into an uncomfortably itinerant life. For some reading this—sitting in a comfortable chair, well rooted in a community, surrounded by close family—the missionary life can seem like an adventure. It can be.

But missionaries are often lonely. They have to say goodbye to their friends and communities every few years. They uproot so frequently that soon it becomes difficult to keep making the effort. After leaving a half dozen communities you've known and loved, how hard would you work in your third language to develop new friendships, which too would pass with your next assignment?

And the travel quickly loses its allure. Miss your third connection, thirty-six hours into your transit around the globe, sit for twelve hours in a developing country's airport, only to then squeeze into an economy-class seat for another eight hours, and then hop on a unair-conditioned bus situated on the equator for six more hours. A good night's sleep is a distant memory, and the idea of adventure quickly dies.

The words *travel* and *travail* both come from the same Latin word for a three-pronged torture device. As any missionary knows, that's not by accident.[3]

Chapter 23

SINGLENESS

When I remarked to Katy just how nomadic her life was during the 1980s and 1990s, her eyes sparkled. "That's the advantage of being single. You haven't got any commitments."

The life Katy led would have been nearly impossible for a family. Gone for three to six months at a time, home for less than a quarter of the year, year-round? Most missionaries in Bible translation have families. At that time, they had to be more planted in a single community.

It's precisely this erratic schedule, living and working everywhere at once, eighty-hour weeks, for sixty years—not as compulsion but as passion—that no married person could have done well while also honoring their spouse and children.

Katy knows this and finds great meaning in this. Though she does not claim to have a call to singleness or a gift of singleness, as many call it, she certainly shows all of its signs. Unlike many in that situation, she never expressed a great pining, a great crying out, a wondering of *Why me, God?*

Katy was open to finding the right man and marrying. It simply never happened, she said. And she was not bothered by it.

When she first told me this, I didn't believe her. People recast their narratives in all sorts of ways to make themselves feel better. Every few weeks, I'd gently approach the subject again. Had she been on dates? Were there boys in school or young men at university she'd had feelings for?

She knew what I was up to. I think she understood I had to keep going back over that territory. Finally, with a glimmer in her eye, she said, "I'm sorry for your story, but there are no romances." Could she be remembering correctly?

And then, in reading through thousands of her personal letters from the time in question, I changed my mind. I believed her. She hardly ever brought up the subject.[1]

By contrast, read other great missionaries of the time. Elisabeth Elliot's journals and letters over the same period minutely detail her dating and courting life in both high school and college. After meeting her future husband Jim, her increasing longing and love for him come to dominate the pages. This seems more the rule than the exception for young single people wanting to find a spouse.

Elisabeth Elliot was not called to singleness. Called or not, Katy Barnwell had the gift.[2] And she finds herself in good company.

In these conversations, people sometimes talk about Saint Augustine, or monks, or Catholic priests. It's easy to forget that our Lord himself was single. Katy also points to the apostle Paul, likely the most influential apostle and author of approximately 24 percent of the New Testament by word count.[3]

"I say to the unmarried and to widows: It is good for them if they remain as I am. But if they do not have self-control, they should marry, since it is better to marry than to burn with desire."[4]

Paul goes on to write that though marriage is good, those who are able to remain single are free to focus more wholly on the Lord.

Those who are married are concerned not only with how to best serve God but also how to serve their spouse and family. This causes a kind of tug-of-war. Though many of the early disciples were married, Paul was not. And this is part of what allowed him to have the same kind of transient existence that, some nineteen centuries later, Katy would.

I want you to be without concerns. The unmarried man is concerned about the things of the Lord—how he may please the Lord. But the married man is concerned about the things of the world—how he may please his wife—and his interests are divided. The unmarried woman or virgin is concerned about the things of the Lord, so that she may be holy both in body and in spirit. But the married woman is concerned about the things of the world—how she may please her husband. I am saying this for your own benefit, not to put a restraint on you, but to promote what is proper and so that you may be devoted to the Lord without distraction.[5]

As little as Katy bothered to talk about it, her call to singleness was not merely a *part* of what made her so influential. It's the *precondition* for her success. Many of the things that distinguish her life and career simply could not have happened if she were a wife and mother as well.

Chapter 24

DREAMING OF A
GREEN CHRISTMAS

K aty's life had become so busy that though she and her team had drafted the Mbembe New Testament as of 1974, her increasing responsibilities took her away from the work of correction, revision, and redrafting. It's hard to train the world to do Bible translation and still make it back to the village where you began a translation yourself.

Today, this wouldn't be a problem. Knowing Katy, she'd be on Zoom at any hour of the night to work with her Mbembe colleagues. But in that era, especially with no access to fax machines in rural Nigeria, she had to be present to do the work.

At this time, she began going to the Mbembe over her Christmas holiday. Given that her trainings, Scripture checking, and conferences were often many-week affairs, bouncing from one place around the globe to another, it rarely made sense to travel all the way to the Mbembe for only a week, just to head off again around the world.

But all bets are off around Christmas. While the rest of the Christian world did not make significant work plans from about December 15 to January 5, Katy spotted her opportunity.

Whenever she could, she took three to four weeks over Christmas to be with the Mbembe. There, she connected with the team she'd worked with to translate. They would review, check, and test Scripture. Testing is an exhausting but necessary process to make sure the translated message communicates what it ought to. When multilingual language geeks who know a good bit of theology do translation at their desks, it doesn't always communicate the same to the expected audience.[1]

By mid-1984, the Mbembe New Testament had been fully tested, checked, drafted, and redrafted. All that was left was for it to be typeset and for the tapes or disks to be sent to Dallas.

Katy returned to the UK where she would have access to the right computers and software to typeset the Mbembe New Testament. And together with Heidi Rosendall, an expert type-setter in minority languages and complex orthographies, they finalized the Mbembe New Testament.

They saved the files to something Katy called "tapes" but on further reflection, they may have been disks. Whatever medium the files were saved on, they were finished and sent from the UK on December 23, 1984. Katy made her goal. She got it done by the end of the year.

Katy was delighted to get the tapes sent when she did. Six days later, on December 29, 1984, her father died. He suffered emphysema. The end was hard. Every day he was less able to breathe than the day before. Katy was glad to be in the UK during his final weeks. Though working on typesetting when she could, she also helped her father and supported her mother during those difficult days.

After his passing, Katy remained for two months to help with the funeral, spend time with family, and make sure her mother was okay.

Katy had a restrained relationship with her father. They loved each other but never quite understood each other. Katy's childhood was clearly marked by the disfavor of not being social enough, pretty enough, or able to do the *right* things for the time—marry at nineteen and have children. Instead, what called her was academia, a PhD, Bible translation, and revolutionizing missions many times over.

Colonel Barnwell wasn't interested and didn't follow Katy's career. What was the point of missionary work? Though her mother and brother would visit Katy on the field, her father and older sister never did.

Much of Katy's greatest contribution to the world of Bible translation occurred during the 1980s. This decade saw Katy crisscrossing Africa and the globe, primarily training others to do the work of translation. She led translation workshops, one-book workshops, translation teams, and linguistic courses. She taught her methods and her book to hundreds of people, year after year.

The students from those days now line the senior leadership levels of Bible translation organizations all over the globe. A family tree of Katy's trainees gets remarkably unwieldy.

But during this time there are no civil wars to escape or espionage accusations. There are no new revolutions in Bible translation, only the continual rolling out of the revolution Katy and her colleagues helped to usher in the previous decade. Though we have less ground to cover here, it certainly does not mean the decade was uneventful. It only means that the rules for good storytelling and good Bible translation leadership are not the same. Faithfully training hundreds—thousands—of people all over the world in translation and linguistics may not carry a story like conflict or danger does, but it carried *the story* of the good news of Jesus of Nazareth to the ends of the earth.

But if they were going to train mother-tongue translators[2] all over the world, how would they help them understand the text they were working with? Mother-tongue speakers know their own language fluently and intuitively. With adequate training in translation principles, they can do good work.

But what if they don't understand the source text—namely, the Bible? From simple questions like, *What in the world is a Levite?* to trickier questions like, *What does "the kingdom of God" refer to? What is sin, justification, sanctification, propitiation, or atonement?* These are matters professional Bible scholars still actively debate. How could we expect those without a formal biblical education to translate terms well if they cannot understand the terms?

If cutting-edge applied linguistics was the major strength of SIL and Wycliffe, biblical scholarship was not. In that era, it was much more common to find senior SIL employees with PhDs and master's degrees in linguistics than in biblical studies. Some had taken a few semesters of Greek and had accumulated much general knowledge about biblical backgrounds, but that was the extent of it.

They could explain what a Levite was, but the notion of how Jesus's preaching on the good news of the kingdom fit together with Paul's preaching of the good news of salvation and how those were in fact both parts of the broader reversal of the curse of sin and death, from now into eternity, may not have been as clear.

"That was a weakness of Wycliffe in the early days," Katy said. "I wish I'd had more formal training in that area."

But Katy made up for it. In pouring through biblical commentaries, Katy and many others realized just how valuable a deep biblical scholarship was to translation. PhD linguists can read biblical commentaries and fully follow along in those texts infamous for being closed off to all but the most educated. But what about mother-tongue translators all over the world?

They too could benefit greatly from senior scholars, but the commentaries were too dense to read, and often they were only published in English or German, sometimes French or Spanish.

But just as Katy translated the difficult concepts of linguistics from Nida, Beekman, and Callow into her *Bible Translation: An Introductory Course in Translation Principles*, why couldn't she and her colleagues do the same for biblical commentaries? Regular people already experience a taste of biblical commentaries in the much shorter and simpler notes in study Bibles. Could a middle ground between a scholarly commentary and study Bible notes be found? Could they communicate biblical scholarship in a way that nonscholars could understand?

Under Katy's leadership, they began the series called "Translator's Notes." It was precisely that—below the level of biblical scholarship but more in-depth than study Bible notes. And they were aimed at local translators and the particular issues they faced.

As described by Katy, "The aim of the Translator's Notes is to put the cookies on the bottom shelf."

Few outside the academy could be expected to read a thousand-page commentary on every book they're translating. But what about a system of concise and exegetically tuned lists of notes to help translators as they translate?

And put the cookies on the bottom shelf, they did.

Katy and a large team of linguists and Bible scholars have published dozens of Translator's Notes manuals. In the early stages before laptops, it was clunky. These would be printed and shipped, or saved on disks and then sent around the world to the relevant teams ad hoc, printed, and used. Then marked up, lost, destroyed.

Not long after, in the early 1990s, Katy had a vision. Instead of a strange curiosity, laptops were becoming affordable enough and powerful enough that Katy understood the potential. A laptop could hold more books than a human being could read in a lifetime. What if each of the thousands of local translators around the world had not just a few resources but a full library? Hundreds, no—thousands of resources from the best publishers in the world? Original languages, commentaries, journals, Translator's Notes, exegetical helps, linguistic helps? This would cost tens of thousands of dollars per copy.

Could there be some other way?

Chapter 25

A JOB OFFER

As wonderfully as Katy had done in Nigeria, and then all of Africa, in the UK and East Asia, South Asia and the Polynesia Islands, there was one country in which she'd not worked much at all: the United States of America.

Wycliffe US was headquartered in California (now Orlando, Florida), and SIL was headquartered in Dallas. And they both had Katy's number.

Katy was the highest-ranking linguist in all of Africa. On the technical and scientific ladder of linguistics, there existed only one post above hers in the entire organization. And that post had an office in the US. And the time was up. The mother ship was calling.

DAVID BENDOR-SAMUEL

At some point in the second half of the 1980s, Katy was asked to consider leaving Africa to take the highest possible promotion in her field—International Translation Coordinator.

She declined. She already had her hands full with Africa. Training African translators and consultants was her life's calling. How could she expand to the whole world?

But it seems there was nobody else within a mile of her qualifications. The person in that role before her simply held on, hoping she'd change her mind. And discreetly, leadership began asking higher-ups all over the world who would do a good job. The same name kept coming up.

On June 23, 1988, David Bendor-Samuel, the international vice president for academic affairs (and the brother of John Bendor-Samuel), wrote to Katy. He began by surmising that she was likely in Nigeria, but since he couldn't know for sure, he would send copies of the letter to Nigeria and the UK because of Katy's nomadic life. Surely he'd catch her within a month or two in one of those countries. Then, after some pleasantries, he writes:

> *I thought it wise however to write now to introduce in a preliminary way a topic which I would like to discuss with you in greater depth when you are here.[1] I hope it won't ruin your peace of mind in the interim, but I would like to discuss again the possibility of your serving as International Translation Coordinator.*
>
> *I haven't forgotten the things you said last time we discussed this. You gave me several reasons which I felt I should accept why I should not consider your name. The need to identify another coordinator still exists, however, and I feel I should ask you to pray about the matter and be ready to discuss the possibility seriously with me in October. Let me briefly give you my reasons for returning to this topic.*
>
> *Ron Olson continues to feel that he should serve as coordinator only for a fairly short interim period. He would like to have the next person take over from him by the fall of '89. He sees the major emphasis of the next few years as needing to be in two areas: first, better preparation of our members*

in Biblical studies and second, training and help
for MTTs.[2] *He continually makes discreet enquiries*
of the people he has contact with concerning whom
they view as suitable to serve as coordinator and the
strengths that person should have. He tells me that
you are the one whom most people view as the best
choice for the position, both in general and in terms
of these specific emphases.[3]

    I know that you were reluctant to consider tak-
ing the coordinator's responsibility because you didn't
want to find yourself involved in trying to lead
into areas where people are not willing to follow.
You were afraid that many of our folk have priori-
ties and values somewhat different from your own.
I have discussed this with Ron and he feels that this
would prove to be much less of a problem than you
anticipate. He feels that the tide is flowing strongly
in the direction of what he perceives as your val-
ues and strengths. Even in Latin America there is
growing recognition of our need to train and help
others to do the translation and also of our need to
"translate for the local church" (i.e., subordinate our
judgment to that of local churches even in areas like
the degree of literalness). Obviously, this is a matter
we should look at very carefully together.[4]

He goes on to assure her that she would have the freedom
to help care for her aging mother. Though the position was in
Dallas, they would even consider moving that role to the UK if
she wanted to take it there. Remote work in the era of the fax
machine, pre-Internet, would not be easy. But they wanted no
one other than Katy. He closed by asking her to pray.

He did not pressure her for a reply. They'd speak in October.

David Bendor-Samuel's letter was a great encouragement to Katy. It's why it's one of the few that survived her many international moves.

It's important for us because it paints a crystal-clear picture of so many things Katy and her peers no longer remember.

Katy was not a climber. She did not set her eyes on achievement and titles. She loved the Mbembe people, the Nigerian people, and would have been more than content to stay in her original assignment. Or to stay in Nigeria. But in a field where promotion is predicated upon knowledge and ability, it's winner takes all. Even if you don't want it, it comes for you anyway.

Katy was offered this role before—the highest technical role in the entire SIL and Wycliffe world. The only thing higher are the C-level leaders like CEO, CFO, and so on. Katy had no interest in these roles because they're not so involved in Bible translation as they are managerial and administrative roles, constantly courting large donors.

When *International Translation Coordinator* was offered to Katy the first time, she turned it down. But her ability was so great, and her leadership so well thought of, that her peers could think of nobody else more suited. Many leaders will resonate with what it feels like to ask the perfect candidate to take on a role and then have them decline. It's exasperating.

Every new name pales in comparison to the one you truly wanted. It's rare, but sometimes going back to the dream candidate yields a yes. And what a relief when they say yes. Katy said yes this second time and inhabited that role for a decade. From 1989 to 1999, she carried the Bible translation world forward many decades.

In the letter we also see her reticence. As mentioned previously, Katy is notoriously inclined to look on the bright side. You can know her for years and never hear a critical remark. Even more, she rarely committed any criticism to writing. But we see here a hint of reported speech. Many did not like the new era of training mother-tongue translators. Asking a seasoned pilot to move aside for the new trainee to take the controls is never popular. And Katy's method, once novel and innovative, was clearly showing itself to be the future of Bible translation.

The role of International Translation Coordinator already presumed a mountain of soft skills including management ability, organization, drive, and hard work. But SIL leaders sensed that in the new International Translation Coordinator, two specialties must be well represented—that of training and equipping mother-tongue translators and increasing the biblical and exegetical skills in the organization, from senior consultants to translators.

Katy helped begin multiple series and helps for translators around the world, distilling commentaries and putting the cookies on the bottom shelf. More than this, she was the de facto leading voice worldwide in training first-language translators and national consultants.

Various branches were more or less on board. Africa and parts of Asia saw the potential, but some branches were hostile. Those who were most conservative were found then, and still, in Latin America. Mexico branch is often referred to as the most traditional of the branches. In some ways, their methods resembled and still resemble Uncle Cam's and Kenneth Pike's in the 1920s–1940s much more than the Nigeria branch in the 1980s.

When I went to train with SIL UND in the summer of 2013 I found there a live debate over the value of training local translators and nonprofessional linguists. Working with The Seed Company, which we'll discuss later, I was excited about partnering with local churches and translators. I was an evangelist for what I thought was an innovative method. But many of the students farther along shamed me and cautioned me against these methods. The right way was still to live in primarily one small community, develop the raw data for a grammar, leave the field for years to complete a PhD, publish a grammar, then go back and work with a language helper or assistant to draft their New Testament.

Because of this hostility toward me, I assumed training national translators and consultants was still hotly debated. I assumed it was new. What I didn't know is that the leaders and many of the more advanced students of SIL UND came almost exclusively from the Mexico branch. I'd stepped into a cul-de-sac thirty years past its resolution. Most of the rest of the world had long since moved on.[5]

It's hard to imagine how difficult it was more than two decades earlier, when only the early adopters were excited about Katy's book and methods.

David Bendor-Samuel says, "Even in Latin America, there is growing recognition of our need to train and help others to do the translation and also of our need to 'translate for the local church.'"[6]

In the traditional model, translation was often embarked on principally by the Western translator. They employed local help, referred to in the now anachronistic and racist-sounding term "language helper," which clearly delineated their place. They were not the translators. They were helpers.

Though many completed New Testaments were celebrated and adopted, it's just as common to hear of a missionary couple spending twenty-five years translating the New Testament, just for the books to sit on a shelf, collecting dust. Without church involvement, Scripture use becomes doomed.

In Latin America, the church was often much less involved, if at all. And if the church never got to champion the translation process, or own the translation process, they'd often keep getting by as they could in the wider trade language.

We don't know why it was different this time, but shortly after that letter, it seems Katy was ready to say yes long before the October conference. It was likely that the context decided it for her. They needed her skill set. And her peers overwhelmingly pointed to her. She was the best candidate. Though she was sad to go, she recognized the calling of her peers and her superiors as the calling of God.

And so, after making a home in Nigeria, it was time for Katy to begin her strangest cross-cultural experience yet. Dallas, Texas.

Chapter 26

INTERNATIONAL
TRANSLATION
COORDINATOR

Katy often remarks that the greatest cross-cultural challenge of her career was learning how to live in Dallas and
work in a bureaucratic office-style environment. From Katy's
PhD study to her work in Nigeria and around the world, she'd
been much more nimble. There was correspondence involved,
but she nearly always worked in small horizontal teams that
functioned organically.

When she arrived in Dallas, this all changed.

She credits her secretary Virginia Velie as her cultural insider.
Katy, ever the academic, was comfortable wearing the same two
to three outfits. This had always worked for her before and was
normal in her world. But Virginia told her, "That just won't do."
In the United States in the late 1980s and early 1990s, women in
leadership had different expectations than academic researchers.

Just as Katy contextualized to Nigeria, she was now in her
early fifties and having to recontextualize to an American office
culture. Virginia took her shopping.

She also had to buy a car. The US and Canada were, especially at the time, some of the only places in the world where car
ownership was a given if you intended to be mobile.[1]

This position had Katy in more of a ranching role than
a shepherding role. She was now shepherding the shepherds.

With this came less time in the field and more time in conference halls, meetings, and under piles of correspondence.

But she maintained as much activity as she could, regularly scheduling training events and checking trips around the world. The adoption of her methods was in full bloom. No longer was it the innovators and the early adopters who were interested in her work. It was now the majority who were adopting her model. The pen had passed to the global church.[2]

In reading through biographies of great people, you often get the sense they were somewhat lonely. Though they may be surrounded by colleagues and acquaintances, they had few friends. Their innate intellectual ability plus their drive to produce sets them apart from their peers. They feel a disconnect.

Just about everybody loved Katy and admired her, but there were not many who were equals. She had photos by the shoebox full of friends and acquaintances. Letters of constant correspondence keeping people up to speed. But few equals. As I read through five decades of her most important correspondence, I couldn't escape the sense that Katy was gracefully waiting for others to catch up. To understand. Always hand-holding—not patronizing but patient. There are few glimpses in her correspondence when she interacted with an equal.

And then the 1990s came.

Katy was chosen by her colleagues for the highest translation role precisely because of her strengths in training national translators, consultants, and her strengths in biblical studies.

The Translator's Notes series was revolutionizing the work of Bible translation yet again. It provided affordable and concise resources national translators could use to produce much better work. It was as if the first and second visits and checking sessions with a senior Bible translation consultant were already finished before their first draft.

But there had been a problem. Teams eager to dive into translation sometimes went ahead, translating each paragraph or book as seemed fit and then, as they approached other books and texts, did the same. When they ran into important theological terms, like *sin* or *salvation*, they may translate it differently and with little memory of how they'd done it the last time.

For the Western reader, these concepts may seem straightforward, but when you approach these concepts from a variety of other cultures and time periods, they get clouded fast. The Western notion of sin, for example, is remarkably contextualized and conditioned to three thousand years of Hebrew, Greek, Roman, and Christian understandings of life, culture, duty, and civilization. Many around the world share none of these cultural backgrounds. And although sin is just as pervasive in their culture, their understanding of it doesn't work the same as a Westerner's. Their concept of sin might be much closer to bringing shame upon their relatives or deceased ancestors. It might be connected with ritual impurity rather than moral impurity. It might have a more collective flavor than an individualized one. Westerners often forget that their Christianity is just as contextualized as African or Asian Christianity.[3]

For the term *salvation*, your religious background preconditions your understanding. Those from an animistic background might view salvation as being delivered from evil spirits and the curses of others. Those from a Buddhist or Hindu background may view salvation as breaking from the cycle of reincarnation, achieving true liberation through the extinguishing of this human life. For them, the world isn't something to be remade or regenerated; rather, it's an illusion to escape.

But in the Bible, creation is good, and humanity is good, marked with the image of God. But both are fallen and scarred, awaiting redemption. Salvation is to be saved from the curse of sin and death and *restored* to the goodness of creation, reconciled to the Creator. *Salvation* is not to have your humanity and its habitat extinguished because it's an illusion but to become even more fully human in the transformed image of God, living forever with him in the new heavens and new earth, which are also good.

One can easily see that how these words (and hundreds of others) are translated is enormously important for those who don't carry the same assumptions about these words. And if someone translates them differently at different times when they ought to be translated the same, new Bible readers are effectively hindered from developing a not only healthy but expressly *Christian* theology.

How do you build a theology of sin if the hundreds, maybe thousands of verses that refer to it are misleading and seem to refer to different things?

How do you develop a soteriology (a theology of salvation) if your translation is not clear about what you're being saved *from*? And saved *toward*?

Translation teams would get many years into a Bible translation only to realize they'd made a mess of these important "key terms." There are hundreds of them, and a translation team has to be especially careful in how they translate any of these terms so that they are interpreted uniformly across the entire canon of Scripture.[4]

As we learned from Katy previously, once the cake is baked, you cannot reverse the process to change the ingredients. By then it's too late.

Katy decided it was time for a master list of key terms. Each would have helpful exegetical research and the many ways a given term could be translated. It would then have helpful tips for translators to choose faithful, accurate, and clear translations that would effectively communicate the sense of that word in the original biblical languages.

Katy and a small team of exegetes and linguists took to the task. But Katy had come by exegesis less formally than her linguistics. She'd taken many classes in her undergraduate, master's, and PhD that aligned with biblical studies. She took night courses and correspondence courses and studied the languages on her own. But at the end of the day, she was a linguist and a translation scholar, not a proper New Testament scholar. And she knew where she needed help.

Around this time, a delightful correspondence began.

D. A. Carson is one of the most respected and prolific Evangelical scholars to live—not only in our time but ever. He earned his PhD at the University of Cambridge and for decades served as professor of New Testament at Trinity Evangelical Divinity School.

Together with Timothy Keller, he founded The Gospel Coalition, possibly one of the only English-speaking media and publication networks to rival *Christianity Today* since its founding.[5] Justin Taylor, the executive vice president of book publishing at Crossway, noted, "Dr. Carson's sheer productivity is nothing less than astonishing. One could become tired just working through the latest numbers: he has written fifty books; 235 articles; 112 book reviews; and forty-six edited books in the various series he edits. Average it out and it comes to about one book written or edited every four months, with one article and two reviews written every six weeks—for three decades."[6]

And those books together sold mountains of copies, from more approachable books for those in the pews, to dense and technical exegetical arguments, to biblical commentaries. He even published a book of sonnets.

His commentary *The Gospel according to John* is widely regarded among pastors and seminarians to be the best commentary—not just on John but the best commentary on any book of the Bible.[7]

Carson was interested in Bible translation and had begun to involve himself, serving from time to time during the summer break from his regular work at the University. And in the course of his volunteer work, he met Katy, learned from her, and served alongside her. Katy did not soon forget his ability, nor did Carson forget Katy's. Their correspondence shows a warm and mutual respect—Barnwell, the eminent translation scholar and Carson, the eminent New Testament scholar.

Though many of the key terms were within Katy's reach, some are so complex that not even expert Bible scholars can agree on the shades of meaning. Remembering Carson, Katy reached out for help. And soon reams of faxes were traveling between Chicago and Dallas as Carson began to help on the Key Biblical Terms list.[8]

Carson's feverish productivity took on these duties in stride. He contributed to an initial list of seventeen key terms but then went on to offer one more per week, approaching close to sixty contributions by the time of publication.

That finished book of more than five hundred pages proved immensely valuable. But it may not have been the most practical. In an age before portable computers and Amazon.com, how do you ship a five-hundred-page book to all the translators around the world?

Chapter 27

TRANSLATOR'S
WORKPLACE

U nder Katy's leadership, SIL's biblical, exegetical, and translation helps continued to grow. But it was grow-ing far faster on the shelf than on the translation table abroad. The Key Biblical Terms book was a great success. They printed a thousand copies and all sold. Academics like D. A. Carson begged for a spare copy—if any were allowed to go to non-SIL workers.[1]

But translators in Nigeria weren't using them unless they were transported and given to them. The same was true all over the world.

How could the knowledge of a three-thousand-volume library be delivered to all the translators of the world? Print simply wouldn't do.

But for the first time in human history, there was a medium that would accomplish the task. The hard drive. The personal computer.

Creating a library of digital tools would be extremely valu-able, and SIL had enough resources to move forward with the planning. But what would make it especially worthwhile would be resources SIL did not own. Namely, biblical commentaries and other valuable books outside SIL's domain.[2]

If you ask Bible scholars of a more Evangelical persuasion (which is dominant in Bible translation) to name the most influential Bible commentaries in their study and walk with God, you will often hear the same titles: Doug Moo's Romans in the NICNT series. Don Carson's John commentary in the Pillar series. Gordon Fee's First Corinthians commentary in the NICNT series, or G. K. Beale's Revelation commentary in the NIGTC series.

The most interesting thing about these lists is that it's easy to assume these heavyweight commentary series, often the most used and cited, are from different publishers. They have different names like The Pillar New Testament Commentary, or New International Commentary on the New Testament, or New International Greek Testament Commentary.

What they often don't know is they all come from the same publisher. Though Lifeway, Zondervan, Baker, B&H, and IVP may seem more like household names in Christian publishing, Eerdmans publishes the lion's share of favorite Bible commentaries and commentary series.

As of this writing, fully seventeen of the twenty-seven books of the New Testament have an Eerdmans commentary listed as number one at bestcommentaries.com. Not only that, but many of the remaining ten happen to be smaller, less used books, and often line the later stages of translation, like 2 Peter and Jude.

If there were a single publisher in the entire English-speaking world that SIL wanted to pitch this idea to, it was Eerdmans. Could they give away the greatest commentaries, each set of which costs well over $1,500 in print? Could they do this for free? How about for thousands of people?

The history of missions is full of ridiculous asks like this. If you give your work away for free, who will buy it? Normally, these requests go nowhere, but not this time.

Eerdmans was delighted. National Bible translators as well as strapped missionary Bible translators all over the world would be able to use their cutting-edge research. Resources that were bound to academic libraries for all of church history could now bless the global Great Commission.

And though Eerdmans was especially thrilled, many other publishers were glad to go along as well. Together, they licensed millions of dollars of hard-earned scholarship to be used for free, or near free in some cases, within SIL's Translator's Workplace software.

And on May 1, 1996, Translator's Workplace launched. According to SIL's website, the collection has "Bibles, Greek and Hebrew texts, dictionaries, commentaries, translation handbooks, articles and other reference materials."[3]

Within six months, Translator's Workplace enjoyed a thousand active users. And it only grew. After Katy's tenure as the International Translation Coordinator, a partnership with Logos Bible Software was made. Why ship all these great resources on DVDs and as PDFs when you could have the power of Logos? Want to see every single use of a difficult Hebrew word in the Old Testament? Easy. Want to see how twelve major translations have treated a difficult passage? No problem. Want to hover over any word to see its verbal parsing and dictionary entry? Want to open many of the best commentaries on a difficult verse in front of you? You got it.

Today, though estimates are hard to come by, it's rare to find anybody in the missionary Bible translation world (organizations like Wycliffe USA, American Bible Society, United Bible Society, The Seed Company, SIL, Pioneer Bible Translators, Lutheran Bible Translators, and Biblica) who does not use TW.

About 85 percent of Bible translation worldwide is accomplished by these organizations.[4] And all over the world, each of those Bible translation workers has a $54,000 library of the best resources on the planet, all for the low price of a one-time $50 fee.[5]

If it weren't for Katy's bold request—ridiculous request, frankly—it's unlikely this project ever would have happened.

Chapter 28

WHAT MAKES A BIBLE TRANSLATION CONSULTANT?

Training national translators was a landmark change in Bible translation. This one change may be Katy's greatest accomplishment. It may be the greatest single step to handing the baton to the global church.

But it would never end there.

Some of those translators would show not just a gift in translating into their own languages but the gifts to help others learn to do the same. They would show remarkable ability in understanding biblical backgrounds and in translating for meaning rather than only form. They were leaders, and they had the ability to unite various denominations in the single task of translating Scripture for the whole of the church.

These national translators were ripe to move on from "translator" to the higher echelons of the translation world—Bible translation consulting. Becoming a Bible translation consultant is *the* prized accomplishment. Like the culmination of the board exams for medical licensure, this is the moment when you officially enter the guild of the rare few. Because of how difficult the position is, and how many hard and soft skills require mastery, it's been a bottleneck in Bible translation since before Katy joined the movement.

The translators who received recognition as consultants were often those who'd spent "a million years" on the field, as one consultant put it.[1] They spent around two decades doing their own New Testaments and showed great skills along the way, like Katy. They were nearly exclusively Westerners, with Western PhDs and Western ancestry.

At some point, they were called up into the rarified ranks as a consultant. This meant they could "check" the translations done by other teams. Every Bible translation done by Wycliffe, SIL, UBS, and many others required a full consultant check before publication. This often meant many weeks in person, extensive notes and checking, then back to drafting and redrafting, more checking, and so on. Eventually, after countless hours, the translation team would have a final consultant check and receive a pass. Their translation was deemed clear, accurate, and faithful to the original. It could go on to publication.

It was noted for decades that the bottleneck in translation workflow was due to the lack of consultants. Many of the teams doing translation work ended up having to twiddle their thumbs while waiting on consultants. More were always needed.

But Katy saw a solution. During her famous one-book workshops, she witnessed eighty translators from twelve different languages helping one another in real time. They were doing the work of Bible translation consulting, but these were Nigerians who would never be recognized under the then-current system.

Many of her Nigerian-trained translators were better at the work of Bible translation consulting than her Western colleagues. But these Nigerian translators didn't have PhDs. They hadn't gone to a *different* country to do their translation work, but they worked in many other languages within their own country.

Like anything in life, raw talent predisposes certain people to certain things. Then hard work makes up the difference. And all over the world, there was a mountain of raw verbal, linguistic, and exegetical talent. But few channels were open before them to become recognized traditionally.

Just as Katy revolutionized what it meant to be a translator, so she would revolutionize what it meant to be a consultant. She'd begun training Nigerians toward the work of consulting as early as 1977. But by the time they were recognized, and translations they'd checked in that role were hitting the press, another decade or more had passed.

And recognizing Nigerians as translation consultants raised eyebrows not only within SIL but in the Bible translation world. What were these non-Western, non-PhD-holding folks who'd lived in Nigeria their whole lives doing calling themselves consultants? What really was a consultant?

It's true, they didn't have the gobs of formal education that many Western translators had, but they natively spoke a handful of Nigerian languages, many of which needed translation. They didn't have formal linguistic training, but they'd spent hundreds of hours receiving instruction, studying Katy's and others' teachings, and then spent thousands of hours at the translation desk.

They did not have formal seminary training, but they had spent thousands of hours poring through commentaries, dictionaries, exegetical helps, and word studies. And many of them had spent those hours next to Katy. They'd learned the craft from the best.

What mattered most was they could do the work. And they were not just getting by. They were often superior to their Western colleagues. Even if they may have had fewer lines on their CVs, many outperformed the Western consultants.[2] For one, they often spoke the languages they were consulting in as a fluent language learned from their youth, as well as Nigerian trade languages like Housa, Igbo, or Yoruba—or all three.

They also looked just like the people they worked with and thoroughly understood their culture. So many Bible translation projects explode when Western and non-Western worldviews meet. Western views of hospitality (or lack thereof), honor, respect, or how money is handled and tracked, all strongly grate against the customs and cultures of much of the rest of the world. But local Bible translation consultants don't share these weaknesses.

And so over time, you had Western so-called "ordinary" linguists rise to the level of consultant because of their mastery of the craft. Even more, non-Western translators were beginning to take on this role as well.

This was not warmly received. According to multiple sources, United Bible Societies (UBS) in particular was not pleased with these changes. Drama mounted on the field as UBS would not recognize certain Bible translations done by SIL as official, begging the question of whether UBS would try to start from scratch and repeat a translation where one had already been completed by Wycliffe.

Reinier de Blois, a former translation consultant with UBS, told me that there were even places where there was doubling. On one side of a village, SIL worked on a translation. On the other side, UBS worked on a different translation in the same language. "They were pure duplicates of one another," he said. "It was obviously very shameful."[3]

Now, some have painted this in a racist or classist way. *If you're not a white man with a PhD, we won't accept your work.* Though we're all sinful human beings, and so some bias along these lines likely played a part, we don't want to paint a simplistic straw man. Race, nationality, and education aside, you'll rarely find *any* industry where the people who've been doing the work the same way for thirty years gladly welcome massive shifts that upend the current model.

It's not as simple as that. It's also divinely inspired Scripture. It's not to be handled lightly. If what we have is working (albeit slowly), why change it? Shouldn't we have the highest possible standards for Bible translation? Can asking for a doctorate possibly be too much when handling God's revealed truth? Why lower our standards in the name of speed?

These are all fair arguments. In the end, they weren't valid, but in the beginning, Katy's opponents simply weren't sure yet. The battle lines had been drawn.

UBS was the more academic and PhD-credentialed organization in biblical studies. And Wycliffe/SIL was more credentialed specifically in linguistics but on the master's level. It was also the larger organization and often the innovator. Now, this may be confusing because SIL linguists were also well educated.

Though at the top of SIL's ranks, they produced some of the most cited linguists and biblical scholars of the twentieth century,[4] the main ranks of SIL tended to be regarded more as "OWLS" or "Ordinary Working Linguists." Now, to a normal person, being trilingual and having a master's degree in linguistics is no ordinary accomplishment. But in a world where everybody has at least those qualifications, the bar is raised. Then, it's the *true* scholars with PhDs and scholarly publications who sometimes look down on their otherwise extremely well-educated, but still less educated, peers.

UBS often fit the higher bar. Their members were more likely to be poached to head academic programs at seminaries and universities. SIL certainly had their share of these but fewer per capita.

It was a hard fight, but Katy would lead the day again on this discussion.

Does a PhD mean somebody would be a good consultant? Not necessarily. Many in the field knew of doctorate-holding colleagues who weren't good at all. But the kind of critical thinking and mental endurance typical of most PhDs makes a good consultant.

Does being a Westerner make one a good consultant? No. In fact, it sometimes predisposes one to be worse.

Does living in the target area for multiple years make one better as a consultant? Of course. How much better a native to the area than a Westerner who's spent a handful of years there?

Over time, with rigorous and systematic questioning like this, it turns out that being Western, or having a PhD, did not a consultant make. What made for a great consultant was a well-nurtured natural gifting, years of experience, multilingualism, years of demonstrating high-quality work under a senior consultant, and being recognized as a strong fit by peers and senior consultants.

Though the battle was hard, Katy won the argument. A good Bible translation consultant is, at the end of the day, one who helps translators produce the best Bible translations.

If your Bible translation training, guidance, checking, and final product exceeds the quality of the German PhD consultant at the other end of the table, you ought to be recognized alongside or even ahead of that person, even if you do not have their credentials.

Katy showed in this way that the work of Bible translation consulting was more akin to the apprenticing process in a blacksmith shop than the theoretical metallurgy one might learn in a chemistry PhD. Apprenticing under a master blacksmith requires loads of learning, mountains of practice, and all under the watchful eye of the senior expert. If your work doesn't cut it, you're helped, redirected, or eventually cut. But if you excel, and rise through the ranks, you too become a master blacksmith someday.

What Katy did for Bible translation was shift the requirements from a time and résumé status to a competency-based approach. How well do you teach, train, revise, check, and ultimately guide teams to do great translation work?

You may be a widow with few resources in a country that would never dream of sending you to the UK for a PhD. But by God, with a few thousand hours of directed practice, you can do this work as well as anybody. What's keeping her from serving as a Bible translation consultant?

UBS recognized Katy and SIL were on the right side of this question, and to their credit, after enough testing had come in that showed senior consultants could not tell a difference between the quality of work produced by one of their consultants and a national consultant, they came to the table.

SIL and UBS sat down and came up with a long list of competencies. What made a Bible translation consultant? And true to Katy's arguments and leadership, the list was primarily based on competency. Education was certainly a significant part of the process, like courses in linguistics, biblical backgrounds, translation theory, and biblical languages. But these were courses the Bible translation movement could offer or send translators away for a few months at a time to undergo—all while actively doing the work of translation. And all while being guided, critiqued, and helped along the way. These were not residential five-year PhD programs that removed translators from their field.

Whatever Katy touched, she remade.

In the 90s, it seems upending what had made a consultant for fifty years was not enough. Building Translator's Workplace and having the guts to ask publishers to give away tens of thousands of dollars of content—to each translator in the world—for free, was not enough.

No. Something else needed building.

Chapter 29

PARATEXT

If Translator's Workplace is the library of resources used by nearly all Bible translators worldwide, Paratext is the drafting desk.

Nobody knows for sure, but when I ask software specialists within Bible translation what percentage of translation drafting happens on Paratext, I've never heard an estimate under 90 percent worldwide. For more than a quarter century, nearly every written translation of any Bible passage around the world has been written in this program.

It's the Microsoft Word of Bible translation—that is, if Open Office, Pages, Google Docs, and Scrivener didn't exist.

At the Bible Translation conference in Dallas in the fall of 2023, I found the Paratext representatives at their table. I approached the table, introduced myself, and mentioned my work on Katy Barnwell. "Oh," they said, "we know that name. She had one of the most shared resources in Paratext for a very long time; still does."

"What resource?" I asked.

"It was the Key Terms list," they said. Of all the great resources Paratext had, it wasn't the full library that Translator's Workplace was. It wasn't meant to be. The list of key terms wasn't in there. So somebody took Katy's key terms list and made a version that played nicely with Paratext. And this external resource got shared like hotcakes all over the world.

That was nice to hear. Katy's resources found a way to crack in. But this certainly couldn't be called a major influence in the program. It was just a single resource. I wondered if they could remember anything else about Katy.

"I thought I heard from somebody . . ." I timidly began, "that Katy was involved in some way in the beginning of Paratext."

Of the three or four at the table, one had taken the lead in responding to me. And by the look on his face, I saw I'd made a mistake.

"Paratext is a UBS product. SIL had nothing to do with it." He may as well have said "period" at the end it was so curt.

It was clear I'd stepped on toes. Even hinting that UBS may not have invented this great program alone was hurtful. We all know the feeling of having a strong accomplishment attributed partly or fully to somebody else. It's not fun.

I learned my place.

But something changed. Just weeks before turning in the first draft of Katy's biography, I checked back to my earliest interviews with Katy. Not the interviews for the biography but the interviews I did for the *Christianity Today* story. And there, clear as day, Katy talked about early involvement, in some capacity, with Paratext. Had Katy misremembered?

I reached out to Reinier de Blois, the coordinator of the Institute for Computer Assisted Publishing with United Bible Societies. He is the inventor of Paratext. In the conflicting reporting I'd turned up, surely he could set me straight.

I asked him a similar question via email. Given the previous interaction, I was careful not to step on his toes. Had UBS prickled at a continual misunderstanding that SIL had developed Paratext? I didn't know the story. So I asked quite deferentially. Did Katy or SIL have anything to do with Paratext?

Nine minutes later, he replied. "Yes, Katy did play an important role in the development of Paratext. Could we meet via Zoom or by phone sometime?"[1]

As it turned out, the representative at the conference table had been wrong.

In 1983, Reinier de Blois moved from the Netherlands to Nigeria. He was unique then in Bible translation because he was a Hebrew scholar and would be working with people from three languages—the Izi, Ikwo, and Ezaa languages—to help them translate the Old Testament.

Though he didn't work near Katy, they bumped into each other at conferences and generally knew each other.

De Blois was "kind of frustrated," he told me. In the New Testament, there were not many resources, but there were *some*. UBS handbooks, exegetical resources, and background materials existed. But hardly anything existed for the Old Testament.

And in 1985, as computers were just beginning to be used in Bible translation, de Blois saw the potential. He traveled to the United States to Taylor University in Indiana. There was a six- to eight-week training in computer programming.

So he got his first computer. Though less powerful, he purchased a laptop so he could easily transport it back to Nigeria. It was a "Sharp PC 5000 with eight lines of screen. It had bubble memory and a little cartridge you'd put in," Reinier told me.[2]

At this training, he happened to pick up a little booklet on a coding language that Gary Simons at SIL had created, "Powerful ideas for text processing: an introduction to computer programming with the PTP language."

"This is really cool," a guy told him as he handed it to him. De Blois read it and began playing with the language to see how he could create tools. Could he make the work of Bible translation easier? Could he coax a computer into showing the original Hebrew, dictionary definitions, as well as the ways major translations like the RSV and NIV had translated these terms?

"I started, and started, and restarted many times," he said. He worked in DOS and found he loved the work of computer programming.[3] He designed fonts for biblical Hebrew, obtained digital copies of the NIV and RSV (the predecessor of the ESV and NRSV and one of the more popular translations of the twentieth century).

He worked on this on and off for years. And by 1994, he felt he had something to share with his colleagues. He worked for a Dutch mission, but his brother worked for United Bible Societies. And in 1994, there was an important conference in Chiang Mai.

If you follow Katy's CV through to 1994, you'll see this: "Representing SIL at UBS Triennial Conference May 8–27 in Thailand."[4]

At the conference, in a breakout session, de Blois demonstrated the software. And Katy sat in attendance.

Katy had an uncanny ability to look twenty years into the future and make it happen *now*. Computers were taking over on the field, and the demand for Old Testament translation was skyrocketing. All over the world, hundreds of communities whose translation projects were begun in the 1930s through the 1950s now enjoyed a full New Testament.

But if, with scissors, you removed all the Old Testament references, citations, and allusions from the New Testament, it would look like you'd stuck your hand into a paper shredder's bin and dragged out the mangy scraps.

Agricultural tribes have described the New Testament as a machete without a handle. A tree without roots. Even though Katy was no programmer or even interested in computers, she knew these two things: Old Testament translation was the next frontier. And so was a radical adoption of computer software.

"She had a lot of vision," de Blois said. That's why she was there in that room that day.

After the demo, Katy was so impressed that she asked Reinier to clear a month from his schedule to fly to Dallas.

What's especially interesting about this is that SIL had been working on a similar program for years. But she saw the potential in his program.

They flew de Blois to Dallas, and he demoed the software. They loved it but didn't like that it ran in such a strange language. PTP was a niche language that was not widely used. He'd have to rewrite the program in Microsoft's Visual Basic.

"But I'm not a developer," he said. "I got this book by accident."

He was wrong. He was a developer. He just didn't know it. This untrained hobbyist was writing code that rivaled the software SIL had struggled to build for years. And they had millions of dollars in salaries and donations to do it with.

And so SIL's programmers, recognizing his brilliance, yet lack of knowledge in standard programming, took two to three weeks to teach him a programming language he did not yet know. Now, for a normal person, this is impossible, but for a multilingual Hebrew scholar who writes code for a hobby, they pulled it off. When people tell me this story, they shake their heads. *Taught a novice hobbyist a whole new language in two weeks. This untrained guy wrote the program the entire world uses.*

De Blois rewrote his program in just weeks in a programming language that just days before, he'd never seen.

If SIL had capitalized on this then, the program would likely be seen as an SIL product. Though de Blois was connected to UBS as a consultant, Katy and SIL had put more organizational energy into the software, diverting the time and resources of their best programmers to spend that month with de Blois.

But this was not the only project on Katy's radar. She had dozens of others that came first. And Reinier was already loosely associated with UBS. Once he learned Visual Basic, he returned to his project and kept working on his program. And other programmers within SIL kept working on theirs.

There was no Zoom then, so many of SIL's leading programmers had not been able to see de Blois's program in action. Not yet.

In 1996 in Mombasa, a Bible translation software conference was held, and all the big organizations sent representatives. There de Blois demoed his program.

Nathan Miles sat entranced in his seat. He was a UBS employee. For years, they'd been working on something called "Project 95." The fact that it was 1996 and they hadn't launched is a sign of how things were going.

"They were all frustrated with [Project] 95," de Blois said. "It was too big, too ambitious, collapsing under its own weight." He described it as software that was meant to do everything, including "brewing you a cup of coffee." It was too much. The best programs often have a specific application. They do one thing well or a few things well. They don't do everything.

Miles found de Blois that night at the conference. "Can we have a look at what you've done?" And like a hacker movie from the 1990s, Nathan Miles, Ron Rother, and other programmers sat at the console, tinkering with it.

"They were trying to break it," de Blois told me.

"What do you mean, they were trying to break it?" I asked.

"They wanted it to crash," he told me. Not to destroy his work but as a sparring partner helps another by keeping them on their feet, making sure their balance is true.

They tried all sorts of things to crash the program. Impossible key combos, messing with the back end, opening too many resources. "But it would not crash," he said. They could not elicit a blue screen.

It was "quite robust," they remarked. Quite an accomplishment from somebody who didn't consider himself a developer.

Until then, SIL had been such a leader in the software space that Nathan Miles, who worked for UBS, was seconded to SIL for a chance to work at their headquarters in their offices.[5] But here under their noses, one of their own Bible translation consultants (rather than the computer programming team) had built the best program in the Bible translation world. Project 95 wasn't going anywhere, and that was clear by then, Miles said.[6]

Having come from the for-profit world in smaller businesses, Miles told me he'd developed a keen ability to detect when a project was shippable and when it might sink the company. Small companies cannot afford to fail. They cannot afford to sink two years of programmers' wages into a product that doesn't ship. It bankrupts the company.

But a large, support-based missionary organization can keep working in perpetuity on a product no matter how useful it is or how many people will use it. Their salaries are not tied to the success of their programs. Their salaries are instead tied to whether or not they can get donors excited about what they're working on. This can lead to taking on projects that sound great but, in reality, are not possible.[7]

SIL was trying to accomplish something with only ten programmers that would usually require a thirty-to-fifty-person team. The reason they got as far as they did, according to Miles, was that they had a few "superprogrammers," and so they made much more progress on the impossible than they should have been able to. But it wasn't enough.

Miles raised concerns with UBS. "I told them based on my experience, I don't believe that this Project 95 will ever ship a working translation app. I can't in good conscience continue to take a paycheck because this product will never be delivered."[8]

UBS promptly withdrew from Project 95 and removed him from the team, reversing his *seconded* status. Once again, they assigned Miles to work primarily for UBS.

SIL leaders were so furious with him that he lost friends. They kicked him out of the office. But there was a silver-haired woman who understood his plight. She welcomed him and offered to have him work out of the translation offices until he could move elsewhere. It was Katy Barnwell.

Miles realized that with SIL trying to reinvent the wheel, they would not be able to do it. Instead of looking to them as the software leaders in Bible translation, this was an opportunity for UBS to take the wheel.

He pitched the idea to the higher-ups at UBS. What if UBS took over the full development of Reinier de Blois's tool and developed it worldwide? UBS was thrilled and agreed. By then it had a name: Paratext.[9]

Sadly, as involved as Katy was in its early stages, de Blois was a bit surprised that she lost interest in it. What he didn't know then is that this was a period of difficulty and conflict for Katy. It was clear she didn't want to continue in this role forever. Though de Blois didn't know it then, Katy hadn't lost interest. She simply had her mental capacity spoken for multiple times over.

If she hadn't been in this position, I doubt she would have let Paratext get away.

UBS went their way, working away on Paratext with a team of three to four developers. SIL meanwhile, rather than recognize the superior product in Paratext, employed about ten programmers on Project 95. SIL programmers had been furious with Miles for his appraisal of Project 95. But one year and about a million dollars in funding later, they came to the same conclusion.[10] They shut the project down.

But they wouldn't give it up. Later, Project 95 was revived as "Phoenix." The name betrays just how poorly the previous program had fared. After Phoenix failed, it was called Santa Fe. After Santa Fe came Lingua Links. After that came Translation Editor. But it was not going well. And most of SIL's employees in the field ignored those programs entirely and used Paratext anyway. It was the better program.

For years, a significant team of SIL programmers had worked to build programs that failed, underperformed, or that few bothered to use. Finally, in 2010, Reinier de Blois became director of UBS's translation software department. At some point, he apparently did recognize that he was a programmer, even if he taught himself along the way.

SIL's team led by Michael Cochran requested a meeting. "You guys have won," he said. De Blois bristled when he heard it. It was never a competition, and he regretted that many thought of it like that.

Cochran went on, de Blois remembers. "We have a request. . . . Can we work together on Paratext? We'll discontinue our Translation Editor."

For UBS it was a no-brainer. Until then, they'd had only three to four people on the entire Paratext team. SIL was the larger organization, and they brought their own salaries. "Absolutely," they said. "It's good for the kingdom that we work together on this," De Blois remembers.

Paratext went from a hobby to the leading software of 90–95 percent of the Bible translation world. It had more than ten thousand active users. The demand this placed on the underresourced program was incredible. The need in the field was much greater than three people could service. SIL's request came just in the nick of time.

Overnight, the Paratext team went from three to four full-time workers to about fifteen full-time employees. Much more appropriate for the software that virtually every Bible translator in the whole world was using.

Teams on the ground, say, in Madagascar, will have Paratext open and running. They check the original languages, as well as the major versions already done in local trade languages, like Malagasy. They discuss, draft, and redraft in Paratext. They add any questions they may have. For many years and still today, they would send/receive their work. Immediately, wherever other team members, consultants, typesetters, or publishers who were associated with the project, they received the updated work. The consultant could then go in and answer questions, interact, and check the quality of their work.

More recently, send/receive, which was *almost* real-time, has given way to genuine real-time collaboration—much like Google docs. With this updated code in Paratext, you can watch in real time where your collaborators are working and what they're typing. Software like this is remarkably complicated. And it's not built by three people.[11]

It's only too bad this merger didn't happen earlier. SIL requested that the middle letters /t/ and /e/ in Paratext be capitalized (ParaTExt, to honor Translation Editor) upon the merger to honor their donors. They'd given millions of dollars over the years to support all those programs that went essentially nowhere. Paratext obliged for a little while. But eventually, they decided it was sort of silly and an eyesore. The letters are once again lowercase.[12]

Katy has an uncanny ability to see potential and see the future. It's why, if you study the changes in Bible translation from the 1960s through today, she seems to have either begun, invented, or stumbled into the center of almost every major movement in Bible translation.

Today, de Blois estimates that about 95 percent of Bible translations are written in Paratext. And long before it was associated with UBS, long before any organization put any real resources into it, Katy saw.

She saw a professional programmer in a Hebrew scholar who never would have entertained the idea. She flew him to Dallas and retasked her people to teach de Blois a living software language, all so that this amazing program might see the light of day and help Bibleless people.

Katy Barnwell is not a computer person. She has not written a line of code in her whole life. Yet all around the world, the two most used Bible translation software programs would not have come into existence without her direct involvement.

"Without Katy," de Blois told me, "there wouldn't have been Paratext. . . . It's easy to say that, because it's absolutely true."[13]

Chapter 30

MAMA KATY: THE MOTHER OF BIBLE TRANSLATION

For all of her other titles, Mama Katy is the term most used for Katy worldwide.

"She is the mother of Bible translation in Africa," said Dr. Olivia Razafinjatoniary, a Malagasy Bible translation consultant serving across the continent of Africa.[1] In the year 2000, she'd just finished her master's in translation. And in a serendipitous encounter on a bus in Nairobi, she happened to tell somebody, "I really want to give back to the Lord what he gave me."[2]

Originally from Madagascar, it so happened that work in Madagascar was to begin shortly. Her information was given to Katy some three thousand miles away in Nigeria. Katy's reach was incredible. Katy got in touch with Razafinjatoniary and began to train her for the work. "She would fly to Madagascar twice a year to train me. I would observe her working, observe other consultants working. She was very encouraging, and she really believed in me from day one. That pushed me to where I am now."[3]

People talk about Katy less as a colleague and more as a family member. "In terms of Bible translation, Katy was the biggest influence in my life. And my desire from day one was to become like her," Razafinjatoniary said. "I dedicated my second master's degree to her."

Katy's trick is that professionally she's unequaled. But she makes you feel like family.

"She's a mother to many," Razafinjatoniary said. "We have been in touch, even now. She knows all about us. We know all about her. When she's sick, we know. When she's well, we know. When she's traveling, we know. We are really in touch, like a family."

Across Africa and the world, the number of people who feel this way about Katy is astounding. Though based in Nigeria and now the UK, Katy's influence is deeply felt worldwide.

Teryl Gonzalez told me that at a recent Bible translation conference, the MC asked for a show of hands. In the auditorium were international Bible translation leaders from all inhabited continents of the world, speaking scores of languages and in charge of hundreds of translation projects.

The presenter did not ask who had read Katy's work. Polls of 100 percent are not very useful. Instead, they asked who had been personally and directly shepherded, helped, ministered to, or trained by Katy. Hundreds of arms shot up. Only a handful of freshman workers were able to keep their hands down. They had not yet had the privilege.

When Teryl Gonzalez was only fifteen, a Bible translation recruiter spoke at a missions conference she attended at Teen Missions in Merritt Island, Florida. She was hooked. Approaching after the talk, she told him that the consultant role he'd barely described at the end—the training, teaching, checking role—that was for her. He patted her on the head and told her to finish high school.

But she did it. A half career of experience and a handful of graduate degrees later, she did it. She's a translation consultant and the strategic quality assurance development consultant for Wycliffe US.

But when she was coming up, there wasn't a track for becoming a consultant other than "spending a million years" on the field, she said. Becoming a consultant was a by-product of a long career, only after you'd finished your own New Testament. "Like an oak, you just grow for 100 years and then you're an oak tree."[4]

But what about young talent who couldn't remain on the field?

"Our second son was born with some real serious medical issues."[5] In a moment, her life changed from missionary and Bible translator overseas to a "stay-at-home mom with pre-schoolers in suburban Seattle. Everything just stopped for a long time," she said.[6] But Katy hadn't forgotten about her.

And Teryl wasn't the only one. Due to medical issues, caring for aging parents or sick children, many people fit to become that oak tree were never able to stay planted abroad for the decades required. But by the mid-90s, in the age of the Internet, laptops, and the passenger jet, couldn't there be a way?

Long before many, Katy saw the essence of a good translation consultant.

As she changed the field from an education-based to a skills-based criteria, there were some unexpected and seren-dipitous results. It meant not only a real path to consultancy for non-Western consultants; it also freed Western consultants who otherwise couldn't live overseas.

It allowed an incredible "return to service" for so many workers who, for one reason or another, could no longer be on the field, said Henry Huang, the former director of Global Strategies at American Bible Society.[7]

"Before the Luke partnership came along, most of these would go home and serve in administrative roles or recruiting roles or something like that, but she felt like that was such a loss of talent and resources. [Katy] began to recruit those people back for a one-language or two-language engagement. . . . It opened up a return of service to the field for consultants who had to return home for whatever reason."[8]

Instead of living overseas full-time, Katy made a way for seasoned translators and consultants to travel to location eight to twelve weeks per year, often in two-to-three-week visits, and otherwise consult via videoconferencing and Bible translation software like Paratext that syncs in real time.

And if veteran consultants could return to service in this capacity, who was to say early career consultants (and say, moms in suburban Seattle) couldn't learn via this same travel model? This also meant Bible translation consultants no longer had to have a spouse with a lifelong calling to the same work. One spouse could be a translation consultant who traveled and worked from home, and the other could work in any other line of work.

By inventing this skills-based growth plan, Katy opened the door for the global church. Many hundreds of Bible translation consultants from the Global South have since been recognized under this system.[9] Only God knows the full extent of the fruit of their labor.

Mama Katy is the mother of modern Bible translation. And because her work equipped the global church with Scripture— by them and for them—she became the mother of something more. In thousands of languages around the world, people carry with them the words of God. The sword of the Spirit.[10] If not for Katy's work, many would never have heard the good news. And as the Word of God goes out, from the church and within the church, it does not return void.[11]

This makes Katy not only the mother of modern Bible translation. For in advancing the very *word* by which the global church carries out the commission of Jesus, it also makes Katy the mother of twenty-first-century missions.

But not everybody considered Katy a mother.

Chapter 31

CONFLICT

F or a sixty-year career, Katy suffered astonishingly little
conflict with her peers. Much of the debate over training nationals to translate into their own languages happened in
papers, journals, and conferences. Day-to-day, Katy did not have
to deal with that soul-sucking conflict among people who share
the same office.

Except for one era.

The late 1990s were difficult years. She'd been SIL's
International Translation Coordinator for nearly a decade. And
she'd accomplished much of what she came to do.

All around the world, the pen (or now the keyboard) had
left the Westerner's hands and was instead in the hands of local
mother-tongue speakers. The outside consultant served in a
helping, training, and checking role rather than as the tip of
the spear. Her idea was no longer the new innovation, but the
modus operandi of much of the Bible translation world.

Translator's Workplace, Paratext, and a mountain of biblical
resources became more available every day. And they were each
run by large and competent teams.

Ever the innovator, it was hard to keep Katy down. She
wanted to try new things, more things. She wanted to keep
revolutionizing Bible translation. But things were comfortable
as they were, *thank you very much.*

SIL, for all its strengths, was becoming increasingly known
as one of the more conventional Bible translation organizations.

With knowing smiles and glances, they are referred to as reticent to change, comfortable with the way things are.[1] And this wasn't a fit for Katy. Not anymore. And it became a problem. For the first and last time in her career, it seems there was a small group of people who would rather not have counted Katy as a colleague. The feeling was mutual.

I reached out to the men who my reporting turned up. The men who had difficulties working with Katy. These are not misogynists or rude men but widely respected leaders in the Bible translation world. Many of them still work in that world, and they've had few problems along the way.

I reached out to all of them. And to a man, none of them replied. Of all the people I reached out to while researching Katy's biography, about 95 percent were glad to interview. But none of these sources would even respond.

I know the son of one of these men and emailed him instead. As a go-between, he asked his father. The answer was quick and straightforward. He "wouldn't want to say anything negative about Katy. Sorry."

Katy is so championed in Bible translation, she's such a hero, that nobody wants to go on record saying anything negative about her. There's a fear that it'd be too easy to turn them into the bad guy. And it would be easy.

It would be easy to imagine the argument in today's time. SIL stifled her innovation. It was a boys' club. And in a short paragraph or two, they are forever seen as the bad guys in Katy's story. But real life is not that simple.

Based on my reporting, it seems Katy *was* hard to work with for a couple of years. And yes, one could easily argue it was only a couple of years within a whole career, but it did happen.

It is telling that these men did not respond to my emails. Contentious, malicious, or narcissistic people don't hesitate to go on record. No, it seems these folks were genuinely hurt and sincerely had a hard time with Katy. But from my seat, it comes across as if they're wise and mature enough to know that when it comes to Katy Barnwell, this is the exception—the aberration—rather than the rule.

For sixty years, Katy has made not just friends but a global family all over the world. They call her mother. How many Western women get called "Mother" by hundreds of people on every inhabited continent?

Everybody loves her—except this small group of her peers from the late 1990s. And though they seem to have fair reasons for those emotions, they don't want to go down in history as some of the few who've had difficulties with Katy. I, for one, can respect that.

Missionary trainings and our church ethos always paint this sort of conflict as *so* unfortunate. If *only* we had done better conflict resolution, or had been less sinful, or prideful, or what have you, maybe none of this ever would have happened. It makes the people involved feel incredibly guilty about having any lasting emotions over difficulties with current or former colleagues.

More conflict resolution training is always needed. But the longer I live, and the more I read, the more I see that occasional conflict is not some terrible failure. It's simply part of the human condition. Some people pair better than others. Some people struggle to work together. And sometimes it's okay to move on.

If you look to your heroes, leaders of the church, from Billy Graham to Mother Teresa, Martin Luther King Jr. to Karl Barth, Jonathan Edwards, John Calvin, Martin Luther, Thomas Aquinas, Bede, Augustine, Jerome, Origen, Polycarp, or Ignatius, you find no different. There is not one of them who did not have serious difficulties with colleagues, or friends, or family. Or all three. And many are recognized as saints.

Even the apostle Paul burned many bridges. Most famously, breaking from Barnabas, his first great friend and colaborer in the church. And all over a dispute about working with John Mark, likely the author of the Gospel of Mark.[2]

John Mark seems to have bailed on Paul just months into the first missionary journey. Having been raised wealthy, and leaving a widowed mother back home, there are various speculations about why he returned, but no one knows.

> After some time had passed, Paul said to Barnabas, "Let's go back and visit the brothers and sisters in every town where we have preached the word of the Lord and see how they're doing." Barnabas wanted to take along John who was called Mark. But Paul insisted that they should not take along this man who had deserted them in Pamphylia and had not gone on with them to the work. They had such a sharp disagreement that they parted company, and Barnabas took Mark with him and sailed off to Cyprus. But Paul chose Silas and departed, after being commended by the brothers and sisters to the grace of the Lord. (Acts 15:36–40)

Barnabas wanted to take him on the second missionary journey. Paul refused to ever work with him again. A major falling-out ensued.

Pastors are quick to draw out the likely reconciliation between Paul and John Mark in Colossians:

> "Aristarchus, my fellow prisoner, sends you greetings, as does Mark, Barnabas's cousin (concerning whom you have received instructions: if he comes to you, welcome him), and so does Jesus who is called Justus."[3]

Though pastors love to point to the reconciliation between Paul and John Mark, they seldom mention the fact that as far as we can tell, Paul and Barnabas never worked together again.[4] They may never have spoken again. We can't know.

Katy has a better track record than many of these great leaders in her relationships, but she was still human. And some combinations of people and temperaments, no matter how saintly, lead to quarreling.

"Katy was fascinating," said Bernie May, founder of The Seed Company. "She'd be in a meeting where everybody decided all one way. Katy would not care. She'd go the other way." He smiled and shook his head. "She marched to a different drumbeat."[5]

"I was in the ITC role for a long time, nearly ten years," Katy told me, "and it was certainly time for a change, both for SIL and for me. I looked forward to a role where I could be more directly involved in Bible translation (training, consulting and checking), not so much 'administration.'"

SIL almost lost her. During that period of discontent, Bernie May told me, American Bible Society offered Katy a job.[6] Steve Sheldon and others didn't want to lose her. Even if their professional relationship was strained, they knew that they had a once-in-a-generation talent. Maybe once in a century—or more.

How could they keep her in the family, even if she moved on from the International Translation Coordinator role?

At this same time another organization in the Wycliffe orbit, a young and hungry organization, was beginning something new. Something more innovative and daring than anything that had been done in a long time. It was called The Seed Company.

They had a lot of bold ideas around financing, projectizing Bible translation, and upending the way things had been done for decades. And now, through a bold partnership with *The Jesus Film*, they were ready to engage in direct translation work. But they didn't know the linguistics. They didn't know translation. They needed a master practitioner to lead the way.

Bernie May spoke with John Watters, SIL's executive director. Did he have anybody he could *second* to help The Seed

Company break out from their role as financing wizards to practitioners of Bible translation? Watters knew just the person.

Katy's reputation preceded her and Bernie May, The Seed Company's founder, knew well who she was. He remembered the telegram prayer requests during the Biafran war three decades earlier. He remembered the two young women lost to communication for nearly a year. He remembered praying for her. And look at all she'd done since.

"You don't want her on your team," somebody at SIL warned him. "She's not a team player. She's a prima donna,"[7] May remembers them saying.

"I don't care if she's a prima donna as long as she can sing," Bernie replied.[8]

He knew he needed somebody with leading talent, and he was willing to take a chance. Depending on who you talk to, this shift from SIL to the early Seed Company is either referred to as something Katy volunteered for or that she was let go from SIL.

At first, I assumed it was a mistake, but enough people said the word *fired* that I stopped assuming this. She kept her SIL credentials and email and so "reassigned" is a more fitting term. But while her reassignment was forceful, Katy was as ready for the change as SIL was. She was ready to be back in the field and to revolutionize it all over again.

Had she been a prima donna? That wasn't Bernie's experience with her at all. Or anybody else I've interviewed. Not even close.[9]

After all the conflicting advice Bernie May had gotten about Katy, he wasn't sure what to believe. It would take him a few months before he realized she was a fabulous colleague and that they would have no issues working together. But in Katy's first few weeks at The Seed Company, he wasn't sure yet.

Katy approached him one day, sort of timid, he described to me in our interview.

"If it's alright, I like to take my month's vacation every December, all at once." She said.

Bernie wasn't sure what to expect. He raised his eyebrows.

"Sure, um, of course!" It was her vacation to use. Why should he have a problem?

She thanked him and turned to leave. Though he probably shouldn't have asked, curiosity got the best of him. Did she like to lie on the beach? Or use up some of the ungodly number of miles she must've racked up? Maybe she had friends she liked to visit, or she went home to the UK?

"Eh-hem," he interrupted her departure. Katy stopped and pivoted. "I'm curious, Katy," May said. "What is it that you do every December?"

"Every December," she said quietly, "I go back to the village where I started, in Nigeria, and spend Christmas with the Mbembe."

Bernie huffed. *This* was how Katy spent her vacation. His mind was made up about her then. He hasn't changed it since.

Katy was an extremely competent, innovative, and fast-moving person. So was Bernie May. I suspect having a boss who could not only keep up but also see the light and champion her innovative ideas had a lot to do with the *supposed* return to the working reputation she'd always enjoyed and would continue to enjoy for the rest of her life. Katy didn't change. Her colleagues changed. Her circumstances changed.

Katy produced work and innovated like a madwoman. Yet she was not mad. She was remarkably kind and hospitable. But she was still human. Even Katy Barnwell can have a couple of rough years.

Chapter 32

THE JESUS FILM

In 1921, a boy was born near Coweta, Oklahoma. His child-hood seemed average enough. Even quaint. Every day he walked to school in a one-room schoolhouse until he was a teenager. He took well to academic learning, leadership, and oratory. After attending university, he moved to Los Angeles and founded a successful confections company.

But upon going to seminary at both Princeton and Fuller Theological Seminary, he met with a crisis. They were the famous words at the end of the Gospel of Matthew:

> All authority has been given to me in heaven and on earth. Go, therefore, and make disciples of all nations, baptizing them in the name of the Father and of the Son and of the Holy Spirit, teaching them to observe everything I have commanded you. And remember, I am with you always, to the end of the age. (Matt. 28:18–20)

He felt he could not go back to his business with a command like that burning in his heart. The command was to make dis-ciples of all nations, and all around him were college students who did not know Christ. He and his wife packed up, moved to the campus of UCLA, and began an evangelism and disciple-ship ministry.

It struck a nerve. In the same era as the Billy Graham evangelistic revival meetings, their ministry to college students gave drink to a parched world. The ministry spread around the country and the world with lightning speed. Soon their organization was serving "inner cities, the military, athletes, political and business leaders, the entertainment industries, and families."[1]

His name was William R. Bright, but his friends called him Bill. The ministry he and his wife, Vonette, founded was named Campus Crusade for Christ.[2] It would go on, Cru says, to become the largest Christian ministry in the world.[3]

When Bright was young, spending most of his time sharing the gospel in Los Angeles, it was only a matter of time before he bumped shoulders with Hollywood types. In most cities in America, young creatives have film ideas, screenplay ideas, or other creative dreams. But in the business of day-to-day life, those dreams fade. But when you're surrounded by the people who write those screenplays, build those props, and make those films, the creative instinct has teeth in a way it may not elsewhere.

Bright wanted to make an artistically compelling *Life of Jesus* that could be dubbed and shown all over the world in people's native languages. Bright then got so inundated with growing Cru that any hopes for developing this feature film were put on pause. But as the decades passed, this idea would not die.

Then in 1976, a non-Christian producer named John Heyman approached Bright because he hoped to do several Bible-related films. He needed funding. Heyman was motivated to adapt Genesis, but it was clear that Bright was especially interested in adapting a Jesus film first. Bright asked Paul Eshleman, the director of Cru's campus ministry, to work with Heyman. After viewing the work Heyman produced based on Luke 1–2, the angelic visit to Mary and the birth narrative of Jesus, Bright was convinced.[4] They had a new ministry on their hands.

Bright enjoyed a superpower for fundraising, and he wasted no time in raising the money needed for the production of a feature-length Jesus film. Hundreds of actors were auditioned, and hundreds alone for the role of Jesus, which fell to a Shakespearean actor named Brian Deacon. The film was shot on location in Israel with a budget of six million dollars.

Rather than dramatize the story of Jesus's life with extra-biblical artistic elements, like *The Chosen* and so many others, they decided to adapt specifically the Gospel of Luke as closely as possible. The film script is nearly verbatim to many sections of the book of Luke.

Bright knew that by adapting only the pure scriptural scenes without embellishment, he'd have a more future-proof and highly translatable film for years and decades to come. And that he has.

After debuting in the United States in 1979, it was dubbed in Hindi and viewed by twenty-one million Indian viewers the following year.[5] The first Jesus Film teams launched in the Philippines to screen the film to as many people as they could.

All over the world, people wanted *The Jesus Film* in their language, and Cru was happy to oblige. By 1984, *The Jesus Film* was available in one hundred languages worldwide. Reports of the success of the film were staggering. Film reels were taken to the most far-flung places, projectors pointed at walls or white sheets, with sheep and goats wandering through the screening areas.

People who'd never before seen a film were seeing and hearing the story of Jesus for the first time in their own languages. And they were following Christ in droves because of it. Cru needed more than simply a way to screen this film. They needed an entire ministry built around translating the film, showing it, and ministering to those who wanted to follow this Jesus they'd just learned about.

In 1985, Cru launched *The Jesus Film* Project, or JFP. It's one of the most effective and successful missionary and evangelistic tools in the history of the church.

By 1997, the film had been viewed one billion times and had been translated into four hundred languages. But there was a problem, and *The Jesus Film* staff knew it. They were running out of languages.

There are approximately 7,164 living languages in the world.[6] However, only 492 of them are listed as "institutional" languages as of this writing. An institutional language enjoys extreme development, literacy, literacy materials, education in the language, newspapers, media, books, and libraries. The government is often run in the language, and important cultural products are printed, shipped, sung, recorded, or otherwise produced in the language.

These are often the largest language groups, and by nature, they often have more resources. But most languages in the world don't fit this description. Many languages are spoken only. They have never been written down in human history and remain unwritten today. They are often small, with a few thousand or hundreds of thousands of speakers instead of tens of millions. They have fewer resources and fewer educated native speakers.

As *The Jesus Film* looked out on the horizon in the late 1990s, they realized they'd picked all the low-hanging fruit. They were quickly closing in on the largest, most spoken, most resourced institutional languages. And they didn't know how to reach the languages outside that designation. Not yet.

Until the late 1990s, *The Jesus Film* Project (JFP) didn't originate translation work. Instead, they "relied on the people who worked on a translation to work on the script for us," said Tom Meiner, chief operating officer of *The Jesus Film*.[7] This meant they could only work in languages that already had a completed New Testament.

The JFP would reach out to translation agencies and ask, "Do you have anybody? Are you working on this language? Do you have somebody who could work on the script of *The Jesus Film* for us?"[8]

If they heard back at all, they were normally pointed in the direction of a Western missionary. Often, Meiner said, that missionary had since retired or moved on to another project. Or they were dead. "And so, we had to wait."[9]

Chris Deckert, the JFP's director of language strategies, told me that if they found a willing translator, they would send "an excel spreadsheet with a little manual that said, 'Hey missionary, if you could translate these lines here into these lines here, and try to keep the syllable count as close as possible because this is lip synced . . .'"[10]

The process was cumbersome. "We'd send off that packet, and maybe a year, two, or three, sometimes they'd get back to us," Deckert said. Worse yet, the work that did come back was unpredictable and often low quality.

The JFP was tired of the runaround. They wanted to "move forward on languages that had no Scripture and no JESUS Film, the largest ones that we could get going," Meiner said.[11] But that meant original translation work. And they didn't do translation. Not then.

But how hard can it be? To outsiders, the complexity isn't apparent—not right away. Though careful not to disparage their work in their interviews, it seemed *The Jesus Film* team made a couple of attempts at translation themselves. It didn't go well.[12] But to their credit, they realized the error quickly.

They were not translators. They didn't do translation. But there were others who could.

And so, Paul Eshleman, the first executive director of *The Jesus Film*, met with leaders from Wycliffe and SIL. Eshleman cast the vision for a partnership to reach the thirty largest remaining languages without a word of Scripture. The translation agencies would do what they do best, and so would *The Jesus Film* crew. The JFP offered to fund the first thirty partnerships. But they needed a partner.

It was a big dream, but who would take on a project this big? It was a risk because it was completely new and experimental.

"At that time, no one was willing to let this be in their house. There was no home for this effort," said Larry Jones, the CEO of The Seed Company and former vice president at SIL. "Wycliffe wasn't sure they were ready to do it. SIL was sure they *weren't* ready to do it."[13]

But together, they all "felt like The Seed Company was the best place to do something more innovative, more creative," Meiner said.[14]

Back then, The Seed Company was a start-up, literally housed in a converted broom closet.[15] Deckert referred to it as "the skunkworks of the Bible translation world," comparing it to NASA's famed R&D department.[16]

The Seed Company was hungry to prove themselves in the world. And like Katy, they sought to pass the translation baton to the global church, employing national translators instead of Westerners. This was such a distinctive that before changing their name to The Seed Company, they were called Partners with Nationals.[17]

The Jesus Film Project finally had a translation partner.

But if they were going to try working simultaneously across dozens of languages at once, employing exclusively non-Western translators, and upending how Bible translation was done for centuries, they better be ready for a storm. Academia rarely takes kindly to new ideas. Bible translation is no different.

As the saying goes, "Science progresses one funeral at a time." This saying is inspired by the theoretical physicist Max Planck, who noted in his *Scientific Autobiography* that "an important scientific innovation rarely makes its way by gradually winning over and converting its opponents: it rarely happens that Saul becomes Paul. What does happen is that its opponents gradually die out, and that the growing generation is familiarized with the ideas from the beginning."[18]

What right did a start-up have to shake things up like that? They would need a leader fit for the task. Whoever led this partnership would require absolute expertise in Bible translation, off-the-charts leadership capabilities, decades of career capital, and when the naysayers came, the impeccable esteem to ward them off. Did Wycliffe or SIL have anybody like that who they could lend out to this project? They had just the person in mind.

And after ten years in the highest technical Bible translation post in the Western world, Katy was ready to get back to the field.

It was time to change history again.

Chapter 33

THE LUKE PARTNERSHIP AND THE CLUSTER MODEL

Giving up her desk at SIL's headquarters in Dallas in the late 1990s, Katy moved back to Nigeria—back home. There was no better place to test out this new idea than in the language-rich, population-dense Nigeria.

Because *The Jesus Film* script comes almost entirely from the Gospel of Luke, the film can be adapted quickly once Luke is finished. Instead of diving into full New Testaments—the norm for that era—Katy planned to assemble translation teams from thirty languages and start them on Luke.[1] Instead of waiting decades for a completed New Testament before producing *The Jesus Film*, they would only have to wait months.

There was another reason she moved back to Nigeria. She had something else she wanted to test.

Though she'd long been a pioneer of the *who*, championing national translators instead of Western linguists, she now wanted to pioneer the *how*. Katy realized that it took her about the same amount of time to train multiple teams as it took to train one. So, instead of working on one language at a time, she wondered, could they do six languages at once? Twelve? What about twenty-five? With this question, said Ernst Wendland, Katy became one of the early pioneers of what we now call the Cluster Model.[2]

In this model, scores of translators from dozens of languages across Nigeria descended on Jos, Katy's home base at the Nigerian Bible Translation Trust.

Rather than deductive instruction, Katy invited them into the water. First, they learned from Katy and the other trainers. Then they learned from one another. By sharing notes and ideas in related languages, dialects, and trade languages, translation became a cohort model, a community practice. Difficult concepts and passages could be collaborated on, and solutions to problems could fly across related languages, hacking years off the time it takes to do a full New Testament.

In just weeks' time, they would develop orthographies[3] for languages that had never been written down in human history. After developing an orthography, they translated the Gospel of Luke, subjecting and testing the dozens of drafts against trained scholars and community testing.

And in two to three years, they had completed the Gospel of Luke. In another month's time, they'd adapt, syllable match, record, and edit *The Jesus Film* in the new language.

This helped revolutionize the category of *Scripture use*, Deckert told me.[4] Some Bible translators have labored for thirty years to produce a New Testament that nobody cared to read. But with the local churches driving the process, those days were over. The local believers led the project and then used *The Jesus Film* and Luke for evangelism, preaching, and teaching. This then catalyzed belief and a desire for more. Almost all of those Luke partnerships turned into larger projects, whether full New Testaments, audio story sets, audio Bibles, full Bibles, etc. And once the craft of translation was learned, the rest of the New Testament could be completed at a much faster clip than Luke.

"It was working all over the world," Deckert said. And The Jesus Film took note. Around 2012, they adopted Katy's model across the globe as their standard method, employing first-language speakers, the Cluster Model, and local church ownership and leadership wherever possible. Under Katy's model, "we almost tripled the number of Jesus Films produced per year," Deckert said. "It was just crazy."[5]

That's three times more work than before Katy's methods. But unlike before, they were no longer working in languages that already benefitted from full New Testaments. They were now working in languages without a word of Scripture. Often those languages had no writing system at all. What she accomplished "is still regarded as nearly miraculous," Larry Jones said.[6]

"It revolutionized the way we did our translations," Deckert said. Their initial goal was thirty languages. With Katy's model, The Jesus Film has now produced in more than seven hundred. The result? "Hundreds and hundreds of millions of people impacted," Deckert said.[7]

And with the original goal pulverized, The Jesus Film needed a better one. They launched Mission 865. The vision, Deckert told me, is to translate and produce The Jesus Film in the 865 remaining world languages with more than fifty thousand native speakers, which previously had no Scripture, by 2025.

With Katy's methods, even despite the disruptions caused by Covid, they're on track to complete Mission 865 on time.[8]

Today, *The Jesus Film* Project has produced 2,153 translated editions.[9] It is by far the most-watched film in human history and is recognized by the Guinness Book of World Records as the "most translated film" in history.[10]

The Jesus Film Project says more than 665 million people worldwide have "indicated decisions for Christ following a film showing."[11] Well over half of those, near four hundred million and counting, were added after the ministry began using Barnwell's methods, according to Deckert.

Even with some padding for optimism, that's a remarkable number. By comparison, Lifeway research estimates 2.2 million people became followers of Jesus at Billy Graham's Crusades.[12] Before even counting the global influence of her written Bible translation work, her influence through *The Jesus Film* means

Katy has a real claim to more than one hundred times the fruit of Billy Graham.

The Seed Company, the young and daring upstart in the Bible translation world, took a chance on *The Jesus Film*. They took a chance on Katy. And they took a chance on the Cluster Model.

And they were nearly crushed by their success. In the space of only a few years, they went from a small R&D innovator to one of the largest players in Bible translation worldwide.

They saw some of the weaknesses of the funding apparatus of the Bible translation movement and vowed to change them. And it worked better than they could have imagined.

Until then, most funding going into Bible translation came in via monthly financial support for Western missionaries. The idea of training nationals around the world was great, but how could you pay them? This often led to Westerners raising extra support to pay them out of their own pockets. Not a great arrangement.

Bernie May decided enough was enough. He brought in leading businessmen and women to serve on the board. These were people who'd served at the C level in Fortune 500 companies. They knew how to get things done.

And unlike traditional ministry, which is hard to measure on a spreadsheet, Bible translation can be measured down to the verse, the letter. It can be projectized.

Now, as in all pendulum swings, there is a worthy critique that projectizing Bible translation overcontextualized the process toward a Western productivity and business model and undercontextualized it to the work of the church. And this is true. And The Seed Company and others have realized this and worked to achieve a healthier balance.

But what's also true is that this was sorely needed at the time. Wycliffe was notorious for how little it seemed they accomplished. In fact, about every five years in the press, you ran into the same article. Some enterprising journalist with a chip on their shoulder would dig into how many millions of dollars Wycliffe took in, yet how little Bible translation was actually produced. Where did all that money and time go?

An article from the *Washington Post* in 1979 reads: "During a recent visit to Mexico by the institute's founder, the education ministry's Nahmad remarked: 'In 40 years, you've had 300 people here with doctorates in linguistics. They have finished only 20 languages and have not helped us train one linguist. But they've produced a lot of Protestants.'"[13]

The article also says, "The officials said they fear that SIL members are spies for the U.S. government and linked with the Central Intelligence Agency."[14] There's that old ghost again, the rumor forever haunting Bible translation.

Though it may be unwise to overly projectize Bible translation, we're also called to be good stewards of God's resources. What on earth were those three hundred linguists doing all those years while not working on Bible translation? All their communities back home sent checks monthly for them to do Bible translation. Their churches weren't against the writing of linguistic articles and grammars, but they'd been baited on Bible translation. It's why they sent funding.

And when that many highly educated people produce so little work, it only gives fodder to the baseless accusations of governmental intelligence work. *Ahh, that must be what they're doing with all that time.*

The Seed Company revolutionized translation by bringing a project approach. Instead of sending self-supported missionaries and allowing them to go at their own pace, The Seed Company raised many millions of dollars from wealthy donors. They then mapped out projects. And together with local leaders, they drew up a plan.

Luke will be drafted by February. Philippians, by April. Consultant check in May, translation workshop in June, etc. Finally, a more task-oriented and accountable system was introduced. As the saying goes, *you are what you measure.* Are you measuring the publication of grammars? Or of Bible translation? As you can imagine, the pace of Bible translation skyrocketed.

Instead of one Western couple spending one lifetime on one New Testament,[15] many teams of people speaking related languages worked together in clusters. They helped one another, advised one another through sticky problems, and avoided errors together. Consultants like Katy were now checking in real time all around the world and flying in for intensive three- to five-week workshops. What used to take twenty-five years or never get finished at all was often happening in just a decade. Sometimes less.

And Katy's output was truly superhuman. Larry Jones, who was the senior vice president of Bible translation for The Seed Company at the time, told me this: "Katy was all on her own— the leading technical expert in Bible translation for The Seed Company in Nigeria, but also the field coordinator who oversaw all of the projects we did there. Really, it was the single largest concentration of projects in any country that we had. . . . Over 20% of all the projects Seed Company was sponsoring at one point were all Nigeria projects. . . . She was directly involved with close to 20%, close to a fifth of all the projects The Seed Company was sponsoring worldwide. At one point in our history, she was personally the steward over nearly a fifth of them. . . . I mean it was incredible."[16]

Katy led, checked, directed, and oversaw 20 percent of The Seed Company's work as they went from incubator to behemoth. If it weren't for her, they would have been crushed under the weight of their own success.

As of this writing, The Seed Company is the fifth largest missionary organization in the US.[17] "The Seed Company never would have happened without her," said Bernie May. Originally, his aim was much smaller. The Seed Company was meant to provide funding to national translators. It was never meant to *be* a translation agency.

"She started our field program." He said. And because of The Seed Company's work, hundreds of languages have Scripture decades before they otherwise would have. Lifetimes before they would have. "Nobody else could have done it," May said.[18]

When Katy was running out of steam at SIL, *The Jesus Film* Project "gave her an opportunity to use her talents. She was being limited where she was," May told me.[19]

He also pointed out the irony. Katy kept wanting to move forward, to progress. To remake Bible translation in a twenty-first-century image. SIL didn't want that. They were comfortable with the way things were. They wanted her out because of it.

But in The Seed Company, she was the lead. And she had no naysayers holding her back, only Bernie May to spur her onward. Her methods were allowed to fly forward, full speed. And it worked. It worked so well, so fast, that The Seed Company quickly eclipsed SIL and many Bible translation organizations in the world.

It even became a problem. The Seed Company was raising more money than it knew what to do with. They didn't have enough translation-side staff to spend it. Bernie May even turned down a half-million-dollar donation because he couldn't fathom a way to spend it.[20] But SIL had a small army of linguists and little funding. The Seed Company quickly realized, why not continue to raise money as well as they did and take on ever more projects, staffing those projects with consultants from SIL and Wycliffe? They were all siblings, after all. If one had consultants and the other had funding, why not share?

Soon, The Seed Company was supporting more translation work than any number of other organizations combined. They worked with the global church, beginning with Luke and *The Jesus Film*, which ignited the local communities and churches. They used Scripture as it was produced and were desperate for more. They trained local translators and local consultants. The local church led.

As soon as Luke and *The Jesus Film* were complete, the projects almost always converted into full New Testaments and full Bible translations. The church and local pastors held local showings of *The Jesus Film*, and viewers followed Jesus in droves. The new believers wanted more. They wanted to hear and read Scripture. Invitations to church followed, where local pastors were preaching from the just-finished Gospel of Luke in the mother tongue. As all of this was happening, the next books were translated and published.

There was a positive feedback loop between Scripture use, Scripture engagement, and Scripture translation. It was a dream come true.

It became harder and harder to ignore that The Seed Company's model was superior. With all the jeers and accusations they'd taken along the way, it would have been easy to play *I told you so*. But they did not.

They humbly carried the torch, shared funds, and invited the other organizations to the massive fundraising table. Instead of hoarding their massive funding pipeline, they turned it into a separate organization, Illuminations, which would share that funding as needed with many of the other Bible translation organizations, like United Bible Societies, Lutheran Bible Society, American Bible Society, Biblica, Pioneer Bible Translators, Deaf Bible Society, and SIL and Wycliffe.

Instead of hoarding their advantage and becoming the clear standout, they slowed, extended a hand, and divested many of their advantages. It was not about them. It was about the Word of God. They'd go farther as a team than by themselves.

They invited the others to join them in a conversation around global best practices. Together, they all came to an accord.

"The whole world adopted The Seed Company's translation policies,"[21] Bernie May told me. Once the other organizations saw how well the model worked, they wanted in. But as a grace, and to avoid the "I told you so," what had denigratingly been called "The Seed Company Model" was no longer referred to by that name.

Instead of calling it The Seed Company Model, it was referred to as the Common Framework.

In 2015, the largest Bible translation organizations in the world, together responsible for about 85 percent of the Bible translation worldwide (names like Wycliffe USA, American Bible Society, United Bible Society, The Seed Company, SIL, Pioneer Bible Translators, Lutheran Bible Translators, and Biblica), banded together to agree on the Common Framework. It was an industry-wide best-practices agreement. According to Every Tribe Every Nation, three of the five pillars of the Common Framework are:

> • "Ownership: The most local expression of the church owns the vision and responsibility for Bible translation in each community.
> • Partnership: Translation goals, products, and plans are determined collaboratively.
> • Accelerated Impact: Short-phased projects seek to develop Scripture products that respond to press-ing ministry needs of the church and are a part of an overall plan to fulfill the Scripture translation needs in a people group."[22]

Look familiar? Instead of Western translation agencies run-ning the process, they would step aside. The global church in its local manifestation would own, direct, perform, and be the "end users" of Bible translation. They would decide which Scripture to translate, what medium—whether audio, written, visual, or sign language—and in which order. The Western partners would act in a consulting and helping role, but the global church would lead.

Forty years earlier, long before it was codified, many of its central tenets were already being practiced by Katy and her colleagues. "That all started in the 1970s," Katy said.[23] It just took the world forty years to catch up.

And global Bible translation organizations united under this method. But make no mistake. What they called the Common Framework used to be called (or sometimes sneered) *The Seed Company Model*. And The Seed Company Model was Katy's model.

Katy had been nudged out of her SIL role because they were not willing to go where she was leading. The irony is that after sending her away and retaining the status quo for another decade, they saw the writing on the wall. As they looked to The Seed Company's model, which was Katy's model, they ended up following her anyway.

Today, what are rebranded as the standard best practices used around the world are largely what Katy and her Nigerian colleagues had been doing since the early 1970s.

Chapter 34

CLIMBING DOWN
THE LADDER

What do you do when you've remade your entire industry again and again? Do you retire? As Katy reached her mid-seventies, she found herself answering this question nearly everywhere she went. Bible translators often work longer than regular people. Their work is their life's calling.

And the world is fortunate Katy did not follow the norm. Some of her greatest achievements would never have happened if she retired at the standard age. Much of her Jesus Film work, the development of the Cluster Model, the training of hundreds of translators and dozens of consultants, and shouldering 20 percent of the workload at one of the largest missionary organizations on the planet never would have happened if she hung it up to collect shells.[1]

But even though Bible translators tend to work longer careers, few are still found working past their mid-seventies.

Katy laughed then. She laughs now in her mid-eighties.[2]

"Will you ever retire?," I ask her.

"What else would I do?," Barnwell said. "Would I just sit and twiddle my thumbs? I enjoy my work, and I'm glad that I can still do it. And I'm very thankful that the physical problems of old age are not in my head so much as in my legs."

Katy is intuitively on to something sociologists are just now beginning to pin down. According to research from Chenkai

Wu at Duke Kunshan University, it seems even after equating for the usual suspects like income, race, gender, and marital status, retiring later correlates with an 11 percent drop in mortality rates.[3]

"Our theory is that a later retirement may actually delay when your physical and cognitive functioning starts to decline, because work keeps your mind and body active. If you stay active and socially engaged, it helps maintain your cognitive and physical abilities."[4]

"There are a lot of social benefits related to working: You're more active, you're more engaged, you're talking with your peers, and so on. Losing those when you retire can be harsh."[5]

Katy is living proof of this. She's still consulting in Bible translation, reading four to five languages at a time on her computer screen, from texts that span three thousand years.

But she's still human.

Somewhere around 2013, at the age of seventy-five, it became evident to Katy that she may not be able to keep up her pace for long. She could still travel and consult. She could still train and check Scripture. But carrying 20 percent of the workload of the fifth largest missionary organization in North America? Maybe not.

At some point, it would become unwise to hold onto those roles—both for her own health and for the sake of the organization. If something were to happen to her, she didn't want to leave the Bible translation world scrambling.

A favorite hypothetical game Bible translators used to play was "How many people do you think it'll take to replace Katy Barnwell?" Most people answered eight to fifteen. Maybe it was time to start training those replacements while she was still sharp and not leave them to pick up the pieces if she were suddenly unable to do the work.

Katy sensed the time was close. She was not as sharp as she'd once been. Her mind, ever the steel trap, let a few things slip through. Then a few more. She could still outdo and outwork any forty-year-old in the organization, but she felt the change.[6]

When this moment comes, it's always hard. But Katy was wise enough to lead the way. She would not be the person, so to speak, whose family had to hide the car keys in the night.

She knew it was time. Time to begin stepping down the ladder.

"Part of her legacy is the graciousness with which she has stepped back," said Larry Jones, the CEO of The Seed Company and her supervisor at the time. "With any person who has been—who is of Katy's stature—it is easy to feel comfortable being in charge and shaping things, and I really admire—it hasn't been without pain for her, but I have seen such a spiritual maturity and humility in her as she has navigated that, and has sought to equip others—both Nigerians and also people from the UK and the United States, to take up, what at one point, she had stewarded so well."[7]

Several years ago, she moved back to her UK home, Goring-on-Thames, about fifty miles west of London. Before Covid, she made regular consulting trips to Nigeria, but with her worsening osteoarthritis, she now stays put in the UK while staying active on Zoom. She jokes that she "travels to Nigeria every day."

But as she's descended the ladder, a poetic conclusion has found her. The churches in the Mbembe area, her original assignment, reached out to her. The church is all grown up there, now, much in thanks to Katy's New Testament work.

Her original Nigerian colleagues are long passed. But that generation's grandchildren had heard the stories. They wanted to work with her. They have only the New Testament, but the New Testament is not enough. For what is a tree without its roots?

Through the Nigeria Bible Translation Trust (NBTT), the churches reached out to her for help. Though once unthinkable, this was the norm now. The local church initiates projects. They call the shots. The next translation would be done by them, for them. But they could use a little help.[8] And who better than Katy Barnwell, the trainer of trainers, the consultant of consultants? The New Testament in their hands, lovingly marked up and dog-eared, owed its existence to Katy and her Nigerian colleagues. And she already knew one of the major dialects of Mbembe.

For Katy, there was no question. There's something about the first translation project. The first people group you work with. They embed deeply into your heart. Katy gladly agreed.

She's working now across three related Mbembe dialects to produce three full Old Testament translations. She's currently sharpening up her Hebrew in her mid-80s. I smile whenever I think of it. She's also training two local consultants and helping to update the New Testament she completed in 1985. For most people, that's too full a plate. For Katy, it's only a fraction of her former workload. But it's enough for now.

Chapter 35

CHURCH-CENTRIC
BIBLE TRANSLATION

Barnwell's long career training first-language translators and putting project ownership into local hands has borne its fruit: Bible translation has become so thoroughly democratized that few today seriously debate whether nationals should lead the translation process.

Instead, in an unrelenting push to make Bible translation faster and cheaper, new reformers have asked different kinds of questions.

Are trained translation consultants really necessary? Couldn't thousands of passionate Christians in Internet cafes work together online to translate a book of the Bible from a major trade language into their first language?

Translation groups—including The Seed Company and Wycliffe Associates—have dabbled with experimental approaches to rapid translation: things like wiki-style community translations; using artificial intelligence, software, and algorithms; or crowdsourcing rather than looking to trained workers or scholarly resources.

In an interview in the *Journal of Translation*, Barnwell criticized the constant quest for a "quick and dirty solution. . . . Quick translations without thorough grounding, careful study, and application of sound translation principles are just a waste of time."[1]

For the most part, the translations these experiments produced have been abysmal. But they have not been fruitless.

"One of the most effective things they were doing was energizing these local communities," said Brian Kelly, The Seed Company's director of Bible translation exploration. "They'd say, 'Hey, wow, we could all be a part of this.'"[2]

Tim Jore works with unfoldingWord, an Orlando, Florida, organization that helps churches around the world translate Scripture themselves. Jore believes the translation industry should focus less on minting new Bibles as if they were a product and focus more on empowering Christian communities to produce their own Bible translations. Historically, he argues, translation has been the work of the church.

"When a new English translation of the Bible is published," Jore wrote in a widely shared paper, "the English lingual church does not look to translation consultants to approve it."[3]

English-speaking church leaders and scholars have the knowledge and the tools they need to approve their own translations. The global church should, too. And it could, Jore argues, if Bible translation organizations shifted their methods away from product-centered thinking and toward equipping the global church to manage its own quality assurance.

This approach is called church-centric Bible translation, and Jore feels it's the logical conclusion of the changes Barnwell set in motion.

Her work "laid an important foundation for the next major transition in Bible translation that is happening all over the world today: Bible translation done by the church to meet their own theological and discipleship needs," Jore told me.[4]

When I asked Barnwell for her thoughts on church-centric translation, she was cautiously optimistic. "The focus on the involvement of churches in the receptor language area is not new and cannot be overemphasized," she said.

But she also stressed the missionary importance of translation "to explore what can be done to promote and support translation work in language areas where there are as yet no believers, no church."

In other words, church-centric translation is great, but who will go to the places with no church? The great test of the church-centric paradigm may not be whether churches can translate Bibles for themselves but whether they expand their translation efforts into regions where there are no believers—without the assistance of Western missionaries or the prompting of their translation organizations.

"We share the same goals," Barnwell said, "to see high-quality translated Scriptures available for every language group as soon as possible."[5]

Chapter 36

JEROME, WYCLIFFE, LUTHER, CAREY, TOWNSEND . . . BARNWELL?

I've spent years thinking about Katy's legacy. The sheer numbers. Many thousands of Bible translations bear her training, her teaching, her shepherding, her students, her methods, her journals, and her textbooks. Hundreds of millions of new global Christians are taught with Bibles that would not exist without Katy. Hundreds of millions of believers came to faith through The Jesus Film. They would not have without Katy.

And Katy did not do this from a corner office. Or from an endowed chair in an ivory tower. It's easy to forget just how challenging her work environment was.

It's a dangerous thing to be a Christian in the Plateau State of Nigeria. There's danger from Boko Haram and other militant groups. "All of my local friends have had relatives or friends or neighbors die. They've had their churches bombed, they've had their offices burned down. [Violence] is pervasive in the north of the country," Teryl Gonzalez said.[1]

Katy's incredible achievements happened against this backdrop.

As a toddler, she escaped underground to avoid Nazi bombing raids. As a young woman, she escaped the Nigerian Civil

War on foot. And by river. Without documents. Six times she was robbed at gunpoint on the roads. Twice her teams were stormed by armed robbers. She spent countless months of her life on planes and buses. Constantly on the move. In danger from bandits, from Boko Haram. In danger from malaria, under attack from her own colleagues over her methods. She labored and toiled and often went without sleep. But through all this, she kept working.

Even using conservative estimates, the number of languages in the world with full Bibles has doubled since the mid-nineties, from 308 in 1996 to 736 as of 2023, according to Wycliffe UK.[2] This happened when Barnwell's trainees and methods were already in full force. Her book was ten years into its third edition by then, used around the globe.

Since then, the number of New Testaments has exploded, and the number of languages with portions of Scripture (but not yet a complete New Testament or Bible) has increased by two thousand.

According to Wycliffe UK, "there is also active translation or preparatory work going on in 2,617 languages in 161 countries. Wycliffe and its partner organization SIL are involved in about three-quarters of this work."[3] Not to mention their other partner organizations that use Katy's teaching and are staffed by her trainees.

"I don't think there's anyone in SIL, Lutheran Bible Translators, UBS, The Seed Company, Pioneer Bible Translators—any of those—who have not been in contact with Katy's thinking, writing, and teaching," said Lynell Zogbo, an author and retired translation consultant in Africa.[4]

Even translation projects not directly interacting with her materials still swim downstream in the global currents set by Barnwell's training, teaching, shepherding, students, methods, and journal articles. As I said before, hundreds of millions of new global Christians are taught with Bibles that might not exist without her.

As Chris Deckert from The Jesus Film said, "Her finger-print is everywhere."[5]

Was there a Bible translator in all of church history with that kind of reach?

When I first thought this, I balked. Surely it's ridiculous to even ask—right? But when I went to the pages of history, I read of the great heroes and their deeds. I placed Katy against them. Each time the contender was underwhelming. My question remained.

I wracked my brain thinking of all the influential Bible translations and their translators. There were single translations which, in their reach, may be more influential than Katy Barnwell's career. Jerome's Latin Vulgate, for example, used by the Roman Catholic Church as its principal translation for more than fifteen hundred years. Or the King James Version. Or Luther's German.

Of course, give Katy's legacy five hundred years to catch up, and then we'll see. In two hundred years, when the beating heart of world Christianity thrums from Nigeria and China, Luther's German may not seem as important anymore. But Katy will have equipped the center of World Christianity to translate their own Scripture.

There are the influential figures who first began major organizations, like Wycliffe Bible Translators (William Cameron Townsend) or laid the theoretical foundation for how we do Bible translation (Eugene Nida), but that's a different kind of influence.

I kept cycling through individual translators across history. Was there a single soul in church history that did as much for Bible translation? For Scripture access?

Was there anybody who for sixty years, caught in a great crux of history, consistently served as the hinge, the before-and-after across many of the largest Christian organizations on earth?

Was there any soul who directly trained translators by the hundreds? Any soul who wrote a book that trained thousands? Any soul who shepherded countless cohorts of Bible translators who then went on to disciple others?

I couldn't find anybody who had such a granular impact on hundreds of translations and also a worldwide foundational impact on thousands. So I asked more than a dozen leaders, scholars, and practitioners.

But after scratching their heads, they reached the same point. "I can't think of anyone who has had a more direct impact on Bible translation in a wider swath of the world than Katy," Larry Jones said.[6]

Only two names in all of church history were consistently mentioned in the same breath as Katy Barnwell—Eugene Nida and William Carey. Not bad company.

Nida laid the foundations for the work of meaning-based Bible translation, a term Katy coined to describe the practical application of Nida's translation theory. He trained translators all over the world and is said to have helped shape translations in more than two hundred languages.[7]

William Carey was a polymath—linguist, translator, anthropologist, founder of schools, publisher, seminary founder, and Bible translator of full or partial Bibles in thirty or more languages.

I might add Kenneth L. Pike, president of SIL from 1942 to 1979, leading linguistic researcher and author, mentor to countless translators, and early ESL pioneer. You may remember having to learn the difference between emic and etic in school—terms he invented. He was nominated sixteen times for the Nobel Peace Prize.[8]

But everybody I interviewed agreed. Nobody has had Katy's hands-on, direct impact. And none had her reach.

"She would die a thousand deaths if you put that in print," said Teryl Gonzalez, one of Katy's former students and now the strategic quality assurance development consultant at Wycliffe US.[9] Katy is painfully humble.

At risk of having Katy remove her blessing from this book (for suspecting I'd make much of her), I asked Katy herself the same question. Had anybody in church history directly influenced as many Bible translation projects as she had—ever?

She frowned, frustrated with me. I had trespassed on unacceptable territory. But I smiled and told her I'd wait. A frown wasn't going to save her.

"Well, it may be true," she admitted regretfully.[10] "But I don't want to talk about that." She reminded me that she never worked alone, and all of her accomplishments happened on teams. She kept saying that it was simply a privilege to serve in what was so often the right place at the right time—to have been placed at the crossroads of history.

If William Carey is the father of modern missions, Katharine Barnwell is one of its mothers.[11] The global church has taken the baton and is far outrunning the West. But the sword of the Spirit at their side? The Word that enables and empowers the mission of God? That was translated according to Katy's training.

As I neared the end of our interviews, I thought there must be something else, something I've forgotten to ask. While this giant, this saint who belongs in the pages of history still walks among us, what would she have for us? What would she teach the world? I asked her what I'd forgotten over our interviews. What did the world need to know?

She shrugged. She had nothing to add. She only wished we could have talked more about *me*.

Chapter 37

PRAY FOR US, MOTHER

Katy had a hip replacement not long after my visit. She's now recovering well, much faster and stronger than expected. Big surprise.

And she's working. I'm reminded of Jesus's words in John 5:17: "My Father is always at his work to this very day, and I too am working."[1]

And she's praying. Always praying.

As she tells me stories about her life, my eyes scan to the books surrounding her. Books on shelves, end tables, leaning against chairs and table legs. There are countless scholarly tomes in her home, including Hebrew grammars and the like. But most of those are on the shelves, highlighted and dog-eared, material she's mastered by now.

The books at the ready, the ones she reaches for without having to get up, treat a subject she dedicated her life to. But it's a subject we can never quite master. These books at hand are books on prayer.

One of her great contributions to the church and the world can never be measured. Her prayer.

I realized then just how monastic Katy's life is. In some ways, her life looks quite the opposite from that of a monastic pursuit. (The Greek word from which we get "monastery" means "to live alone.")

A nun, for example, may spend much of her day in prayer, solitude, and reciting the Liturgy of the Hours. Some are more outwardly oriented and service oriented, but many monastics throughout history have been quite cloistered (hence the term) from the wider world.

Katy was often so mobile she had no true home, itinerantly living five weeks in one country, three in the next, eight in the next, for an entire year at a time, entertaining visitors nearly round the clock outside of her eighty-hour working weeks.

But there is another vein. Nuns often take vows of chastity and poverty, of obedience to their particular order. And their lives are dedicated to the denial of self in service of prayer and the service of others.

This strikes me as quite fitting to Katy. She never married, but God had something else for her.

She lived in a kind of poverty, having no interest in earthly goods. She raised enough money to work in Africa. That was good enough. And long after her organizations established more middle-class requirements for financial support raising, Katy wouldn't bother. She had her daily bread. While others had to leave the field to make sure their earning and retirement packages were meeting standards, Katy's leaders looked the other way for her. She could not be bothered by it. She had no plans to retire. And though not a monastic, she's gone on in this way, serving the world of Bible translation for sixty years.

Around the world, she was known as the mother of Bible translation. The Mother Teresa of Bible translation. Mama Katy. And sometimes now, Grandma Katy. But she was also known for her prayer.

I'm reminded of James, the brother of Jesus and author of the New Testament letter bearing his name.

The early church historian Hegesippus, who lived just after the apostles' lifetimes, wrote that James "was in the habit of entering alone into the temple, and was frequently found upon his knees begging forgiveness for the people, so that his knees became hard like those of a camel, in consequence of his constantly bending them in his worship of God, and asking forgiveness for the people."[2]

Katy has not been able to kneel well for some time now, due to arthritis. But if she could, she'd share this affliction with James, the brother of our Lord.

People know this about her. They go out of their way to ask her to pray for them.

On the way from Jos to Abuja, crammed together with a few too many people in a car a bit less than roadworthy, Larry Jones remembers a tense moment.

"That road has many checkpoints where military [personnel] stop the car, ask questions of the driver, take a look in," Jones said.[3] At one of the many military checkpoints, a soldier with an automatic rifle on his shoulder halted the car.

He scanned the passengers, but Katy was sardined between two people in back. The soldier didn't see her. He began to interrogate the driver. The tone was curt. Tense.

The soldier bent down and scanned the passengers again, catching someone he seemed to have missed the first time.

"He leaned over, with his head into the window," gun barrel trailing him into the car, Jones said. When the soldier's eyes landed on Barnwell, "his demeanor changed almost 180 degrees."

The soldier flashed a huge smile and said, "Pray for us, Mother."

EPILOGUE

Because I live in the US, Katy and I did some of our interviewing over Zoom and some fact-checking via email. For the *Christianity Today* article, this was more than fine. But as I swam deeper into the book, it became clear I needed full days with Katy. Many of them. And if she'd allow it, a read through any and all relevant files she'd kept.

My publisher, B&H Publishing, graciously supported me in a weeklong trip to Goring-on-Thames, where I could interview Katy directly. Because of my work as a professor, the only time that worked for both of us was Christmas break just after the holiday itself. Fortunately, it's about the only time of the year when Bible translation shuts down. Katy could make time for me then.

I flew, trained, and walked to her, staying at a quaint English hotel in the village, about an eight-minute walk from Katy's house.

We quickly developed a rhythm. I'd walk to her place around 9:00 a.m. We'd spend the day talking. I'd run two simultaneous recordings and take notes until my fingers disintegrated. We'd break. I'd look through her photo albums and files. It soon became clear that she had more files than I'd expected, despite her many moves, and I would not be able to go through all of them in person.

With my smartphone, I began taking pictures of decades of correspondence and personal letters. I could go through them once I returned to the States.

I moved things for her, fetched things, cleaned dishes, and made us some of our meals. As she walked with her walker in a certain direction, I'd regularly jump up to remove something from her path.

At one point, after a particularly hospitable couple of hours, Katy turned to me and said, "You're very good at living." I smiled. What a peculiar turn of phrase. I asked her what she meant. "Well, you're very good at knowing what needs to be done and doing it."

Now, my wife may tell you otherwise. Better said, whatever I do know, I've learned from her. It struck me then that I'm not particularly helpful but that Katy has never had someone around, not all day. Not to do the dishes. And not to make her a meal. Ever since Pat left in the early 1970s, she's been alone.

As our time was winding down on the last day, I could tell she was a bit distracted. What had been an undivided focus from her would now falter. Her attention would break as she checked email or dashed off a message. Katy's friend Leoni Bouwer once referred to this as Katy's "screen-saver face, for when she is preoccupied with something else while having to be present in an unrelated context."[1] On that day, Katy would occasionally ask me a question like "And your flight isn't delayed? You've checked?"

What was she anxious about?

This behavior might be normal enough in our society. But after a zeroed-in week of ten-to-twelve-hour days of questions from one of the most doggedly curious people you'll ever meet (eh hem) and one of the most knowledgeable people you could meet (Katy), the sudden breaks and fading attention didn't go unnoticed. Finally, curiosity got the better of me.

"What do you have going on there?" I asked innocently, gesturing to her computer.

"Ah, right." She reckoned she was caught. "Well, I'm coordinating with John Afro. We'll be doing some Scripture checking over Zoom, and we're trying to get organized."[2]

She didn't want to come across as impolite. I was her guest. She wanted me to feel that I was her only priority throughout my time with her.

But with her questions about my flight, I had my suspicions. After a week of grueling interviews, *there was no way—she couldn't be planning what I thought she was.*

Scripture checking, she'd said. What they call a *consultant check*. I nodded my head. "Nice. Which book?"

"Romans."

"Ooo," I said.

She cast a glance at me from the corner of her eye and nodded. We both knew what I meant. It's a tough one. Together with the letter to the Hebrews, it's a toss-up for the meatiest theological book in the entire New Testament.[3]

Of course, I didn't mind one bit if she went to work after I left. I found the idea fitting. And charming. And I suspected that's what she was up to as she wrote with her Mbembe colleagues. But after the week we'd had, going through her timeline down to the month and the week, and checking under every rock, there was no way. She must be planning this Scripture check a few days from now, I thought. After a rest—surely.

Her phone rang. It was a WhatsApp call, the app that seemingly everybody outside the US uses for all personal communication.

I stepped out of the room to give her some semblance of privacy. But I was only in the kitchen. And there is no door.

African conversations require three times the pleasantries than in my part of the world. I listened as Katy inquired of his family, health, and even livestock. But as their conversation concluded, the real reason for the call surfaced. With the emails and schedules flying both ways, John Afro was calling to make sure they were on the same page.

"Right, I cannot do 1:00. But 3:00 should be just fine. I have a visitor, but he'll be on his way by then. Okay, talk to you soon. Yes, 3:00 o'clock."[4]

I smirked and shook my head. At eighty-five, she wouldn't even rest after the week we'd had. The Word of God awaited. I found this charming, but for the sake of her decorum, I pretended not to hear.

Katy and I hugged. A friend and leader from her church named David van den Broek snapped a few pictures of us. Then we two missionaries, awfully overpracticed in saying goodbyes, said goodbye to each other. I do wonder if I'll get to see her again in person, this side of the new heavens and the new earth.

As I went on my way and made my connections, I thought to check my watch. 3:05 p.m. I thought of Katy, laptop open, sitting in her recliner, Paratext and Translator's Workplace both set to Romans 1. Her African colleague on the phone, peering into Romans 1 through the same software programs, neither of which would exist without her.

The Word of God would not wait.

It was time to get to work.

THE KATY BARNWELL
SCHOLARSHIP FUND

T hough not a goal of this book, I feel it would be a great opportunity missed not to mention that in Katy's honor, a scholarship has been opened in her name to help train African Bible translators. This is the link as of now, but I'm sure a quick search for *SIL Katy Barnwell Scholarship* would turn up the right link should this one eventually go out of use. https://www.sil.org/give/projects

WITH GRATITUDE

To my wife Aubrey, for putting up with me being a "writer" for the many years I had nothing, and then almost nothing to show for it.

My agent, Mary DeMuth, who was one of the principal voices I read on the craft of writing when I first recognized I wanted to be a writer. I'm so honored to be represented by you now.

My editor, **Ashley Gorman** at B&H, for immediately seeing the potential in a biography of Katy Barnwell and fighting for it. I pray we can work together again!

My editor **Clarissa Dufresne,** for your biography wizardry and editorial help.

To Capital City Church in St. Paul, Minnesota, for your friendship and encouragement. I doubt we should ever find a church community like you again.

Andy Olsen, my long-suffering editor at *Christianity Today*. Thanks for taking a gamble on Katy's story. It was a risk to run the longest article of this millennium on something a bit dense and technical—not to mention about a relatively unsung Bible translator's story, but you saw the potential.

After writing a piece with a publication, then losing the editor, and having this happen over and over, you were my rescue. Thank you for reaching out directly after my previous editor moved on so that I wasn't lost to the slush pile of the generic pitch line. I'm convinced nobody anywhere reads those at any publication.

Pitching the print managing editor (at the time) directly was such an honor. And thus began a wonderful partnership. For all the long nights and near novella-length manuscripts—"pieces of this length"—thank you.

Russell Moore, for your wisdom and guidance, even when those stances were not popular. For many of us, you are a lifeline. Thank you for your leadership at *Christianity Today* and for being willing to write the foreword for this book.

Caleb Lindgren, for taking a chance on me in 2019 as a relatively unknown writer. Thank you for seeing the potential in my first drafts and telling me to "swing for the fences." I'll never forget that first cover story.

Dr. Craig Ott, my PhD advisor. When I first inquired at Trinity Evangelical Divinity School, I didn't think I was worthy of a PhD. It seemed a kind of alien degree fit for superhuman people. So I inquired about a DMin, a terminal degree more fit for pastors, missionaries, and those outside the academy.

Dr. Ott looked at my CV, writing sample, research interests, and missionary background, and took the trouble to call me. He told me I'd applied for the wrong program. The PhD in Intercultural Studies (Missiology) was not only within my reach but a better fit, he said.

Entering that program while writing for *Christianity Today* are two of the proudest points in my career. In part, it's what allowed me to become a professor and to have the know-how and writing expertise to write Katy's story.

Dr. Harold Netland, thank you for the encouragement, guidance, and camaraderie. And for being a friend.

Dr. Karen Jones, the chair of my department at Huntington University, for leading the search committee and championing me as the right candidate for professor of missions and Old Testament. I'll be forever grateful and in your debt!

Dr. Luke Fetters, my dean, and my colleagues in the Christian Thought and Practice Department at Huntington University. Your support and camaraderie have been invaluable.

Brendan Kalish, librarian researcher extraordinaire who traipsed into archival libraries all around London for me.

My mother, Nancy Monson, whose research ability and attention to detail rival any archivist's. Upon hearing that I would not have time to read through the nearly one thousand of Katy's personal letters and still finish the book on deadline, she not only volunteered but relished the chance to read all of them. She then took notes on certain themes and flagged other letters for me to read in full. Many gems, anecdotes, and historical details surfaced from these letters.

My father, Les Monson, for being the number one encourager of my writing career.

Pamela Burkholder, the archivist at SIL who turned up fantastic information I couldn't find on my own in the SIL archives.

Boone Aldridge, author and historian and to my mind, the de facto chronicler of Bible translation history in the twentieth century. Thank you for the regular help, from email responses, fact-checking, and archive help along the way.

Dr. Dale Lemke, for bringing me on as an adjunct professor at the University of Northwestern, St. Paul and, even more, for recommending me for my current position at Huntington University.

Arthur Lightbody, for your splendid four-hour archival interview of Katy Barnwell circa 2011. While writing the *Christianity Today* piece, I was saddened that so many specific details of her early ministry were lost. Then these videos, recorded while still in her later prime, were as detailed and specific as you'd imagine a PhD linguist would be. That interview was incredible and has allowed much of the narrative of her early years to be sourced by Katy herself. Thanks, Arthur, for allowing me to forego most footnotes, avoiding the clutter, and cite that interview alongside my own simply with quotation marks.

To those who long ago told me I could write—**my brother Matt Monson, Betsy Grams, Cheryl Whitchurch, Micah Darling, Kate Madson, Glenn and Chris Jensen,** and I'm sure a few more who I've forgotten.

To **Greg Mathews,** the finest teacher of my entire life. You pointed out my intellectual curiosity and named it in a way nobody else ever had. You also nourished it like few others have. Thank you.

To those who especially nourished my growth in Christ from an early age. **Pastor Harvey Nelson, Dave Schlack, Karen Ackman, Isabelle Wayne,** and so many others. You know who you are.

Stephen Payne, for meticulously cataloging the last twenty years of Katy's email updates and suggesting material for her story. Thank you for the photos as well. You are a biographer's dream.

To all who took time to interview whose names go unmentioned here.

Finally, to all who've spent their lives sharing the good news of Jesus. It's such beautiful work. And it's so hard. God bless you for it.

> "And everyone who has left houses or brothers or sisters or father or mother or children or fields because of my name will receive a hundred times more and will inherit eternal life." (Matt. 19:29)

NOTES

Preface

1. SIL used to stand for Summer Institute of Linguistics, but now it's simply SIL, pronounced by its letters, not "sill."

2. When people talk about the "great missionaries," they normally mean the great Western missionaries of the past five hundred years. I believe Katy belongs on this list. And because she so thoroughly democratized missions and Bible translation and equipped the local church, she's done more to pass the baton (and therefore close that "From the West to the Rest" chapter) than anyone. This would make her the last of the great Western missionaries from that era—from roughly 1500 to 2000.

Chapter 1

1. Danjuma Gambo, interview with Jordan Monson, July 18, 2022.

2. Andy Kellogg, interview with Jordan Monson, March 3, 2022.

3. Kellogg, interview.

4. Kellogg, interview. As well as reporting from my interviews with Katy.

5. Kellogg, interview.

6. Kellogg, interview.

7. At the time of publication (May 2025), she's still working full-time in Bible translation at age eighty-six!

Chapter 2

1. From the Medes and Persian engineers diverting the Euphrates River and walking under the impregnable walls of Babylon in the riverbed down through today, engineers are often the agents of chaos that allow victory, not better soldiers. In fact, less-talented militaries are often able to win because of engineering advantages.

2. Though Katy did not have a close relationship with her father, the praise he received in the army bears an uncanny resemblance to the praise Katy herself would receive decades later. Military records show that Colonel Barnwell was put in charge of "reconstruction of 200 miles of track and more than 100 bridges demolished by the enemy and Allied bombing." He was described as "indefatigable" in his problem-solving and leadership, a "model of efficiency," and as showing "tireless energy and determination." He was awarded the MID, MBE, OBE by the British government, and by the United States, a Bronze Star. Without his leadership, the recommendation states that the Eighth Army would not have been able to advance from Cassino to the Po River (which is about half of the length of Italy).

3. Interview with Katy Barnwell. Given the scores of interviews I've had with Katy over two to three years, I will not clutter the text with needless footnotes all pointing back to her. Information about Katy's early life and family, unless otherwise noted, comes from my interviews with Katy herself.

4. "The Blitz: The Bombing of Britain in WWII," *WWII Explained*, https://ww2explained.com/the-blitz-the-bombing-of-britain-in-wwii.

5. This nearly yearlong season of the UK standing alone against the Nazis is often referred to as the "Darkest Hour."

Chapter 3

1. Michael Barnwell, interview with Jordan Monson, May 22, 2024.

2. Barnwell, interview.

3. Curiously, they neglect to mention that this man, now spelled Ignacy Jan Paderewski, was also the recent prime minister of Poland. After his political career, he returned to performing.

4. "Lionell Powell, Impresario, Dead," *New York Times*, December 24, 1931, https://www.nytimes.com/1931/12/24/archives/lionel-powell-impresario-dead-staged-more-than-15000-concerts-and.html.

5. "Mr. Lionel Powell Dead," *The Argus*, Melbourne, January 22, 1932, http://nla.gov.au/nla.news-article4418932.

6. "Lionell Powell, Impresario, Dead."

7. I want to be careful not to make a straw man here. You'll scarcely find a family without sibling quarreling like this. This doesn't make Ann bad; it simply marks her as the oldest.

8. Katharine Barnwell, "The Birds' Morning Concert," Rotherham High School magazine, 1951.

9. Mary Aickin Rothschild, "To Scout or to Guide? The Girl Scout-Boy Scout Controversy, 1912–1941," *Frontiers: A Journal of Women Studie* 6, no. 3 (Autumn 1981): 115–21, https://www.jstor.org/stable/3346224.

10. Rothschild, "To Scout or to Guide?"

11. Rothschild, "To Scout or to Guide?"

Chapter 4

1. Michael Barnwell, interview with Jordan Monson, May 22, 2024. In all of these quotations, Michael calls Katy "Rine," pronounced "Rin." This is how Michael pronounced Katharine while a toddler, and it stuck for the whole family. It's how Katy signed all of her letters back home. But in Bible translation, everybody knows her as Katy, or Mama Katy.

2. Barnwell, interview.

3. This would prove true as the Barnwell children scattered all over the world. Ann's husband worked in the tea industry in Sri Lanka and then Kenya, Michael worked and played cricket in South Africa, and Katy lived many decades in Nigeria. Though "not a fan of the foreigner," as Michael told me, their father did go through the trouble to visit Ann abroad. He never visited Michael or Katy. Ann and Katy never visited each other abroad, even though for many years, they were both in Africa. However, Katy's mother and younger brother both made sure to visit Katy in Ovonum, the most rural and developing area in Nigeria she lived in.

4. Paul Bolton, "Education: Historical Statistics," *House of Commons Library, Social and General Statistics*, November 27, 2012, https://research-briefings.files.parliament.uk/documents/SN04252/SN04252.pdf.

5. Jenny Rowe, "The Fight for Rights: The History of Women at Cambridge University," *Britain Magazine*, September 4, 2019, https://www.britain-magazine.com/features/history-of-women-at-cambridge-university.

Chapter 5

1. Interview with Katy Barnwell, Arthur Lightbody, archival interview, 2011. Besides my own interviews with Katy, this four-hour interview is the source I consult most for her direct quotations. In order to avoid an undue number of endnotes all pointing to these interviews, Lightbody welcomed me to simply mention this at the first citation and in the acknowledgments and otherwise quote Katy as is. Unless otherwise noted, citations from Katy come from my interviews or, if not mine, Lightbody's archival interview. These archival videos allow Katy to tell much of her own story when her memory was even sharper than now.

2. In the US and many other English-speaking countries, this ministry is called InterVarsity.

3. Note: The biographer's dilemma is to faithfully cast both the subject's own testimony as well as the facts surrounding their life. Katy's testimony is that she had a true awakening of faith in college. And this is true. But if you asked her friends or community in secondary school if she had a vibrant faith, they likely would have said yes. Both can be true. You see this with C. S. Lewis and other major figures. Testimony "narratives" are always much simpler than the real story.

Through many iterations and speeches in front of churches, missionaries are encouraged to tell a brief testimony of their faith. This requires simplification and repetition. Over the years, these testimonies tend to *become* the story rather than simply refer to the complexity of the whole story. When you dig into the past, you find it's more complicated. My testimony involves becoming serious about my faith when a seventeen-year-old, but running into school papers I did at age fourteen and fifteen and so on, I find that though my story is true enough, the slide into committed faith was much longer and more perceptible than my two-minute testimony would give credit for.

We might say Katy was a Christian who went from being a committed believer to a zealous pre-missionary. She had an awakening, a turning experience. But it's not as if she was not a Christian before this. This might be called an awakening to the cost of discipleship.

4. Barry Didcock, "Scottish Panoramas: the Student Pier Walk of St. Andrews University," *The Herald*, October 31, 2020, https://www.heraldscotland.com/news/18828412.scottish-panoramas-student-pier-walk-st-andrews-university.

5. To hear an example of this whistle speech, George Cowan is on video demonstrating this on YouTube, accessed August 18, 2024, https://www.youtube.com/watch?v=Hvw9sN2fN8A "Mazatec Whistle Talk—Dr. George Cowan."

6. "Foreign Language Training," United States Department of State (blog), accessed May 7, 2024, https://www.state.gov/foreign-language-training.

7. The women understood the whistle speech, but it was not customary for them to use it themselves. George M. Cowan, "Mazateco Whistle Speech." Language 24, no. 3 (1948): 280–86, https://doi.org/10.2307/410362.

8. Cowan, "Mazateco Whistle Speech."

9. SIL International, "George Cowan: SIL Linguist, Mexico," February 16, 2017, https://www.sil.org/linguistics/george-cowan-sil-linguist-mexico.

10. Printing Cowan's words on a page does not do him justice. He was a masterful speaker. George M. Cowan, "Feast or Crumbs," 2011, https://vimeo.com/20862487.

11. Matthew 28:19–20

12. One of the most reported anecdotes (though possibly apocryphal) in all of modern Bible translation history comes from the founding challenge given to William Cameron Townsend (Uncle Cam) as a young man. Boone Aldridge and Gary Simons tell this well: "In 1917, Townsend arrived in Guatemala as a Bible salesman. The standard practice of selling Spanish Bibles to the Kaqchikel, K'iche', Mam, and other indigenous peoples who spoke little or no Spanish proved frustrating. Townsend later recalled that Guatemala's indigenous inhabitants kept asking, if not in these exact words, something like: "If your God is so powerful, why doesn't he speak my language?" Staggered by the implications of this question, Townsend blazed a new path in missions." Boone Aldridge and Gary Simons, "Kenneth Pike and the Making of Wycliffe Bible Translators and SIL International," *Christianity Today*, February 2, 2018, https://www.christianitytoday.com/history/2018/february/kenneth-pike-sil-wycliffe.html.

13. Romans 10:14

Chapter 6

1. Unless otherwise noted, sourcing for this John Bendor-Samuel background comes from his Wycliffe bio, "John Bendor-Samuel," accessed August 18, 2024, https://web.archive.org/web/20120313082933/http://wycliffe.org.uk/docs/wyc-jbs-bio.pdf.

2. "John Bendor-Samuel" bio.

3. "John Bendor-Samuel" bio.

4. Interestingly, Uncle Cam would never set foot in Africa during his lifetime. Source: Boone Aldridge and Bob Creson, *For the Gospel's Sake: The Rise of the Wycliffe Bible Translators and the Summer Institute of Linguistics* (Grand Rapids: Eerdmans, 2018).

5. "John Bendor-Samuel" bio.

6. Drew Maust and Lynell Zogbo, "Bible Translation: An Interview with Katy Barnwell," *Journal of Translation* 17, no. 1 (2021): 1–12, https://www.sil.org/resources/publications/entry/91195.

7. In the 1990s, this was no longer the case. While everybody else in the world had been trying to unite around trade languages, SIL faithfully kept working to develop local minority languages. Then, when it became clear that this method was the best for achieving the kinds of goals nations are interested in, SIL saw a boon. Everybody in the world wanted minority

language development and literacy, and SIL was by far the biggest player in that field.

8. "Nigeria," *Ethnologue*, accessed May 11, 2024, https://www.ethnologue.com/country/NG.

Chapter 7

1. 1 Corinthians 14:26–33

Chapter 8

1. At the time, London was the second or third largest city in the world, depending on how the metro area was counted. New York City was first and Tokyo, second or third. Today, both Western cities are dwarfed by Tokyo and many others in the Global South.

2. Billy Graham, "John Stott—the 2005 TIME 100," *Time*, April 18, 2005, https://web.archive.org/web/20170302185311/http:/content.time.com/time/specials/packages/article/0,28804,1972656_1972717_1974108,00.html. He was listed as eighty-two of one hundred and his write-up was done by Billy Graham himself.

3. Although, I hope by the end of this book, another name might be added to that list.

4. Stott often made this distinction and compared these commissions.

5. In fact, most Protestant and Roman Catholic churches around the world never lost this both-hands distinction. This was a North American error.

6. This whole section on Stott is sourced from Dudley-Smith's wonderful biography: Timothy Dudley-Smith, *John Stott: A Global Ministry: A Biography of the Later Years* (Downers Grove, Ill: IVP, 2001), 150–222.

7. Dudley-Smith, *John Stott*.

8. 1 Corinthians 15:55 KJV

9. Even so-called Christian empires know the leveling power of the Bible. The British Empire itself would not allow its subjects in India to read Mary's Magnificat in Luke 1. D. L. Mayfield, "Perspective | Mary's 'Magnificat' in the Bible Is Revolutionary. Some Evangelicals Silence Her," *Washington Post*, December 20, 2018, https://www.washingtonpost.com/religion/2018/12/20/marys-magnificat-bible-is-revolutionary-so-evangelicals-silence-it. There's a fear in millions of people reading these words: "He has toppled the mighty from their thrones and exalted the lowly. He has satisfied the hungry with good things and sent the rich away empty" (Luke 1:52–53).

10. In response to the Universal Declaration of Human Rights, many Muslim countries have responded with their own document, the "Cairo Declaration on Human Rights in Islam." Article 24 reminds its readers that "all the rights and freedoms stipulated in this Declaration are subject to the Islamic Shari'ah [Law]," https://en.wikisource.org/wiki/Cairo_Declaration_on_Human_Rights_in_Islam.

11. Matthew 25:35–40

12. Matthew 25:40

Chapter 9

1. First Thessalonians 2–3; Acts 18:1–4. To think of Paul as a leatherworker more generally is probably more likely, according to the most respected biblical Greek dictionary. William Arndt, et al., *A Greek-English Lexicon of the New Testament and Other Early Christian Literature* (Chicago: University of Chicago Press, 2000), 928–29.

2. As I write, CNN has Zurich as the most expensive city on earth. Tamara Hardingham-Gill, "The World's Most Expensive Cities in Which to Live in 2023," CNN, December 7, 2023, https://www.cnn.com/2023/11/30/travel/the-worlds-most-expensive-cities-to-live-in-for-2023/index.html.

3. There aren't great statistics on this. It changes according to country and what kind of mission organization is in view. But this is the predominant pattern. Those who take too long are often encouraged to reassess their calling.

4. Katy's pastor, Nigel Gordon-Potts, told me this story during my visit on December 31, 2023. This is how he began to realize how important she was in Bible translation.

Chapter 10

1. Andrew Gardner, email to Jordan Monson, February 23, 2024.

2. Rodney Stark, *The Rise of Christianity: How the Obscure, Marginal Jesus Movement Became the Dominant Religious Force in the Western World in a Few Centuries* (San Francisco: HarperSanFrancisco, 1997).

3. Origen, "Origen against Celsus," in *Fathers of the Third Century: Tertullian, Part Fourth; Minucius Felix; Commodian; Origen, Parts First and Second*, vol. 4; *The Ante-Nicene Fathers*, ed. Alexander Roberts, James Donaldson, and A. Cleveland Coxe, trans. Frederick Crombie (Buffalo, NY: Christian Literature Company, 1885), 4482.

4. Stark, *The Rise of Christianity*.

Chapter 11

1. "Glasgow and Ships of the Clyde," https://shipsoftheclyde.com/ships/show?id=4481.

2. I've read this from several people, including veterans, but wasn't able to dig up the sources. So, I spoke with Courtney G. Stufflebeam, PhD, a Licensed Clinical Psychologist and National Health Service Psychologist within the Veterans Affairs system. She confirmed that "Sudden changes often lead to increased feelings of anxiety," "easing into change allows for more sustainable transition, which allows people to feel a sense of control," and that "social support [acts as a] stress buffer." The shared experience of WWII soldiers in contrast to Vietnam soldiers likely helped them to "navigate through challenging new situations."

3. I'm not intending to draw a comparison between missions and war, but the fact that having a significant amount of time to separate different and trying circumstances from those that are familiar is helpful to the human psyche.

4. Katharine Barnwell, newsletter to friends, family, and supporters, January 28, 1965.

5. Patricia Leigh, email to Jordan Monson, April 11, 2024. Note: Pat (whose maiden name Revill gets more ink here) sent me a forty-four hundred-word email, almost a small memoir or autobiography of those years. Her memory of those times is sharper than Katy's, so it was extremely helpful. All citations from Pat come from this email unless otherwise noted.

6. They likely stopped in Lagos, which provides good context for the memory.

7. Leigh, email.

8. Barnwell, newsletter.

9. Barnwell, newsletter.

10. Christianity, Islam, and Buddhism are often referred to as the three great missionary faiths of the world. Charles E. Farhadian, *Introducing World Religions: A Christian Engagement* (Grand Rapids, MI: Baker Academic, 2015).

11. For example, the Embassy of the Blessed Kingdom of God for All Nations, pastored by Sunday Adelaja, began in the 1990s in Kyiv and, before the Russia-Ukraine war, boasted twenty-five thousand members in Kyiv alone, not counting their many church plants. The Kingsway International Christian Centre in London, pastored by Matthew Ashimolowo, is just over thirty years old and has between eight thousand and twelve thousand weekly attenders.

12. On anthropology growing out of mission work, see Timothy Larsen, *The Slain God: Anthropologists and the Christian Faith* (Oxford: Oxford University Press, 2016). On tribes much preferring incarnational missionaries who help and serve them rather than anthropologists who are apt to take notes, take naked video footage, then leave to make their careers on that data and footage without so much as a penny going back to the tribe. See Mark Andrew Ritchie, *Spirit of the Rainforest, 3rd ed.: A Yanomamö Shaman's Story* (Island Lake Press, 2018).

13. As we'll see later, much of this is due to Katy Barnwell herself.

14. Barnwell, newsletter. As to her final words in quotes, this may be a line from a hymn, or it may be riffing on Isaiah 62:7 or other similar passages.

Chapter 12

1. I've spoken with dozens of retired missionaries about Jungle Camp over the years. Some of this is sourced from the agreement of those untold conversations with people whose names I've long forgotten. More direct sourcing comes from Mickey Richards, "Chapter 20: Jungle Training Camp," *A Joyful Life in God's Hands: The Mickey Richards Story,* November 27, 2014, https://mickeyrichards.wordpress.com/2014/11/27/chapter-20-jungle-training-camp-2.

2. Richards, "Jungle Training Camp."

3. Richards, "Jungle Training Camp."

4. Richards, who I've cited regarding Jungle Camp, went on to serve in the Philippines.

5. Special thanks to the historian Dr. Alice T. Ott for pointing me to this source and for sharing the slides! William Holman Bentley, *Pioneering on the Congo*, vol. 2 (Grand Rapids: Revell, 1900), 429–30.

6. Alice T. Ott, *Turning Points in the Expansion of Christianity: From Pentecost to the Present* (Grand Rapids: Baker Academic, 2021).

7. Katharine Barnwell, letter fragment, early 1965 but the date is missing. Given its placement in the archive, the mention of the dry season, the various fruits in season, and what Katy and Pat were up to, this is undoubtedly referring to her Jungle Camp training in February/March 1965.

8. Barnwell, letter fragment, lightly edited. This surviving fragment has typos and edits in pen. I suspect it was the draft that after editorial changes would be sent to her supporters. So I've cleaned up anything the Wycliffe editors would have before mailing it out.

9. Barnwell, letter fragment. Igala was the local language in that region.

10. Barnwell, letter fragment.

11. She claims only twice, but given the number of anecdotes I received in my reporting about times when she had malaria (and how resilient she was), I wouldn't be surprised if the correct number was four to ten times.

Chapter 13

1. Patricia Leigh, email to Jordan Monson, April 11, 2024.

2. This process is called "exposure." More on Mary's influence on ending infanticide can be found here: David Lishilinimle Imbua, "Robbing Others to Pay Mary Slessor: Unearthing the Authentic Heroes and Heroines of the Abolition of Twin-Killing in Calabar," *African Economic History* 41 (2013): 139–58, https://www.jstor.org/stable/43863309.

3. This term *mother tongue* is somewhat contentious. There have been various attempts to change this to "first language," "native language," "heart language," and any number of other options. Just as "mother tongue" fails to correctly describe the strongest or most resonant language for somebody who grew up without a mother, or raised primarily by another relative, or after their long education, is more comfortable in a wider trade language than their village language, so the other terms all likewise fail in similar ways. I will at times use the term *mother tongue* and later, *mother-tongue translator*, because the term *mother tongue* has been in use for centuries, is widely understood, and is not pedantically interpreted as *necessarily* the mother's language. Despite the attempts to get away from this term, it is stubborn, and most people I interviewed continued to use *mother tongue* and the abbreviation MTT, mother-tongue translator. Because of this, I will use the term like most of my interviewees did.

4. This theology of translation has its roots in the incarnation. Just as God translated himself to us in Jesus, that we might see and know and hear him face-to-face, without the veil, so must his Word continue to go out, unveiled. For Vatican II's rulings on this, see Pope Paul VI, *Sacrosanctum Concilium*, December 4, 1963, https://www.vatican.va/archive/hist_councils/ii_vatican_council/documents/vat-ii_const_19631204_sacrosanctum-concilium_en.html.

5. This *emic* and *etic* description, known the world over and memorized in undergraduate courses, was coined by Kenneth Pike, one of the brightest linguists of the twentieth century, president of SIL, and colleague and friend to Katharine Barnwell. The terms themselves come from a shortening of the linguistic sciences of phonetics and phonemics—notice the second half of those words. Phonetics involves the more external and objective description of the sounds available to any given language. You can give a good phonetic description of a language you don't speak. Phonemics is

more complicated and isn't fully accessible unless you're a fluent and, often, a native speaker. Hence, the insider/outsider descriptions.

6. "Nigeria," *Ethnologue*, accessed May 11, 2024, https://www.ethnologue.com/country/NG.

7. Katharine Barnwell, newsletter, April 2, 1965.

8. Leigh, email.

9. Katy Barnwell, letter to her mother, March 27, 1965.

10. Barnwell, letter to her mother. The colony was such a success that leprosy was completely healed in the area. Katy and her mother were able to be in attendance for the celebration and the closing of the colony.

11. Leigh, email.

12. What linguists refer to as African American Vernacular English, or AAVE.

13. Katy Barnwell, letter to John Bendor-Samuel, March 29, 1965 (as well as interviews with Barnwell). Note: Katy writes and tells about this quote in various places. Each quote from Mr. Arrobo is the same in spirit, but the wording varies slightly. I've done my best to harmonize these reports into one quote here.

14. Katy Barnwell, archival interview with Arthur Lightbody, 2011.

Chapter 14

1. Katy Barnwell, archival interview with Arthur Lightbody, 2011.

2. The word *mzungu* is used in much of Eastern Africa to the same effect—though the word derives from the word for a wandering spirit rather than a priest.

3. Note: To read of missionaries having meals prepared by others can rub some the wrong way. This is simply the wrong way to think of it in a higher hospitality culture. To arrive in an economically poor yet hospitable culture where people want to work, want to serve, want to help, and then hoard your resources, insisting on doing all those things alone that others could do, is often seen as selfish and antisocial.

4. Patricia Leigh, email to Jordan Monson, April 11, 2024.

5. Leigh, email.

Chapter 15

1. As an example: dictionary: ˈdikSHə͟nerē \\ or confuse: kənˈfyo͞oz.

2. His name is spelled in three ways throughout Pat and Katy's correspondence, and I follow their various spellings: Livinius, Livinus, and Levinus. Given he was named in a culture and language without an

alphabet, I suspect all three work just as well for how his name was actually pronounced. This is how spelling often works in oral cultures.

3. Cal Newport, *Deep Work: Rules for Focused Success in a Distracted World* (New York: Grand Central Publishing, 2016). Note: Newport is a computer scientist at Georgetown, not a psychologist. That said, he cites good psychological research on this. But given that research is outside my field, I thought it best to cite Newport rather than retrace his steps on this point.

4. Katharine Grace Lowry Barnwell, "A Grammatical Description of Mbembe (Adun Dialect)—a Cross River Language," (PhD thesis, SOAS University of London, 1969), 64–66, https://eprints.soas.ac.uk/29013/1/10673257.pdf.

5. Though not one to cite Wikipedia, this is the most concise explanation of this tongue twister I found. "Tone (Linguistics)," accessed February 19, 2024, Wikipedia, https://en.wikipedia.org/w/index.php?title=Tone_(linguistics)&oldid=1222430480.

6. Katharine Barnwell, "The Noun Class System in Mbembe," *Journal of West African Languages*, VI, I (1969), 51–58, https://journalofwestafricanlanguages.org/index.php/downloads?task=download.send&id=81&catid=16&m=0.

Chapter 16

1. During the editing phase when I sent Katy the working version of the cover of this book, she protested. She wasn't thrilled that the book would have her picture—on her biography. This is simply who Katy is.

2. Katharine Barnwell, *Seed for the Sower* (Merstham, Surrey: Wycliffe Bible Translators, 1968), 8.

3. Katy Barnwell, letter to prayer partners, March 1966.

4. Katharine Barnwell, *Seed for the Sower*, 10.

5. She explores these thoughts even in published form: "So far no Mbembe has gone to University, very few even to secondary school. There is one young Mbembe teacher who is qualified and anxious to go to University, but where are the fees to come from?" Katharine Barnwell, *Seed for the Sower*, 10.

6. This is Mark 1:1 in what's called a *back translation*—that is, the Mbembe verse translated back into English.

7. Katy will be pained to see herself using this word *helpers*. It presupposes the Westerner as the primary translator. This was the method and terminology used around the world, as well as the method she was trained in. It's hard to blame her. Before you can revolutionize something, you often

need to master the status quo. But soon, she would do more than anybody to correct this—not only in her own translation work but in that of the whole world.

8. Katy Barnwell, newsletter update, May 1967.

9. Barnwell, newsletter update.

10. Katy used this cake analogy many times in writing and in my interviews.

Chapter 17

1. "Why Were the Sides in the Nigerian Civil War So Weird?," *History Matters*, YouTube, 2022, https://www.youtube.com/watch?v=rae3AC4kWjU.

2. About 109 million Punjabis live in Pakistan, and thirty-eight million in India due to this zany border.

3. *An Honest Explanation of the Nigerian Civil War | The Biafran Story*, NewAfrica, YouTube, 2020, https://www.youtube.com/watch?v=7JCvIvb8PpY.

4. *An Honest Explanation of the Nigerian Civil War.*

5. *An Honest Explanation of the Nigerian Civil War.*

6. *An Honest Explanation of the Nigerian Civil War.* From the Cleveland Clinic: "Kwashiorkor is a type of malnutrition characterized by severe protein deficiency. It causes fluid retention and a swollen, distended abdomen. Kwashiorkor most commonly affects children, particularly in developing countries with high levels of poverty and food insecurity. People with kwashiorkor may have food to eat, but not enough protein," https://my.clevelandclinic.org/health/diseases/23099-kwashiorkor.

7. Samuel Fury Childs Daly, *A History of the Republic of Biafra: Law, Crime, and the Nigerian Civil War* (Cambridge, UK: Cambridge University Press, 2020).

8. Patricia Leigh, email to Jordan Monson, April 11, 2024.

9. Katy Barnwell, prayer letter (pre-edited copy, undated but likely April or May 1967).

10. Barnwell, prayer letter.

11. Unfortunately, this year behind the communication curtain allowed a foot for hagiography. I heard a source tell an astounding story, that Katy was held hostage by armed guards for weeks. But over the weeks, the grace within her was so strong that her captors became Christians and let her go. What a story. But unfortunately, it was too good to be true. Both Katy and Pat said this never happened.

12. As the New Testament scholar Mark Strauss writes, fully 93 percent of Mark is found in either Matthew or Luke. The best understanding of this is that Matthew and Luke used Mark as one of their sources and then added additional material Mark didn't have. Mark Strauss, *Four Portraits, One Jesus: A Survey of Jesus and the Gospels*, 2nd ed. (Grand Rapids: Zondervan Academic, 2020), 65.

13. Marcus E. Raichle and Debra A. Gusnard, "Appraising the Brain's Energy Budget," *Proceedings of the National Academy of Sciences of the United States of America*, July 29, 2002, https://doi.org/10.1073/pnas.172399499.

14. Patricia Leigh, email to Jordan Monson, April 11, 2024.

15. Andrew Gardner, email to Jordan Monson, February 23, 2024.

16. Leigh, email.

17. Leigh, email.

18. Leigh, email.

Chapter 18

1. As discussed earlier, Katy often led me to believe she was led by others. But whenever I talked to those others, they would laugh and steer me straight. I imagine Katy was the leader of the two.

2. Philippians 2:7 note: the term "emptied himself" for ἐκένωσεν is tricky, but it's often how we translate it best. Cf. CSB, ESV, NRSV, NASB, LEB, etc.

3. Eliza Griswold, *The Tenth Parallel: Dispatches from the Fault Line between Christianity and Islam* (Farrar, Straus and Giroux, 2010), 220ff. Kindle edition. For more on this, see Andrew Walls, *The Missionary Movement in Christian History: Studies in the Transmission of Faith*, 1st ed. (Maryknoll, NY: Orbis Books, 1996).

4. Griswold, *The Tenth Parallel*, 221–22.

5. Griswold, *The Tenth Parallel*, 222.

6. Andrew Walls, *The Missionary Movement in Christian History*.

7. Revelation 7:10

8. 1 Corinthians 9:19–22 NIV

9. Patricia Leigh, email to Jordan Monson, April 11, 2024.

Chapter 19

1. Here she refers to those who died in the war.

2. Katy Barnwell, newsletter to supporters, April 1970.

3. Statistics on this vary depending on organization and specialization, and I've seen no rigorous scientific data from any missionary organization.

That said, data from many organizations and experience in the missions world supports this. Two to four years seems average. Those who last more than five are the exception. Few who become overseas missionaries are still overseas in ten to fifteen years doing the direct work. If they've stayed with their organization, they're more than likely back in their home country helping to manage or fill the administrative ranks. Even if missionaries stay with their organization, active mission work has an incredible attrition rate.

4. Danjuma Gambo, interview with Jordan Monson, July 18, 2022.

5. "How Does Memory Work?," *ScienceDaily*, May 17, 2016, https://www.sciencedaily.com/releases/2016/05/160517131928.htm.

6. "How Does Memory Work?"

7. Philippians 3:13

8. Mr. Oyama, who helped with the translation, and Egor Oyama, in whose compound Katy and Pat lived, were different people and not related. Oyama is a common surname in that area.

9. Still today, many locals who show a spark for translation, and continue to show great promise and work ethic, will use Bible translation funding and scholarships to move all the way through a master's or PhD, helping in Bible translation along the way. But once they have the degree, many other posts within universities, ministries, or the government offer better compensation.

10. Teryl Gonzalez, interview with Jordan Monson, January 18, 2022.

11. Gonzalez, interview.

12. Katy Barnwell, newsletter.

13. Boone Aldridge, *Kenneth L. Pike: An Evangelical Mind* (Eugene, OR: Pickwick Publications, Kindle ed.), 92.

14. Patricia Leigh, email to Jordan Monson, April 11, 2024.

Chapter 20

1. Or many others I'm forgetting to mention.

2. Ron Stanford, Nigeria Branch proposed policy statement, November 1971.

3. Stanford, Nigeria Branch proposed policy statement.

4. This is one of three or four sources I found most thrilling to uncover in all of my research. As a missiologist, it's remarkable. Nigeria branch was incredibly ahead of its time. It's on the level of digging up a fifty-year-old time capsule with an iPhone inside.

5. Ernst Wendland, interview with Jordan Monson, January 25, 2022.

6. Of all Katy's accomplishments that she plays down or ignores, coining the term "meaning-based translation" is about the one exception. It's one of the few things she takes pride in and is not shy about mentioning.

7. Its original 1975 title was "Bible Translation: An Introductory Course for Mother-tongue Translators."

8. Hugh Steven, *Yours to Finish the Task: The Memoirs of W. Cameron Townsend, Part Four: 1947–1982* (Hugh Steven, 2013), 228.

9. The principal reason for the fourth edition was to spend significantly more time on Old Testament translation issues. Since the mid 1980s, so many translation projects around the world have finished the New Testament. Now, they want guidance with tricky Old Testament problems.

10. Wendland, interview.

11. Wendland, interview.

12. Wendland, interview.

13. This is mostly by design. They send the translated file into closed countries for printing and necessarily lose track of it. It takes on a life of its own then.

14. Wycliffe Bible Translators, "State of the Bible," accessed May 16, 2024, https://wycliffe.org.uk/home/resources/state-of-the-bible. Note: This page is regularly updated with new stats and old ones are gotten rid of. The graph I used for this statistic, showing how many total languages were engaged by year, no longer appears, but this stat was correct and current as of October 2022 when the *Christianity Today* cover story published. It's certainly only grown since then.

Chapter 21

1. Nigeria Bible Translation Trust, *Strategic Plan 1998–2007*, Archives. Note: In this internal document kept by the NBTT, they have the history of the founding of the NBTT, which is where this information is sourced.

2. "Institute Shut," *Daily Times* (Lagos), May 6, 1976.

3. "Institute Shut," *Daily Times*.

4. When I worked in São Tomé, an island about 250 miles out at sea from West Africa's mainland coast, there was a large radio station that broadcast American-programmed content to much of West Africa. Local missionaries told me not to visit or get to know anybody in the station's orbit. The price for being mistaken as associated with US intelligence is simply too high. Though there may be folks there who could be great ex-pat friends on the field, they were off-limits.

5. Matthew 19:29–30

6. Julia Cass, "Just Bible Translators? Colombians Have Doubts," *Boston Globe*, March 8, 1981.

7. Cass, "Just Bible Translators?"

8. Diana Shaw, "The Temptation of Tom Dooley," *Los Angeles Times*, December 15, 1991, https://www.latimes.com/archives/la-xpm-1991-12-15-tm-868-story.html.

9. "Eisenhower Again Named 'Most Admired Man' for the Ninth Straight Year," *The Tampa Tribune*, December 25, 1960.

10. Shaw, "The Temptation of Tom Dooley."

11. Shaw, "The Temptation of Tom Dooley."

12. Paula Herbut, "Another Cross to B . . . CIA Involvement . . . : The New Missionaries, Part 2," *Philadelphia Bulletin*, May 4, 1981. Note: This is a "sanitized copy approved for release" that I obtained from the CIA archives. Its title is obscured (not on purpose); likely by a sticky note or something covering part of the title when it was copied, https://www.cia.gov/readingroom/docs/CIA-RDP90-00806R000201050011-1.pdf.

13. Herbut, "Another Cross."

14. In doing due diligence, I've assumed this is a lead worth pursuing and tried to get people to betray any evidence. Nothing.

15. Danjuma Gambo, interview with Jordan Monson, July 18, 2022.

16. Lamin Sanneh, *Translating the Message: The Missionary Impact on Culture*, (American Society of Missiology, Book 42) (Maryknoll, NY: Orbis Books, Kindle Edition, 2009), 35–36.

Chapter 22

1. That is, the newly formed Nigeria Bible Translation Trust.

2. Her fiftieth anniversary was in 2013, but the timeline was requested in 2011 in her forty-eighth year.

3. For the curious, the word traces back like this: "'labor, toil,' mid-13c., from Old French travail 'work, labor, toil, suffering or painful effort, trouble; arduous journey' (12c.), from travailler 'to toil, labor,' originally 'to trouble, torture, torment,' from Vulgar Latin *tripaliare 'to torture,' from *tripalium (in Late Latin trepalium) 'instrument of torture,' probably from Latin tripalis 'having three stakes.'" Source: "travel," Online Etymology Dictionary, https://www.etymonline.com/word/travel#etymonline_v_16914, "travail," online *Etymology Dictionary*, https://www.etymonline.com/word/travail.

Chapter 23

1. For all the skeptics reading this, it's not that she never brings it up. That might paint a picture of active avoidance. She'll mention casually here and there that she's working as a single person or that traveling alone posits certain dangers. It's not a taboo topic for her, nor does she avoid it. She simply doesn't make much of it. Being single was never her identity. Instead, it's a nearly forgotten reality.

2. Paul calls this a *gift* in 1 Corinthians 7:7.

3. According to Doug Enick, Paul wrote 23.5 percent of the New Testament: "The New Testament's Most Prolific Authors," blog post, December 11, 2017, http://dougenick.blogspot.com/2017/12/the-new-testaments-most-prolific-authors.html#. This number does not count Hebrews, which neither I nor most scholars would assign to Pauline authorship. Why? (1) The author of Hebrews does not open the letter with a self-designation, as does every other letter from Paul. (2) The style is shockingly different. It's simply not Paul's voice. (3) The smoking gun, Hebrews 2:3, clearly designates the author as a second-generation hearer. This writer heard the good news from *others* who knew the Lord. This author did not know Jesus. But Paul is adamant throughout his letters that he received his gospel directly from the Lord. He would never place himself as a second-generation hearer.

4. 1 Corinthians 7:8–9

5. 1 Corinthians 7:32–35

Chapter 24

1. Sometimes people start laughing uncontrollably because of some inappropriate oversight the translators have made. This process has saved many an innuendo and taboo from entering the translation.

2. The term *mother tongue* is surrounded by strong debates and difficulties. See chapter 13, footnote 3.

Chapter 25

1. That is, in Dallas for a conference in October that same year.

2. That is, mother-tongue translators.

3. Katy's peers in important positions around the world pointed to her as the right person for the top technical job at SIL.

4. David Bendor-Samuel, letter to Katy Barnwell, June 23, 1988.

5. To nuance this, I'm sure some will cry foul. "This is a straw man. This is unfair." And it's true that the senior leaders engaged with more nuance around this issue, especially in writing. But when the mics are

turned off and the presses are no longer running, people's real attitudes come out around lunch tables and in lectures. And this attitude, even if nuanced when needed to be among the leaders, finds its way deep into the acolytes and employees not in leadership. They are the ones who then apply the status quo and peer pressure. The vitriol I experienced as an advocate of this method was intense. I was marked as heretical or at least heterodox, a problem. It was clearly the students headed toward the traditional model (one couple, one people group, one grammar, one New Testament, one lifetime) who were championed. And because this model is dying and in part because the numbers were dwindling, the SIL UND school shut down not long after.

6. Bendor-Samuel, letter to Katy Barnwell. Many linguists have a short memory on this subject. In response to this critique of some of the Latin American branches, I've heard some say Westerners never did the translating. It was always the (anachronistic and racist-sounding) "language helper." Of course, the name "language helper" betrays their argument, as does any journal or conference paper published in those decades. Incidentally, so does DBS's letter here. In the traditional model, the Westerner held the pen. In Katy's model, the pen, that tiny baton, was passed to national translators (MTTs) with the outside consultant offering help, technical expertise, and linguistic and biblical background.

Chapter 26

1. There are rare exceptions like New York City or Toronto, but not many. Most American infrastructure grew up after the automobile (or has been radically remade in its image).

2. The adoption of new technology is often shown on a graph. In the graph linked below, 2.5 percent of the population are called *innovators*. They are the ones to create new methods. The next 13.5 percent are called *early adopters*. They are the ones trying out and weighing new methods and technology. Once this group approves of a method and finds it useful, the *early majority* (34%) takes it on. After them, the *late majority* (34%). What's left is the 16 percent of *laggards* who keep holding onto the old methods. This shift to indigenous leadership follows the same trajectory. If the late 1960s and 1970s represents *innovators*, the 1980s represents *early adopters*. By the 1990s, we're well into the majority. When I began studying linguistics in 2013, I was dealing mostly with the laggards. See this link for the graph I'm referencing: "Diffusion of Innovation Theory," DoD, Anthrax, and the Internet, https://www.ou.edu/deptcomm/dodjcc/groups/99A2/

theories.htm#:~:text=Innovators%20are%20the%20first%202.5,are%20
called%20the%20early%20majority.

3. Westerners often have this notion that our Christianity is the "basic," "true," or "foundational" Christianity. Any other culture requires contextualization. But Western Christianity is just as contextualized. We just don't see it like this because it's one of the early contextualizations and happened to become the dominant global variety. The good news was first preached to Hebrew people with little education. From there, it spread east, south, north, and west, and took on different terms and expressions to do so. The variety that spread West, which came to dominate much later, contextualized to Greek categories, philosophy, as well as Roman hierarchy, law, and economy. Out of this, a great Western culture marrying Greek and Roman thought to Hebrew and Christian thought was produced. The creeds, as important as they are, were created largely to answer or bat down heresies or heterodoxies that were Western issues and responses originating from their cognitive landscape, which the rest of the world did not share. Christians to the east of Jerusalem shared few of these presuppositions and the way they practiced and proclaimed their faith was quite different because of this.

4. This doesn't mean these terms always have to be translated the same way. They simply have to be translated purposefully. Many modern translations will translate the Greek word σάρξ (sarx) in around two dozen ways in order to convey the Greek meaning in modern English, from "flesh" to "sinful nature," to "meat," to "sensual," "body," "physical," "earthly," and so on.

5. As a writer for *Christianity Today (CT)*, I tip my hat to *CT*. *CT* excels in excellent and deeply researched journalism and news coverage. The Gospel Coalition does not publish much journalism or news coverage but thrives as a theological resource and in editorial and opinion writing.

6. Justin Taylor, "D. A. Carson Publications," *The Gospel Coalition*, June 3, 2009, https://www.thegospelcoalition.org/blogs/justin-taylor/d-carson-publications. Note: This statistic is as of 2009. The numbers are surely significantly higher now.

7. When checking resources like bestcommentaries.com, Logos Bible Software, Amazon, and so on, Carson's *John* commentary sits at or near the top.

8. For those curious, the most difficult terms Katy asked for help on were *baptize, believe, bless, body, church, clean, covenant, fellowship, flesh, forgive, Gentile, glory, grace, holy, Israel/Jew, just,* and *kingdom of God.*

Chapter 27

1. D. A. Carson, letter to Katy Barnwell, March 14, 1995.

2. A biblical commentary is a book thoroughly explaining and expounding on a biblical book. It's written by lifelong scholars of the work in question. They summarize the best of the two-thousand- to three-thousand-year history of interpretation and give valuable exegetical and historical arguments for how best to interpret tricky passages. They are one of the most impressive scholarly resources in any field.

3. SIL International, "Translator's Workplace," May 7, 2019, https://www.sil.org/resources/publications/tw.

4. Freddy Boswell, Samuel Chiang, Bob Creson, Carl Moeller, Michael Perreau, and Roy Peterson, "Accelerating Accuracy: The Bible Translation Challenge," *Christianity Today*, November 6, 2015, https://www.christianitytoday.com/ct/2015/november-web-only/every-tribe-every-nation-mast-translation.html.

5. As of this writing, there are 1,793 scholarly resources in TW. Some, like commentaries, are expensive. Others, not so expensive. I've taken an estimate at $30 per resource to get this figure of $53,790.

Chapter 28

1. This is from Teryl Gonzalez, whose story features more heavily in a later chapter.

2. Katharine Barnwell, "A Handbook for Translation Consultants," *SIL Global*, 2009, accessed August 20, 2024, https://www.sil.org/resources/archives/49201.

3. Reinier De Blois, interview with Jordan Monson, April 4, 2024.

4. For example, Kenneth Pike and Eugene Nida, cited every day by linguists and Bible scholars alike.

Chapter 29

1. Reinier de Blois, email to Jordan Monson, March 26, 2024.

2. Reinier de Blois, interview with Jordan Monson, April 4, 2024. Unless otherwise noted, all quotes from de Blois cite back to this interview.

3. For those unfamiliar, DOS did not work on mouse clicks but a mostly blank screen in which a command line of code and computer prompts were entered.

4. This comes from Katy's CV which she drafted for her fiftieth anniversary with Wycliffe.

5. *Seconded* (pronounced sec-OND-ed) is a term commonly used in the missions world when one organization assigns their employee to work

closely together with, or in the primary interest of, another, though their funding still comes through the original organization.

6. Nathan Miles, interview with Jordan Monson, April 9, 2024.

7. Miles, interview with Jordan Monson.

8. Miles, interview with Jordan Monson.

9. As a professor, I teach biblical Greek. I was charmed that a Hebrew guy named his program such a Greek name. The preposition *para* plus the accusative case often means "along," "near," or "by the side of" as in something that "goes along with the text." I quickly gave a gloss like this, and Reinier blinked. "No, I meant it as 'Parallel texts.'" As you scrolled in the biblical languages, all the other texts would scroll in sync with the one you changed. I suppose both explanations work, and the word parallel comes from the root I describe, but his idea is of course the truer explanation of the name.

10. I include the support-raising totals in this approximate figure. Ten full-time programmers' salaries, benefits, retirement, etc, plus other project funding.

11. For more on this, the "video introduction to Paratext" on their homepage is interesting and will no doubt be updated as the years go on: Paratext, https://paratext.org.

12. De Blois, interview with Jordan Monson.

13. De Blois, interview with Jordan Monson.

Chapter 30

1. Olivia Razafinjatoniary, interview with Jordan Monson, March 1, 2022.

2. Razafinjatoniary, interview.

3. Razafinjatoniary, interview. Unless otherwise noted all quotes from Razafinjatoniary come from this interview.

4. Teryl Gonzalez, interview with Jordan Monson, January 18, 2022.

5. Gonzalez, interview.

6. Gonzalez, interview.

7. Henry Huang, interview with Jordan Monson, February 17, 2022.

8. Huang, interview.

9. According to Larry Jones, former CEO of The Seed Company.

10. Ephesians 6:17

11. Isaiah 55:11

Chapter 31

1. I point to no specific source here, but this came up dozens of times in my reporting—from people inside and outside SIL and worldwide. It's a consistent reputation.

2. John Mark knew Peter well and attended the same house church in John Mark's mother's home (Acts 12:12). Many scholars believe Peter was the primary source for John Mark's Gospel.

3. Colossians 4:10–11

4. Paul briefly mentions Barnabas when he's making an unrelated argument in 1 Corinthians 9, but to assume that means they were on great terms is beyond the text. Paul's simply listing married evangelists, and Barnabas comes to mind as an example.

5. Bernie May, interview with Jordan Monson, October 23, 2023.

6. May, interview.

7. May, interview.

8. *Prima donna* is Italian for "first lady" and comes from the opera term for a leading singer/actress. It's commonly thought of as a pre-Madonna which oddly enough, also points in a singing direction, but this is not correct.

9. It's still baffling to me that so many had trouble with Katy during this two-year period, and there's not a hint of this in the rest of her sixty-year career, only praise and love.

Chapter 32

1. Unless otherwise noted, the following biographical details are sourced from Bright's bio at Cru.org. "Bill Bright," *Cru*, accessed March 28, 2024, https://www.cru.org/us/en/about/billbright/profile.html.

2. Now called simply "Cru" to avoid the unsavory ties to the Crusades.

3. By this, they mean the largest parachurch salaried ministry. There are, of course, larger denominations, churches, and volunteer networks.

4. John G. Turner, *Bill Bright and Campus Crusade for Christ: The Renewal of Evangelicalism in Postwar America* (Chapel Hill: University of North Carolina Press, 2009).

5. Many of these stats and the history are taken from "The History of Jesus Film Project®," *The Jesus Film* Project, accessed May 10, 2024, https://www.jesusfilm.org/about/history.

6. "Languages of the World," *Ethnologue*, accessed May 30, 2024, https://www.ethnologue.com.

7. Tom Meiner, interview with Jordan Monson, March 21, 2022.

8. Meiner, interview.

9. Meiner, interview.

10. Chris Deckert, interview with Jordan Monson, March 21, 2022.

11. Meiner, interview.

12. I can't say this with certainty, but reading between the lines at things said and unsaid, it seemed likely to me that the motivation to reach out to Wycliffe and SIL was not only the diminishing number of institutional languages but the fallout of some of the JFP's unsuccessful attempts at translation.

13. Larry Jones, interview with Jordan Monson, January 27, 2022. Larry Jones was CEO of The Seed Company at the time of this interview and the time of writing. He has since handed the baton to the next CEO.

14. Meiner, interview.

15. I've been scolded a few times for saying this by people who simply can't imagine this could be true. That's the remarkable thing, though—it is true. It really was a broom closet.

16. Deckert, interview.

17. Bernie May, interview with Jordan Monson, October 23, 2024. Interestingly, the people at Partners International asked them to change their name because of how similar it was to theirs. Though early Seed Company employees didn't want to, Bernie obliged his friends at Partners International. Instead, Partners with Nationals became The Seed Company. This was serendipitous because only weeks later they received a cease-and-desist letter from some kind of sex worker company in England that apparently had the former name.

18. Max Planck, *Scientific Autobiography and Other Papers* (New York: Philosophical Library, 1950), 97.

Note: Though evident in all fields, Einstein may be the most perfect example. His relativity upended physics. Then, some decades later, after he'd become the establishment, he refused to accept quantum mechanics. Also, the Bible scholar in me has to point out that he is correct but wrong about the Saul —> Paul misunderstanding of his day, which is still often repeated from pulpits. Paul never took on the name Paul after his "conversion." Paul had the names Saul and Paul from birth throughout his whole life. Depending on whether he was in a Greco-Roman or a Hebrew context, he used one or the other. See my cover story together with Mark Fairchild at *Christianity Today* in May 2024 for more on this.

Chapter 33

1. The original idea to reach the largest thirty languages without a word of Scripture was wonderful, but it didn't quite work out the way it was planned. Many of these groups were scattered around the world in closed countries or creative access areas. It would also be impossible to attempt the "cluster" model Katy wanted to try if they split their efforts. Katy proposed working on some of those languages in Nigeria, along with the other largest languages in Nigeria. Once the proof of concept was established, they'd keep doing the same all over the world. They have long since hit those original thirty from the goal, but they made adaptations to that original goal in the process.

2. Ernst Wendland, interview with Jordan Monson, January 25, 2022.

3. That is, alphabets and writing systems.

4. Chris Deckert, interview with Jordan Monson, March 21, 2022.

5. Deckert, interview.

6. Larry Jones, interview with Jordan Monson, January 27, 2022.

7. Deckert, interview.

8. This interview took place in 2022. In October of 2024, Deckert updated me that Covid has set him back, but not by much. They expect to reach this goal within a year or two. As a silver lining, they were able to "finish a record number of smaller languages in the process of pursuing M865.

9. These and the following stats are taken from "Jesus Film Project Ministry Statistics," Jesus Film Project, https://www.jesusfilm.org/partners/resources/strategies/statistics as of May 2024, but they're constantly being updated.

10. "The History of Jesus Film Project," *The Jesus Film* Project, accessed May 10, 2024, https://www.jesusfilm.org/about/history.

11. "Jesus Film Project Ministry Statistics."

12. Aaron Earls, "Billy Graham's Life & Ministry by the Numbers," Lifeway Research, February 21, 2018. https://research.lifeway.com/2018/02/21/billy-grahams-life-ministry-by-the-numbers.

13. Marlise Simons, "American Missionaries under Pressure to Leave Mexico," *Washington Post*, July 20, 1979, https://www.washingtonpost.com/archive/local/1979/07/20/american-missionaries-under-pressure-to-leave-mexico/8b23d30c-0762-4419-ae86-7edbf3632d50.

14. Simons, "American Missionaries under Pressure to Leave Mexico."

15. This used to be a kind of slogan: one couple, one New Testament, one lifetime.

16. Jones, interview.

17. "50 Largest Missions and Bible Translation Organizations," MinistryWatch, April 1, 2021, https://ministrywatch.com/50-largest-missions-and-bible-translation-organizations.

18. Bernie May, interview with Jordan Monson, October 23, 2023.

19. May, interview.

20. May, interview.

21. May, interview.

22. "What We Do," *Every Tribe, Every Nation*, accessed May 16, 2024, https://eten.bible/what-we-do.

23. Drew Maust and Lynell Zogbo, "Bible Translation: An Interview with Katy Barnwell," *Journal of Translation*, 17, no. 1 (2021): 1–12, https://www.sil.org/resources/publications/entry/91195.

Chapter 34

1. Here I allude to a famous John Piper quote. Katy enjoyed his books and teachings, and I wouldn't doubt that his teachings on retirement are part of the reason she continues to work to this day. One example of Piper's fervor: "O God, don't let me waste my final years! Don't let me buy the American dream of retirement—month after month of leisure and play and hobbies and putzing around in the garage and rearranging the furniture and golfing and fishing and sitting and watching television. Lord, please have mercy on me. Spare me this curse." John Piper, *Rethinking Retirement: Finishing Life for the Glory of Christ* (Wheaton, IL: Crossway, 2009), 27.

2. I'm reminded of the Proverbs 31 woman, far more industrious and with far more agency than many Leave-It-to-Beaver style Evangelical interpretations would be comfortable with. "Strength and honor are her clothing, and she can laugh at the time to come. Her mouth speaks wisdom, and loving instruction is on her tongue" (Prov. 31:25–26).

3. Nicole Torres, "You're Likely to Live Longer if You Retire after 65," *Harvard Business Review*, October 1, 2016, https://hbr.org/2016/10/youre-likely-to-live-longer-if-you-retire-after-65.

4. Torres, "You're Likely to Live Longer if You Retire after 65."

5. Torres, "You're Likely to Live Longer if You Retire after 65."

6. As an example, certain colleagues had been waiting on Katy's latest revisions of the Luke Partnership training materials. They wanted to make these available for distribution to those around the world who were interested in this new model of training new teams of national translators. But Katy couldn't let them go. Her taste for near-perfection had not waned, but her ability to accomplish that work on top of everything else was no longer up to the task. She was too busy. After attempting over several years

to acquire these materials, with no delivery, the highest levels of The Seed Company leadership signed off on accessing the latest training materials directly from the backups kept in the company server. This grieved Katy very much. But it's a sign that she had too much on her plate. Note: I fact-checked this with a source who wished to remain anonymous. They helped to edit this note, rewriting certain phrases or sentences for accuracy and clarity.

7. Larry Jones, interview with Jordan Monson, January 27, 2022.

8. The local church initiative, plus reaching out through NBTT, were either methods or organizations that Katy helped create. It's uncanny to see just how institutional her innovations have become.

Chapter 35

1. Drew Maust and Lynell Zogbo, "Bible Translation: An Interview with Katy Barnwell," *Journal of Translation*, 17, no. 1 (2021): 1–12, https://www.sil.org/resources/publications/entry/91195.

2. Brian Kelly, interview with Jordan Monson, August 5, 2022.

3. Tim Jore, "From Unreached to Established: Church-centric Bible Translation and the Establishing of the Church in Every People Group," January 1, 2018, https://www.academia.edu/36662901/From_Unreached_to_Established_Church_Centric_Bible_Translation_and_the_Establishing_of_the_Church_in_Every_People_Group.

4. Tim Jore, email interview with Jordan Monson, August 17, 2022.

5. There's a debate about how revolutionary church-centric Bible translation really is. On one side, it's the culmination of Bible translation. The global church will run with the baton and not need to consult with any outside consultant. Just as institutionalized languages (like English) don't seek outside approval when their own scholars produce a translation. On the other side, they say this is impractical. For noninstitutional languages with few or no biblical or linguistics scholars, you need the consultant-checking process to ensure faithfulness to Scripture. One source (who wishes to remain anonymous) called CCBT a marketing scheme to repackage what they were already doing. They compared it to dishwasher detergent pods. It's the same thing they've been doing for a long time but packaged and marketed differently. I suspect the truth is between the two poles. Only the future will tell. What is sure is that Katy Barnwell built the many foundations that CCBT will rely on as we move into the future.

Chapter 36

1. Teryl Gonzalez, interview with Jordan Monson, January 18, 2022.

2. Wycliffe Bible Translators, "State of the Bible," accessed May 16, 2024, https://wycliffe.org.uk/home/resources/state-of-the-bible.

3. Wycliffe Bible Translators, "State of the Bible."

4. Drew Maust and Lynell Zogbo, "Bible Translation: An Interview with Katy Barnwell," *Journal of Translation*, 17, no. 1 (2021): 1–12, https://www.sil.org/resources/publications/entry/91195.

5. Chris Deckert, interview with Jordan Monson, March 21, 2022.

6. Larry Jones, interview with Jordan Monson, January 27, 2022. Jones served both at high levels within SIL and then with The Seed Company as senior VP and finally president and CEO until 2024.

7. David Neff, "Interview: Eugene Nida on Meaning-Full Translations," October 7, 2002, https://www.christianitytoday.com/ct/2002/october7/2.46.html.

8. Boone Aldridge, *Kenneth L. Pike: An Evangelical Mind* (Eugene, OR: Pickwick Publications, 2021).

9. Gonzalez, interview with Jordan Monson.

10. Notice, she did not admit she may be the most influential, only that "it may be true." That is, what I was implying may be true—that it's her. In more than one hundred hours of interviews with Katy, this was her most uncomfortable response, much more than about conflict or potential romances.

11. Other women to receive this title include Rebecca Freundlich Protten, Ann Hasseltine Judson, Charlotte "Lottie" Moon, and Amy Carmichael.

Chapter 37

1. New International Version (NIV)

2. Hegesippus is lost to history, but some of his work was quoted directly in other ancient church sources. This quote is preserved for us in Eusebius of Caesarea: "The Church History of Eusebius," in *Eusebius: Church History, Life of Constantine the Great, and Oration in Praise of Constantine*, vol. 1, eds. Philip Schaff and Henry Wace; trans. Arthur Cushman McGiffert; A Select Library of the Nicene and Post-Nicene Fathers of the Christian Church, Second Series (New York: Christian Literature Company, 1890), 1125.

3. Larry Jones, interview with Jordan Monson, January 27, 2022.

Epilogue

1. This was related in a card that friends and colleagues put together for her fiftieth anniversary as a Wycliffe member.

2. John Afro is one of the senior Mbembe translators in Nigeria.

3. I tip my hat to Hebrews in this debate.

4. In the UK, Katy happens to be in the same time zone as the Cross River State in Nigeria.

ALSO
AVAILABLE

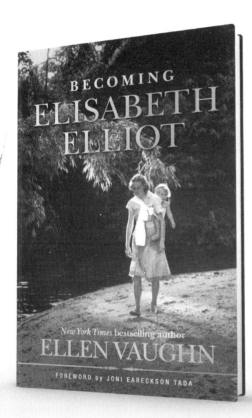

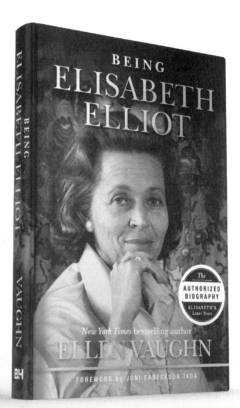

Kids need HEROES!

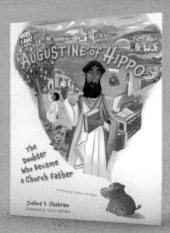

Introduce the kids in your life to heroes of the faith!